99 WAYS
TO CUT, SEW & DECK OUT
YOUR DENIM

Faith Blakeney, Justina Blakeney &
Ellen Schultz of Compai
Photography by Kira Lillie

C⊗MPAI

POTTER
CRAFT

NEW YORK

Published in the United States by Potter Craft, an imprint of the Crown Publishing Group, a division of Random House, Inc., New York.

www.crownpublishing.com

www.pottercraft.com

Potter Craft Newsletter
Sign up at www.pottercraftnews.com to get information about new books, receive free patterns, and enter contests to win free stuff.

POTTER CRAFT & Colophon and POTTER & Colophon are registered trademarks of Random House, Inc.

Library of Congress Cataloging-in-Publication Data

Blakeney, Faith.

99 ways to cut, sew & deck out your denim / by Faith Blakeney, Justina Blakeney & Ellen Schultz. — 1st ed.

    p. cm.

 Includes index.

ISBN-13: 978-0-307-35170-8 (hardcover : alk. paper) 1. Denim. 2. Tailoring. 3. Clothing and dress—Remaking. I. Blakeney, Justina. II. Schultz, Ellen, 1980- III. Title.

TT557.B53 2007

646'.11—dc22

2006028322

ISBN: 978-0-307-35170-8

Printed in China

Cover design by Sarit Melmet
Graphic Design by Sarit Melmed & Compai

10 9 8 7 6 5 4 3 2 1

First Edition

introduction

Denim's been around since the seventeenth century, when it got its name from the Frenchman Serge de Nimmes. Since its birth, it's taken a long journey from the gold mines of San Francisco to the catwalks of Paris and Tokyo. Denim jeans are now an indispensable item in everyone's wardrobe. There is a reason why they are so friggin' popular. Denim is comfortable, wearable, versatile, accessible—need we say more?

Jeans are, in fact, **the most popular clothing product in the whole entire world** (maybe the universe). While your wardrobe surely contains several of your favorite pairs, we would be willing to bet that it also contains a few pairs that were long since abandoned to the deep dark depths of your closet. This book will endow you with the power to revamp even your hooptiest pair of jeans—and not only yours, but yo' mama's and papa's and best friends' boyfriends'—you get the point? It's easy and fun and cheap and ecofriendly and ever so hip.

This, my friend, is not your run of the mill, do-it-yourself manual. This book is a silent mentor, providing you with the essential (and nonessential) tools to become a denim doctor, a recycling magician, a jean genie. *Theme music begins now . . .

attention!!!

Before initiating this adventure there are a few invaluable things to keep in MIND, HEART and SPIRIT.

Sewing denim can be both CHALLENGING and GRATIFYING. Some of the same qualities that make it such a desirable fabric (that is, its durability and resistance) can also make it difficult to sew. Arm yourself with the proper needles, for both hand sewing and machine sewing, and remember that patience is a virtue. (And watch out for rivets and zippers!) For those of you who have the first book in this series, 99 Ways to Cut, Sew, Trim & Tie your T-shirt into Something Special, know that for this book we took it up a notch . . . this one is slightly more advanced than the T-shirt book.

Read through the instructions for each project and the corresponding technical drawings before beginning. It's essential to understand each step in order to calculate dimensions and ensure a proper fit. We assume, for this book, the use of a sewing machine. Though it is not required, it is definitely a time-saver.

The glossary of techniques is a PRICELESS TREASURE of little sewing lessons for big results. For any of you who have tried sewing before, only to find yourself in hair-pulling desperation after just moments of exalted CREATIVITY, this glossary will be your savior. USE IT, and use it wisely.

The **bold-faced** words are a reference to the **glossary of techniques** that can be found in the back of the book. We recommend that everyone—novices and pros alike—read through it before beginning, while you're creating, and when you're done (just for fun!).

Remember, when cutting up, that DENIM is a PRECIOUS MATERIAL; it is not to be wasted! When instructed to cut, cut carefully. You may need the pieces later, if not for the project you're working on at the moment, perhaps for the next one. And if not for the next one, you can use it as a tissue the next time you have a cold (ha-ha!).

We presume the use of a basic 501 type jean. For most projects, other types of jeans will work fine. Make sure to choose the right jeans for the project. (Many projects only need jean scraps, despite calling for 1 pair of jeans.)

Estimates for quantity of fabric, elastic, and so on, are just that—estimates. We tried to err on the side of excess—better too much than too little—but depending on your size you may need to slightly reconsider our estimates.

In case you haven't noticed, we've packed a ton of essential information into this little teeny-tiny itsy-bitsy book. Please forgive us and do take your time when reviewing instructions, technical drawings, the glossary, and, of course, this page. MAY THE FORCE BE WITH YOU.

Stars signify level of difficulty ✳=easy; ✳✳✳✳=difficult

contents

introduction
attention

#1
caitlin

backless top

You'll need
1 pair of jeans

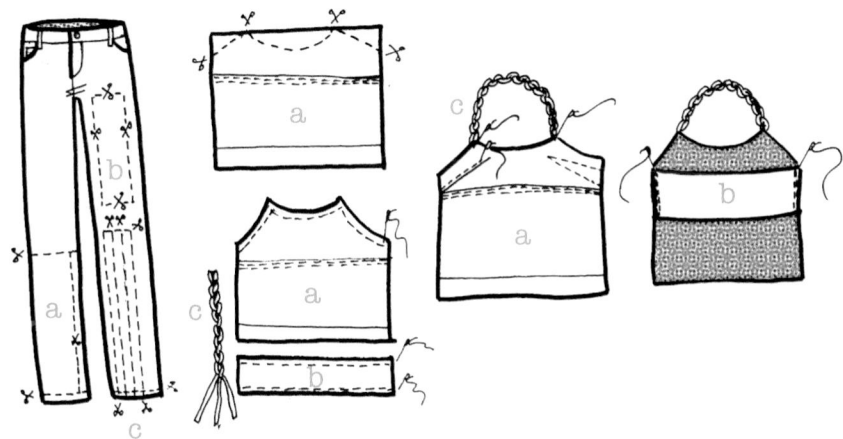

1. cut hems off both legs, cut off one jean leg at knee (a)
2. cut (a) open in front, 2 inches/(5cm) from inseam
3. cut out rectangle (b) (be sure that length of (a) and (b) is equal to circumference of your bust)
4. cut 3 thin strips from front bottom of leg (c) (long enough to use as halter neck; remember braiding requires extra length!), braid strips together
5. cut indicated neckline out of (a)
6. sew **flat hem** around (a), leaving bottom unhemmed
7. **sew darts** into each side of (a) in front
8. **hand stitch** braid (c) onto (a) where indicated.
9. **flat hem** (b) on top and bottom then **clean finish sew** onto (a) at sides

lawanda

jeans with
appliqués

You'll need
1 pair of jeans
3 vintage buttons
2 pieces of fabric 12 x 18 inches (30 x 46cm)

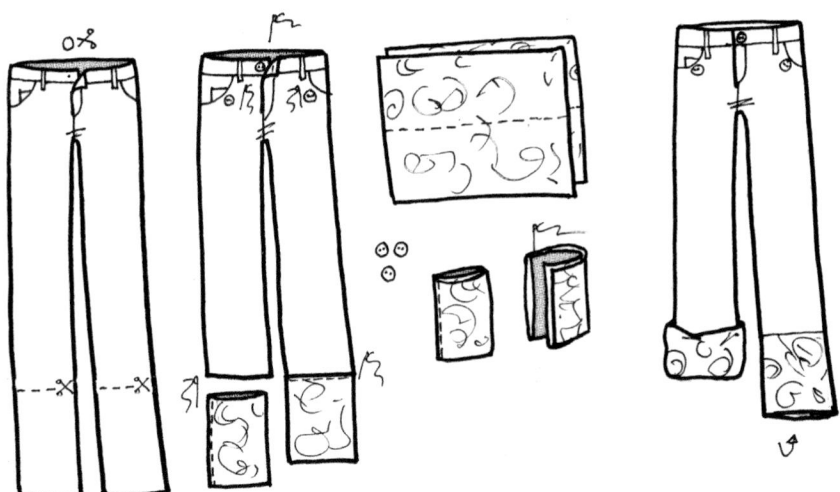

1. cut off button on waistband (may be a little difficult, but you can do it!)
2. cut off both legs at capri length
3. **sew on buttons** where indicated
4. fold both pieces of fabric in half
5. **clean finish sew** each folded piece of fabric into a tube
6. **clean finish sew** each piece onto legs of jeans
7. fold up new funky hems as desired!

#3

hille

slippers

You'll need
1 pair of high-waisted jeans

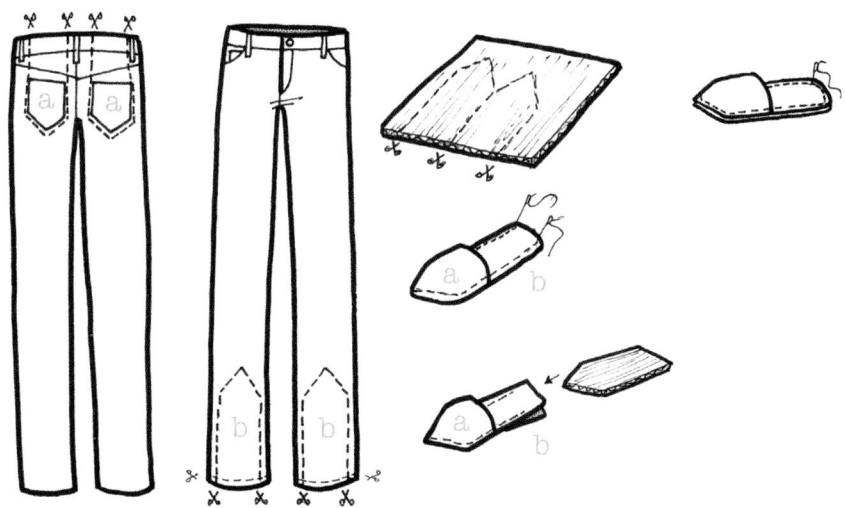

1. before you start cutting, place feet into back pockets to ensure a good fit
2. cut out back pockets (a), add seam allowance
3. cut out same shape from front bottoms of each leg of jeans (b) (avoid bottom hem)
4. cut out same shapes in cardboard (minus seam allowance)
5. sew together (a) and (b), leaving back heel open
6. insert cardboard into both slippers, sew heel closed, and slip them on

#4

piper

blazer

You'll need
2 pairs of jeans
1 vintage button

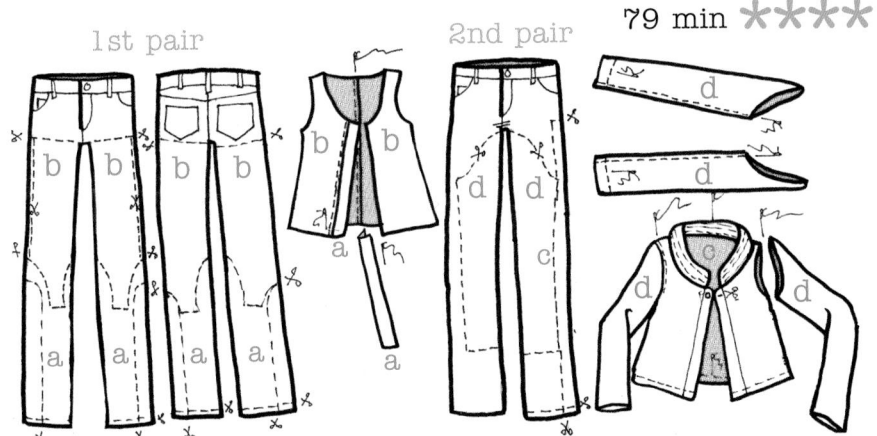

1. on 1st pair of jeans cut off hems, cut out strips (a) on side seams of both legs, front and back
2. on same pair, cut off legs at crotch, eliminate side seams and cut shapes (b) from legs in front and back (ATTN: these shapes are different!) use **pattern tech.**
3. cut long strip on side seam of 2nd pair of jeans (c)
4. **clean finish sew** pieces (b) together on sides and shoulders
5. sew (a) onto (b) using **covered hem technique**
6. cut out general sleeve shapes (d) from front and back of 2nd pair of jeans using **pattern technique**
7. **clean finish sew** sleeves closed (d), **flat hem** wrist, and **clean finish sew** to piece (b)
8. sew strip (c) to neckline of piece (b), using **covered hem technique** and **flat hem** bottom of (b)

5

mammina
dog jacket

You'll need
1 pair of jeans
1 small dog

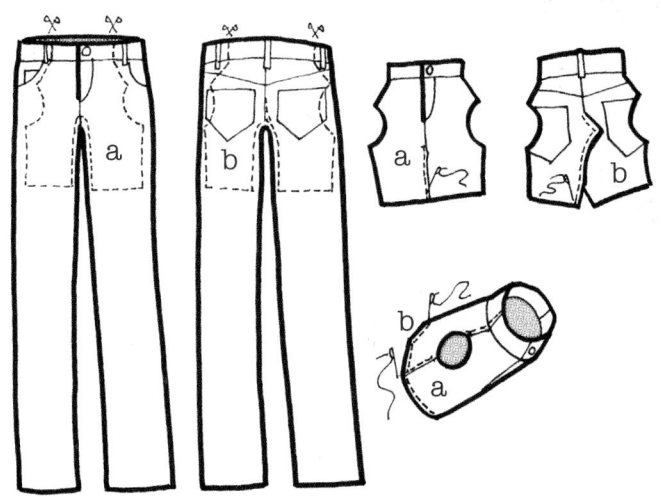

1. cut out general forms (a) and (b) as indicated, making sure that the width of (a) plus (b) is equal to the circumference of your dog's waist—adding seam allowance all around edges
2. **clean finish sew** crotch together on (a)
3. **flatten crotch** to sew pieces (b) together
4. **clean finish sew** (a) and (b) together (ATTN: do not sew arm, neck, or body holes closed)
5. **flat hem** armholes and bottom edge of jacket

#6

jenny

balloon skirt

You'll need
1 pair of jeans

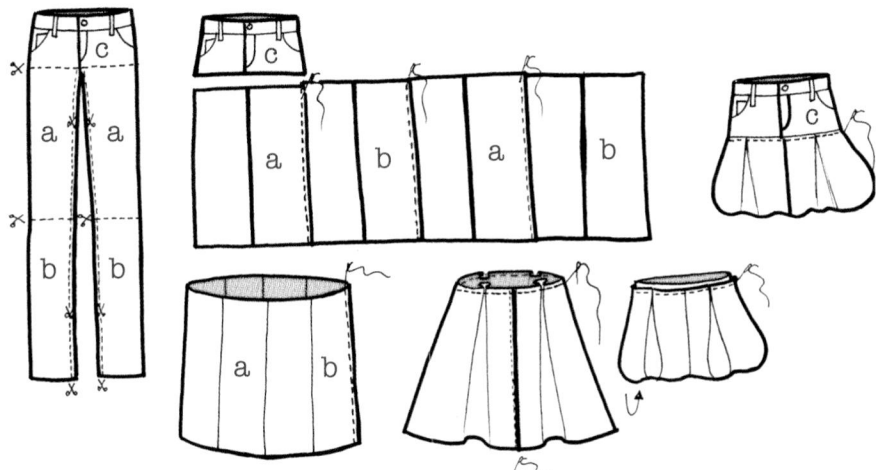

1. cut open legs, eliminating inseams
2. cut legs off at knee, then cut legs off just above crotch
3. **clean finish sew** together pieces (a) and pieces (b) as indicated
4. **clean finish sew** together to form a tube
5. stitch around 1 edge of the tube, adding 4 **inverted pleats** [ATTN: make sure that the new circumference of the tube is the same size as the circumference of bottom edge of (c)]
6. fold under tube, then stitch and **gather** edges together on the outside, as shown
7. **clean finish sew** top of folded tube and bottom edge of (c) together (ATTN: layers will be thick, so sew with care)

#7

leann

shopping bag

You'll need
1 pair of jeans

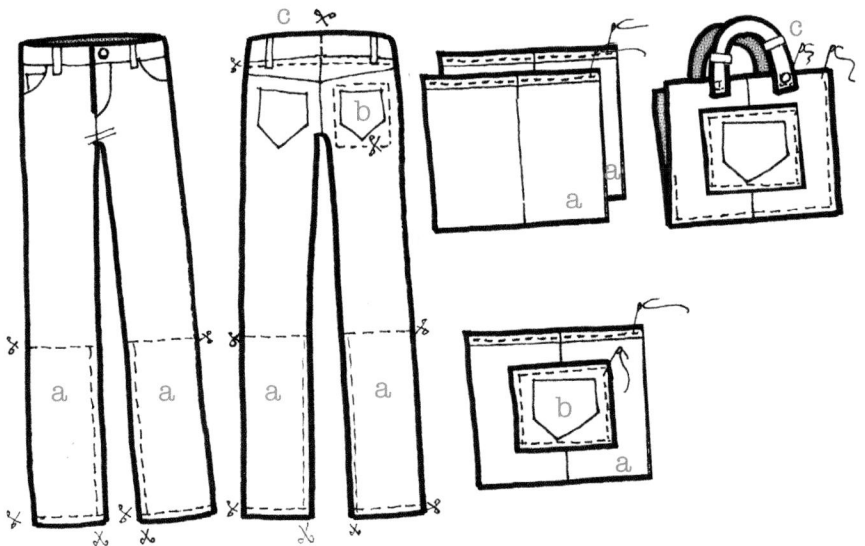

1. cut hem off both legs, then cut legs off below the knee
2. cut open (a) and (a), eliminating inseams
3. hem top edges of (a), as indicated
4. cut out square around pocket (b) and stitch it onto (a) center front
5. **clean finish sew** edges and bottom of bag of (a) together, leaving top open
6. cut off waistband (c) then cut in 2 pieces
7. stitch waistband (c) onto each side of bag, creating handles as shown

#8

maya

minishorts with frills

You'll need
1 pair of jeans

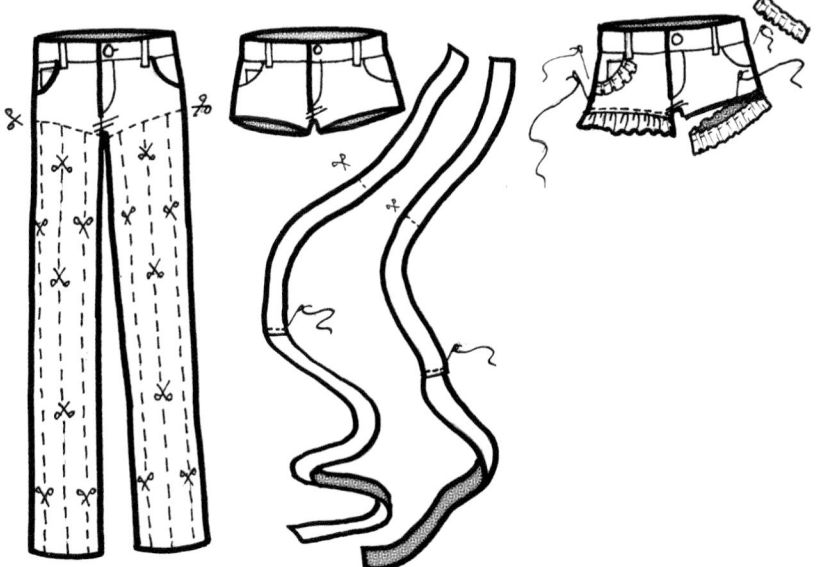

1. cut legs off just below crotch to make shorts
2. cut 2 strips from each leg in front, avoiding seams and hems
3. cut about 8 inches (20cm) off each strip
4. **clean finish sew** remaining strips together to make 2 long strips of equal length, then sew ends together to form a band, **gather** bands
5. **clean finish sew** gathered bands to bottom of shorts then **top stitch** for clean look

#9

bianca

belt

You'll need
1 pair of jeans
1 ribbon that is 1 inch (2.5 cm) longer than the waist of the jeans

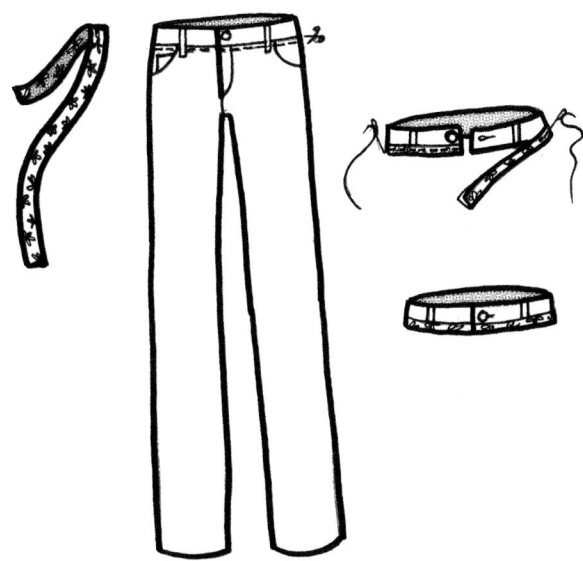

1. cut off waistband
2. use **covered hem technique** to sew ribbon onto waistband (watch out when sewing over beltloops!)
3. fold in ends of ribbon and **top stitch** closed

#10
benjamine

heating pad

You'll need
1 pair of jeans
1 box of rice

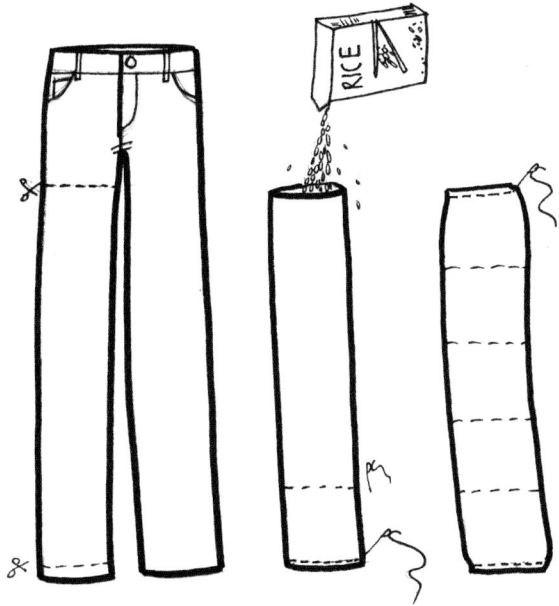

1. cut off 1 leg of jeans
2. **clean finish sew** 1 edge
3. fill about 5 inches (13cm) with rice, and **top stitch** closed
4. repeat until you reach the top.
5. **top stitch** other end closed, folding in raw edges.
6. put in microwave for 15 seconds and apply to back for pain relief! ahhhhh...

#11

sofia

skirt with
gathered bottom

You'll need
1 pair of jeans
1 piece of fabric 2 yards (2m)
   long (width depends on desired length of skirt)

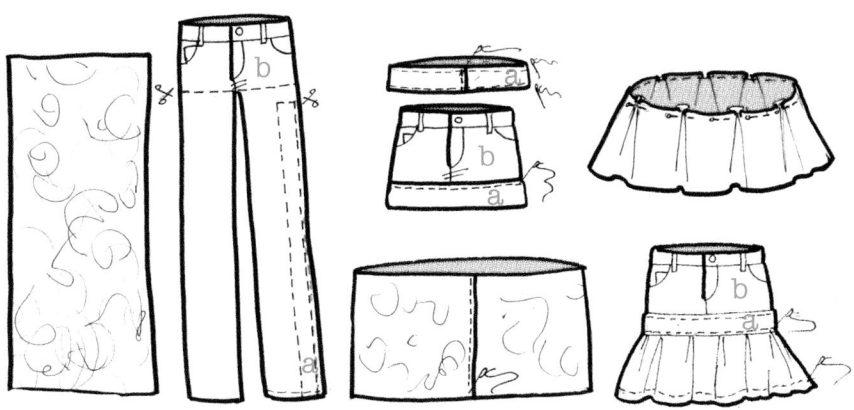

1. cut legs off just above crotch
2. cut 3-inch (8cm) strips from front and back of 1 leg (a), eliminating hem
3. **clean finish sew** strips together at both ends, making sure the band created has the same circumference as the bottom edge of (b), **hem flat**
4. **top stitch** strip (a) onto (b)
5. **clean finish sew** fabric together to create a tube
6. **top stitch** around one edge of the tube, adding 10 **inverted pleats** [ATTN: make sure that the new circumference of the tube is the same size as the circumference of bottom edge of (a)]
7. **top stitch** bottom edge of (a) onto pleated fabric
8. **rolled hem** bottom edge of skirt for a clean look

12

hedvig

madonna
mittens

You'll need
1 pair of jeans
1 piece of fabric 6 feet (2m) x 5 inches (13cm)

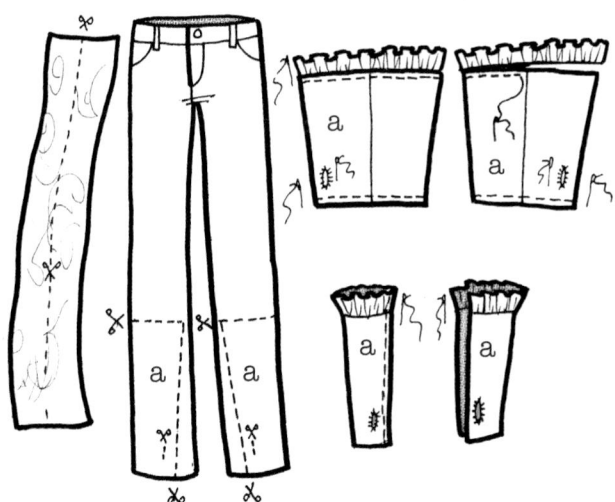

1. cut pieces (a) from front and back of each leg (make sure you have ample width to put your hand in after sewing!)
2. cut out 1 thumb hole in front on each piece (a), then finish edges using **eyelet technique**
3. cut fabric into 2 long strips and **flat hem** 1 long edge on each piece (a), then **gather** each strip
4. **clean finish sew** gathered strips onto wider end of each piece (a), then **top stitch**
5. sew each piece into a long tube

#13

crysell

letterholder

You'll need
1 pair of jeans

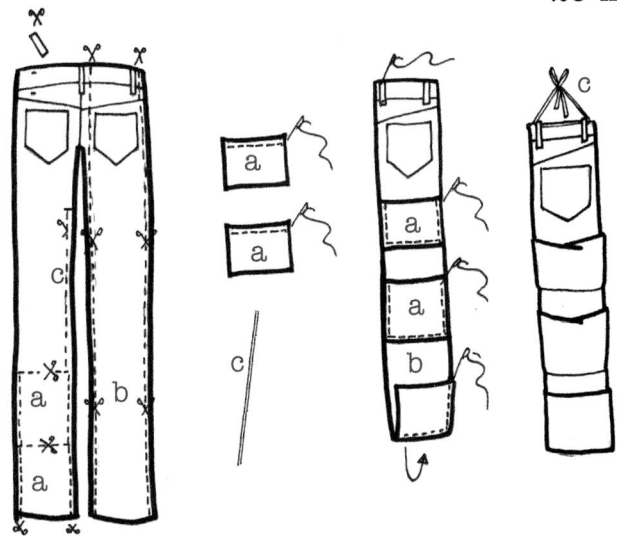

1. cut out 2 squares (a) from 1 leg (maximize width, a good length is 4 inches [10cm]), **flat hem** edges
2. cut out back of other leg from top to bottom (b) (again, make sure to maximize width)
3. cut out inseam (c)
4. cut off 1 belt loop, and **top stitch** back on where indicated
5. fold bottom of leg up 4 inches (10cm) to create pocket, **top stitch** sides closed
6. **top stitch** bottom and sides of squares (a) onto (b), where indicated
7. tie string through belt loops and hang on the wall

14

tessa

tiny top

You'll need
1 pair of jeans, preferably stretch

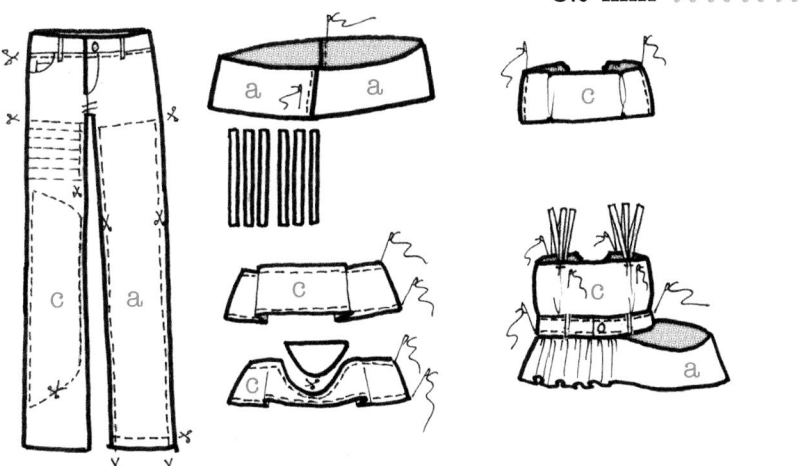

1. cut off right leg below crotch (a) eliminate seams and hem, then cut off waistband (b) below belt loops
2. sew pieces (a) into big tube as shown
3. cut out 6 thin strips from left leg on front and back
4. cut out indicated shape from left leg on front and back, creating pieces (c)
5. cut out semicircle from 1 of pieces (c), as shown
6. pin and stitch down pleats on pieces (c) where indicated, then **flat hem** edges
7. **clean finish sew** pieces (c) together into a tube
8. **clean finish sew** tube (c) onto waistband
9. **clean finish sew** (a) to waistband while **gathering**
10. stitch 3 strips onto either side of piece (c) front and back, creating shoulder straps

#15

frida

culottes

You'll need
1 pair of jeans

1. cut legs off at knees
2. cut 2 long slits in sides of jeans at side seams as indicated
3. cut 2 long slits in back center of both legs of jeans
4. cut the remaining legs in half diagonally, creating 4 long triangles (a)
5. insert and **clean finish sew** (a) pieces into the 4 slits (like huge darts)
6. trim bottom to even edge, **roll hem** for a more refined look

#16
kathy

funky top

You'll need
1 pair of jeans
1 piece of fabric 16 × 6 inches
(41 × 15 cm)

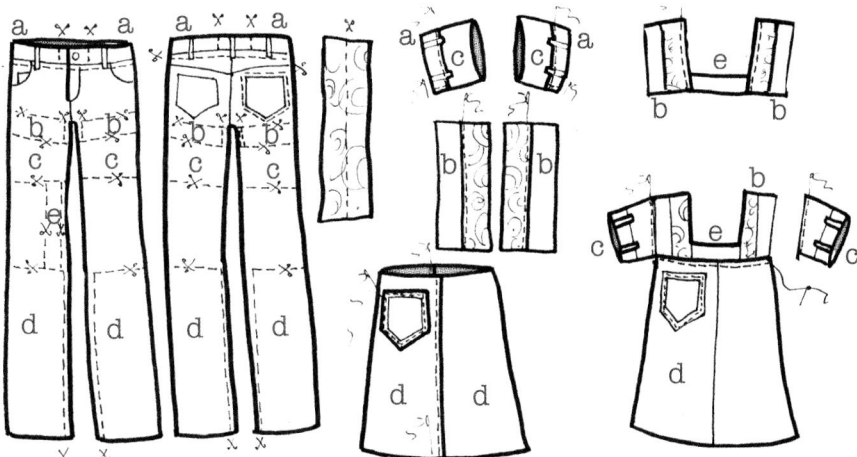

1. cut off waistband, then cut out pieces (a)
2. cut out strips (b) from front and back, avoid inseams
3. cut out pieces (c) in front and back, creating 2 tubes
4. **clean finish sew** pieces (a) closed and onto tubes (c)
5. cut fabric strip in half lengthwise and **clean finish sew** onto strip (b), **hem flat**, then fold in half lengthwise, repeat
6. cut out rectangles (d), **clean finish sew** them into tube
7. cut out back pocket, leave seam allowance, **top stitch** to (d)
8. cut out piece (e) and **flat hem** 1 long side, **clean finish sew** piece (e) to either side of fabric on pieces (b), uniting the top piece, and **clean finish sew** onto tube (d)
9. **clean finish sew** each sleeve (c) to both sides of (b)

#17

miki

vest

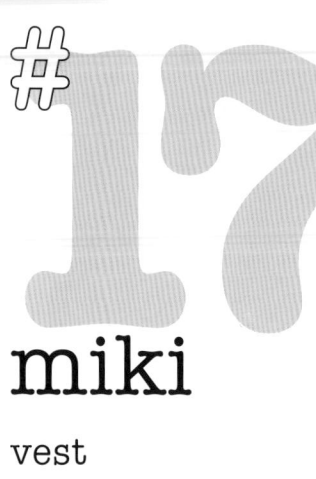

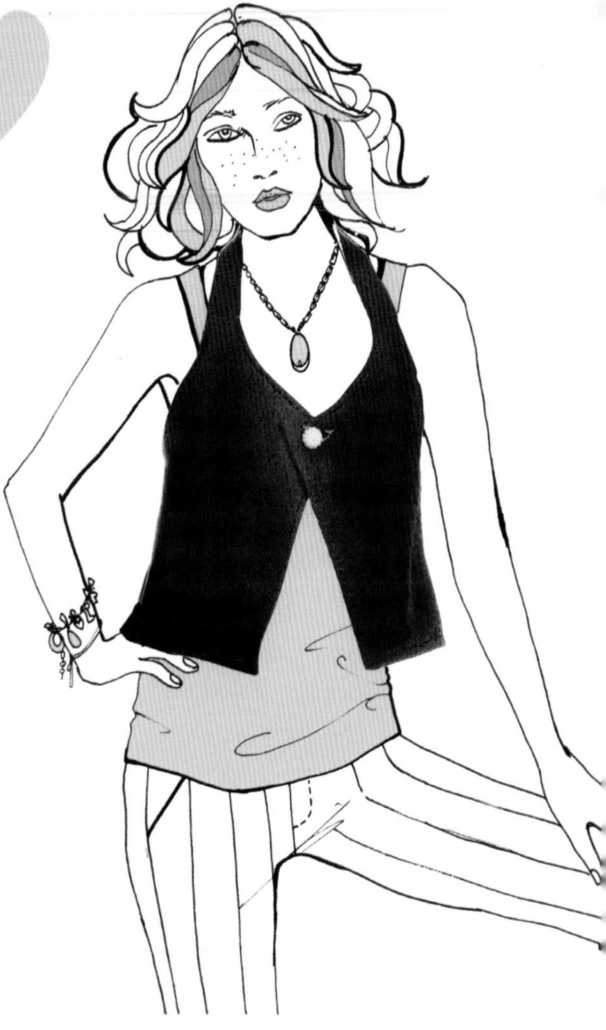

You'll need
1 pair of jeans
1 vintage button

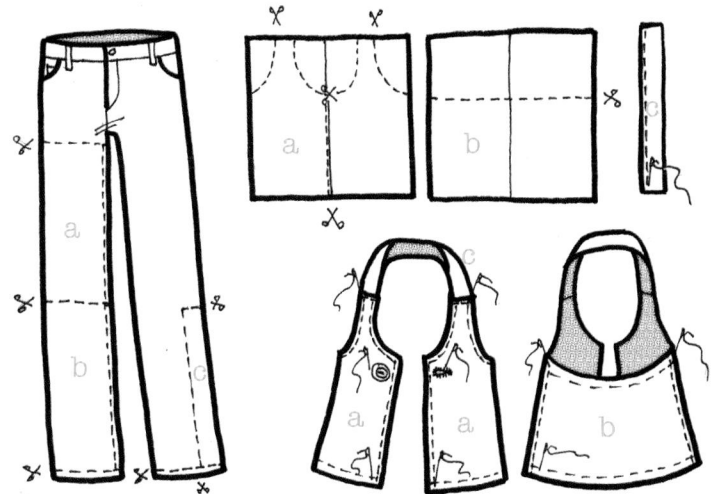

1. eliminate hems, then cut 1 leg off below crotch
2. cut off inseam and then cut that leg in half
3. cut strip (c) from front and back of other leg
4. fold strip (c) in half, as shown, and sew closed
5. cut out (a), use **pattern technique** and (b), as shown, making sure that the height of piece (b) is equal to that of (a) at the base of the armhole
6. cut (a) open in center front (eliminating seam), sew (c) onto (a) as indicated
7. **make eyelet** on right side, **sew button** on left side
8. sew back piece (b) to (a) on sides, **flat hem** around all remaining raw edges

#18

carla

strapless top

You'll need
1 pair of jeans
1 piece of fabric
   36 (92cm) x 10 inches (25cm)

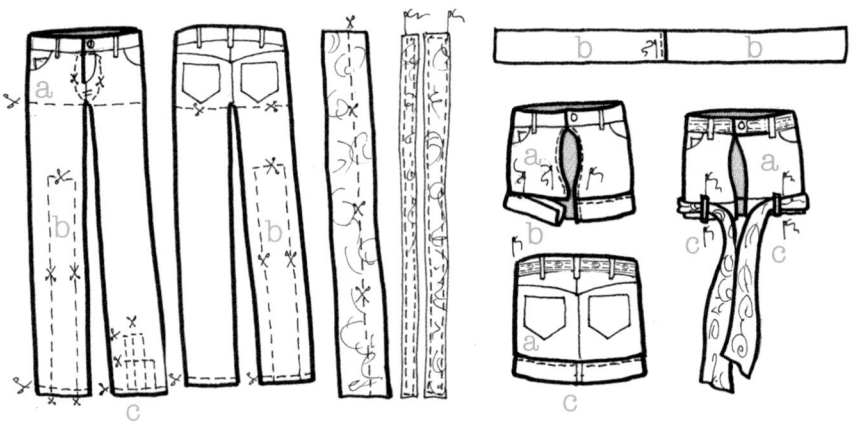

1. cut off legs at crotch, then cut out zipper/button fly, leaving top button intact (a)
2. cut long thick strip (b) from 1 leg in front and back, eliminating hem, and sew into band
3. cut 5 itsy-bitsy strips (c) out of other leg in front, eliminating hem, as shown
4. sew tube (b) onto bottom of (a) using **covered hem technique**
5. **top stitch** 5 itsy-bitsy strips (c) around bottom edge of (a) as belt loops
6. cut fabric in half lengthwise and **flat hem**
7. stitch 1 fabric strip around original waistband
8. thread fabric through belt loops on bottom and tie

#19

rosy

jeans with patches

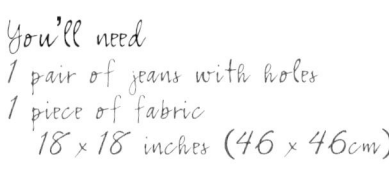

You'll need
1 pair of jeans with holes
1 piece of fabric
   18 x 18 inches (46 x 46cm)

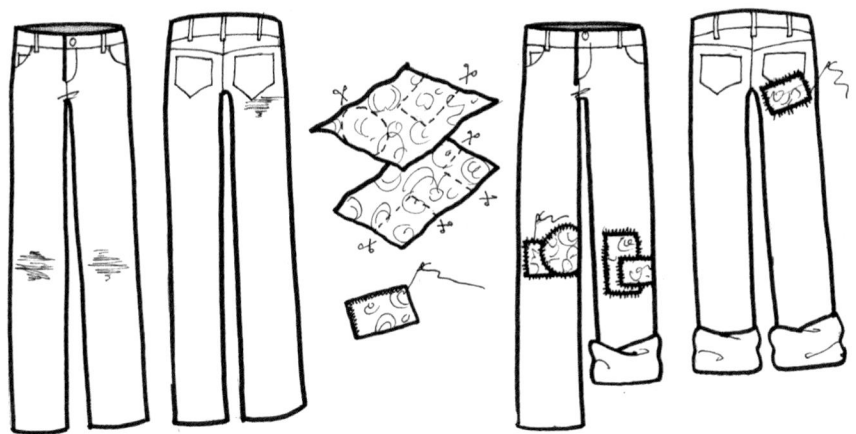

1. cut fabric into desired dimensions and shapes for
   patches, leaving seam allowance (make sure they're
   large enough to cover holes)
2. **zigzag stitch** around patches
3. place patches onto jeans where you see fit, and pin
   patches over the holes
4. **hand stitch** patches onto jeans
5. fold up bottom of jeans to complete that vagabond
   look!

#20

anaïs

visor

You'll need
1 pair of jeans
1 strip of fabric
    1 inch × 12 inches
    (2.5 × 30cm)

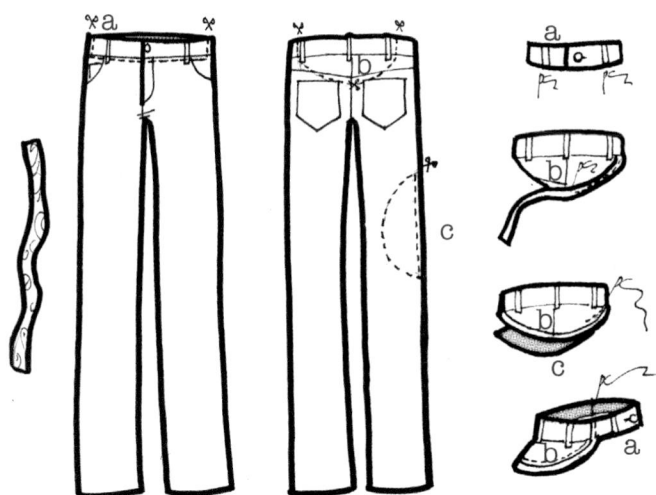

1. cut off waistband in front (a)
2. cut out (b) as indicated
3. cut out (c) as indicated in back, leaving seam allowance on flat side [ATTN: (c) should be the same size as (b) plus seam allowance]
4. sew the fabric strip onto (b) using **covered hem technique**
5. stitch (c) onto the bottom side and below the waistband of (b) for extra support
6. **clean finish sew** (a) onto sides of waistband (b)

#21

beth

book cover

You'll need
1 pair of jeans
fabric glue or hot glue
your favorite book

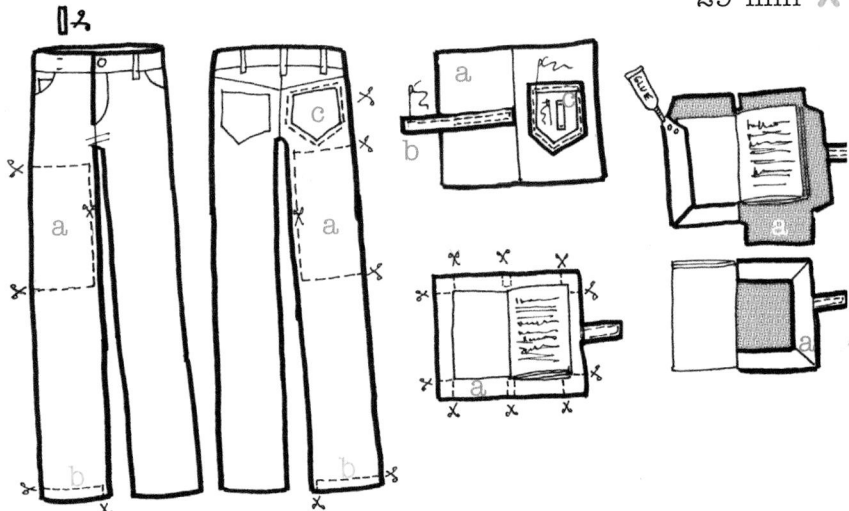

1. cut out (a) in front and back to the dimension of your book plus 1 inch (2.5cm) for seam allowance (you may need to cut out extra jean and sew it on, depending on the size of your book)
2. cut off hem (b) on 1 leg in front and back
3. cut out pocket (c), leaving seam allowance around the edge; cut off 1 belt loop while you're at it
4. stitch strip (b) onto (a) where indicated
5. stitch pocket (c) and belt loop onto (a) as shown
6. place book onto (a) then cut 1-inch (2.5cm) slits, eliminating corners and tabs for the book's binding
7. glue corners of (a) and fold edges over inside of front book cover, repeat on inside of back cover

22

charlie

dog collar and leash

You'll need
1 pair of jeans
12-inch ribbon (30 cm)
a dog

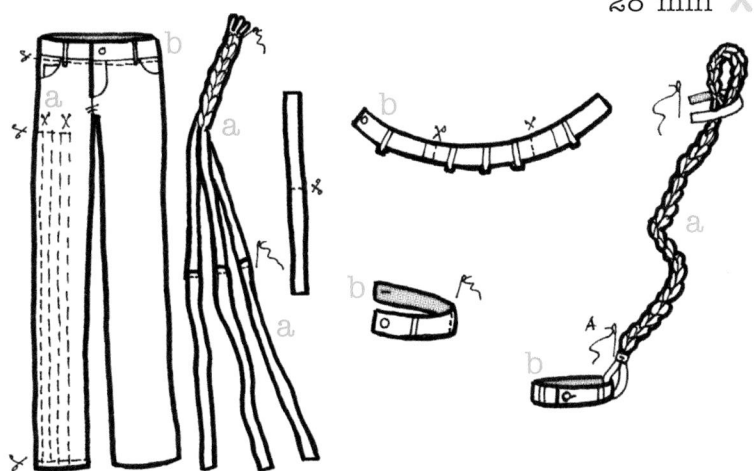

1. eliminate hem from leg, then cut it into 6 long strips (a) (3 in front, 3 in back)
2. sew 6 long strips (a) into 3 superlong strips
3. make braid and sew closed on each end
4. cut ribbon in half, loop it, and **top stitch** it onto 1 end of braid (a)
5. make loop with other end of braid, secure by wrapping other ribbon around and **top stitching** it closed
6. cut off waistband (b)
7. if necessary, cut out center piece of waistband to accommodate the neck of your canine friend, then **clean finish sew** back together, leaving the original button and eyelet
8. slip leash onto collar, grab your dog, and get walkin'

#23

chelsea
minijacket

You'll need
1 pair of jeans
3 inches (8 cm) of velcro
1 tie

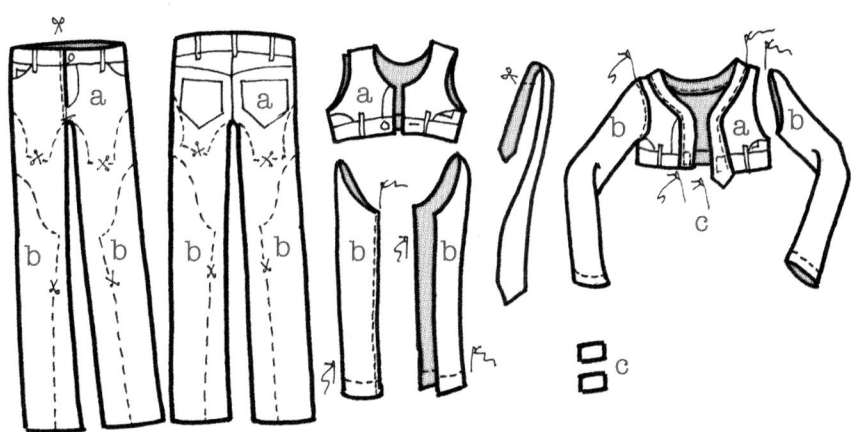

1. cut out (a) and pieces (b) as indicated, in front and back, using **pattern technique** to make sure the measurements allow a customized fit
2. **clean finish sew** front and back shoulders together (a)
3. **clean finish sew** pieces (b) into sleeves
4. **clean finish sew** sleeves (b) onto (a)
5. **top stitch** tie onto jacket neckline as shown
6. trim skinny end of tie if too long and **hem flat** raw edge
7. **top stitch** velcro pieces (c) onto outside of bottom left side, and onto reverse side of bottom right side of (a)

#24

joanne

double-waisted
skirt

You'll need
2 pairs of jeans

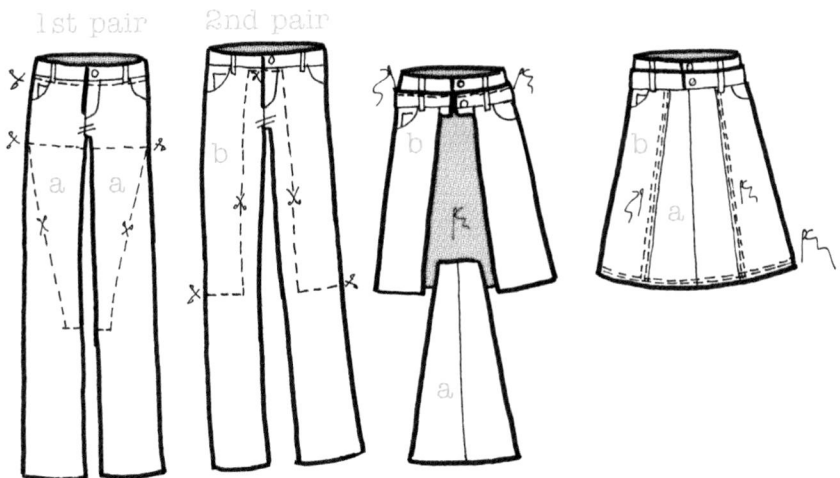

1. cut off waistband from 1st pair of jeans below belt loops
2. with the same pair, cut out indicated shapes (a) from each leg in front and back
3. take 2nd pair of jeans and cut (b) in front and back, making sure to keep the waistband attached
4. **top stitch** waistband of 1st pair of jeans onto (b) (beware of thick seams and belt loops!)
5. insert pieces (a) into front and back of skirt and sew with **double stitch**
6. **roll hem** bottom, then **top stitch** bottom

#25
margaret
yoga bag

You'll need
1 pair of jeans

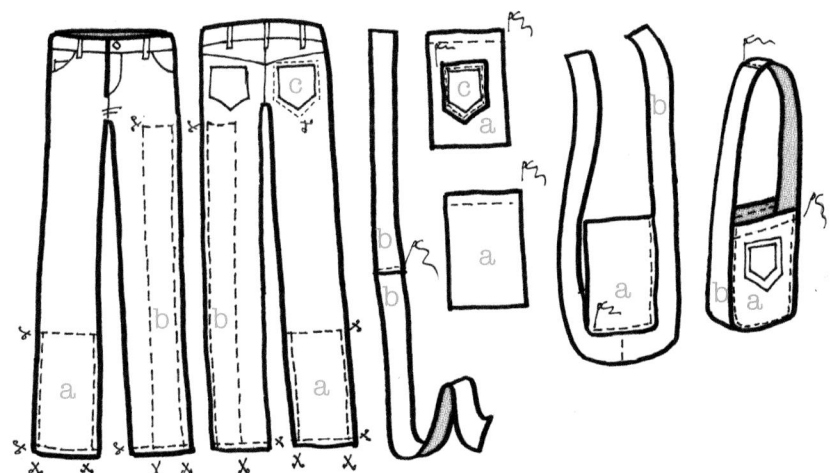

1. cut rectangles (a) from front and back of jeans (eliminating seams and hems)
2. cut strips (b) in front and back, then **clean finish sew** the 2 strips into 1 long strip
3. cut out back pocket (leaving seam allowance) and **top stitch** onto front center of 1 of the (a) pieces
4. **roll hem** top of both (a) pieces
5. **clean finish sew** strip (b) around (a)
6. **clean finish sew** remaining (a) piece onto other side of strip (ATTN: make sure the pocket ends up on the outside)
7. **clean finish sew** strip (b) closed

#26

elana

jeans with embroidery

You'll need
1 pair of jeans
embroidery thread and needle
1 vintage button

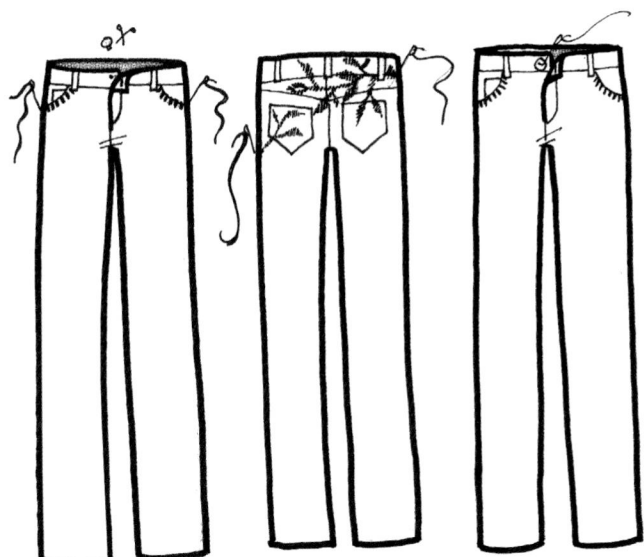

1. cut off existing button (may be a little difficult, but you can do it!)
2. **blanket stitch** around front side pocket
3. draw a fabulous design onto jeans with pen to help you with next step (take liberties with the design and placement)
4. stitch over your design (make sure not to sew pockets closed!) using **embroidery stitch**
5. **sew vintage button** next to hole where button used to be (make sure that you can button up jeans properly)

#27

dawn

top with appliqués

You'll need
1 pair of jeans
1 piece of fabric 30 x 7 inches
  (76 x 18 cm)

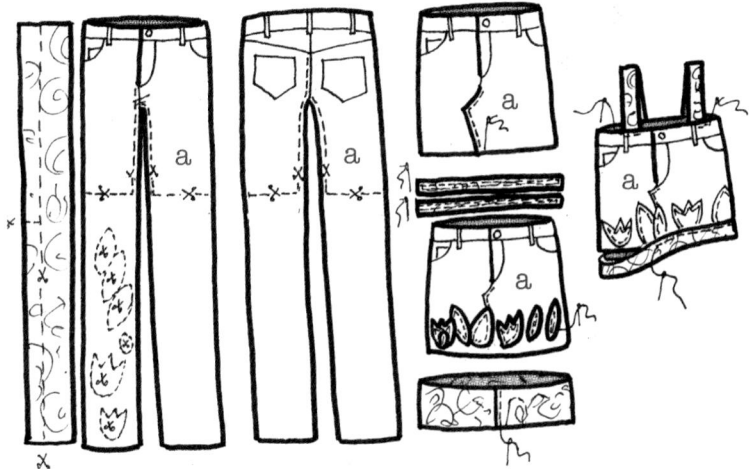

1. cut legs off above the knee and eliminate inseam
2. cut and **flatten crotch**, pin and stitch closed
3. cut out leaves from remaining jeans
4. pin then **hand stitch** leaves 1 inch (2.5cm) from bottom of (a)
5. cut fabric in half lengthwise, creating 2 strips (2 inches [5cm] wide and 5 inches [13cm] long)
6. measure circumference of bottom edge of (a), cut fabric to same length, adding 1 inch (2.5cm) seam allowance, sew strip closed to create tube
7. cut remaining strip into 2 (widthwise), **flat hem** edges
8. sew tube onto bottom of (a) use **covered hem tech.**
9. stitch short strips onto (a) as shoulder straps

#28

28

lilith

laundry bag

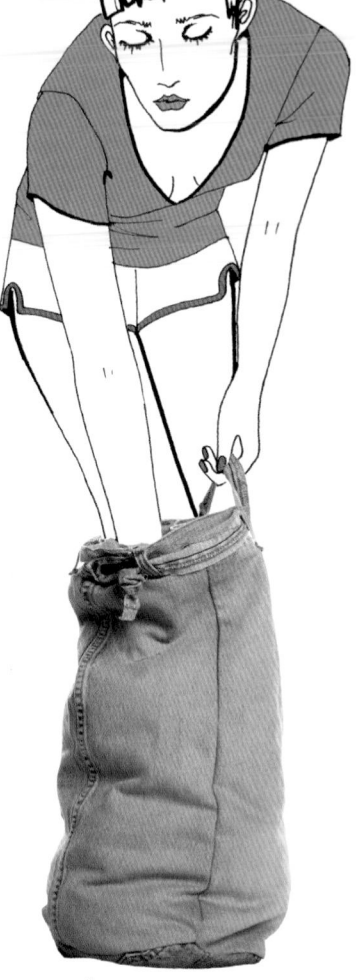

You'll need
1 pair of jeans ... the bigger the jeans the bigger the bag

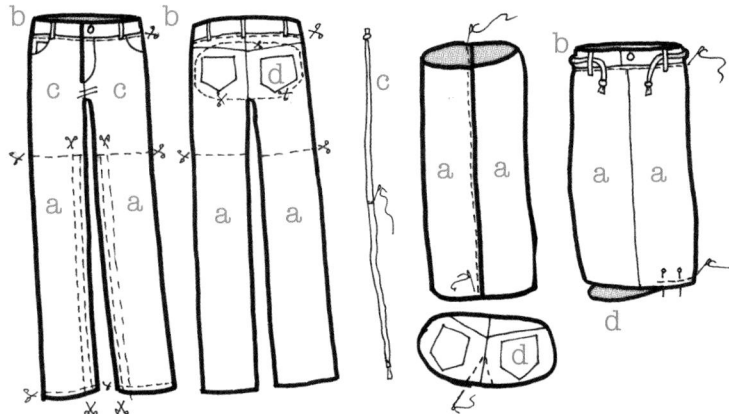

1. cut off bottom hem and cut off legs at midthigh (a)
2. cut off waistband, leave loops attached on top (b)
3. cut 2 long thin strips, 1 from each leg on front (c)
4. cut out (d) as shown
5. **clean finish sew** (a) pieces together into big tube
6. resize waistband to equal the circumference of tube (adding or cutting away jean as necessary)
7. **top stitch** waistband onto tube
8. stitch bottom of belt loops onto tube
9. **sew dart** into center seam of (d) to create flat oval
10. pin (d) onto bottom of tube, matching up the seams, then **clean finish sew** closed
11. sew 2 strips into 1 long strip, tie knots at each end and thread through belt loops

#29

cornelia

miniskirt

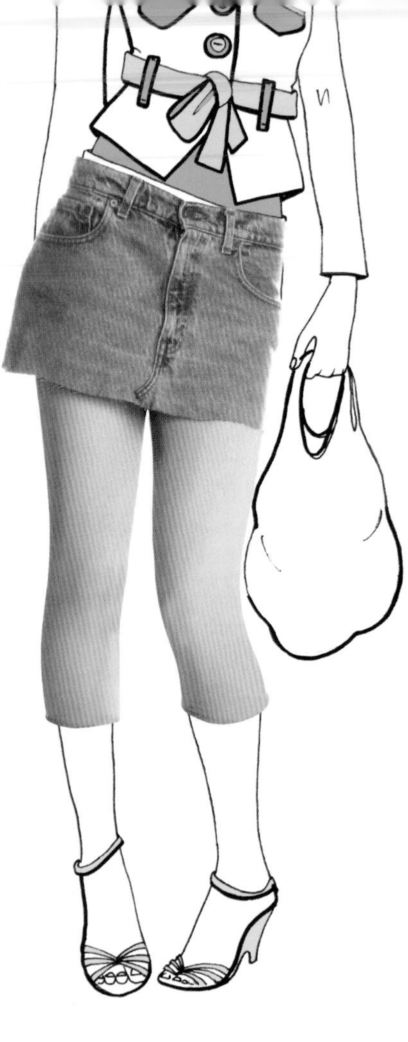

You'll need
1 pair of jeans
1 pair of tights

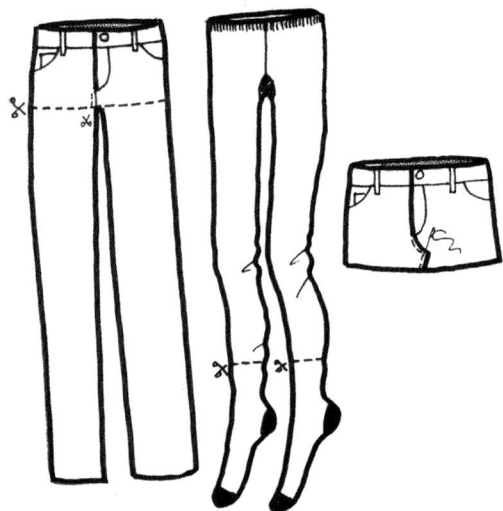

1. cut legs off jeans at crotch
2. cut and **flatten crotch** on both sides, then pin and stitch closed
3. cut feet off tights at ankle
4. use a pin to fray bottom edges of skirt
5. put tights and skirt on, and run out of the house before yo' mama sees you!

#30

ida

clutch bag

You'll need
1 pair of jeans
1 tie

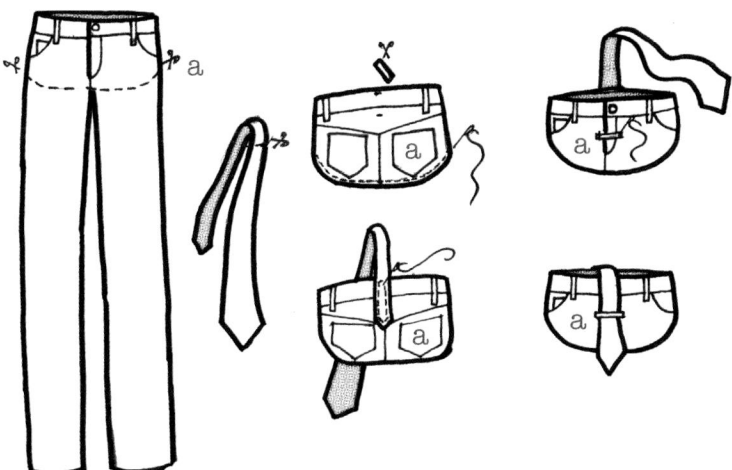

1. cut legs off at crotch as indicated (ATTN: leave front pocket linings intact)
2. **clean finish sew** bottom of (a) closed
3. unstitch center back belt loop
4. cut tie to appropriate length—probably about 2 feet (61cm)—eliminating thin part of tie
5. **top stitch** tie onto back of (a) as indicated, folding in raw edges
6. **top stitch** belt loop onto front of (a) at center and thread tie through belt loop to close your funky new clutch!

#31

lena

vest with hood

You'll need
1 pair of jeans
2 vintage buttons
jersey fabric 18 x 18 inches
    (46 x 46cm)

1. cut out rectangles (a), then **flat hem** on 3 sides
2. cut pieces (b) from front using **pattern technique**
3. sew pieces (b) together at center as shown
4. cut out pieces (c) from back using **pattern technique**
5. cut out small rectangle (d) [3 x 1 1/2 inches (8 x 4cm)]
6. **flat hem** (d) and **sew buttons** onto either side
7. fold jersey in half, cut out piece (e) and 2 strips (f)
8. sew strips (f) to front of (c) using **covered hem technique**
9. **clean finish sew** pieces (c) to (b) on sides and shoulders
10. **flat hem** long straight edge of (e), then sew rounded edges together to create hood; sew hood onto vest
11. **clean finish sew** (a) pieces to bottom of (c), leave slit
12. **clean finish sew** (d) piece onto back, where shown

#32

mark

pillow

You'll need
1 pair of jeans (preferably old, soft ones)
stuffing (try recycling the stuffing from an old cushion)

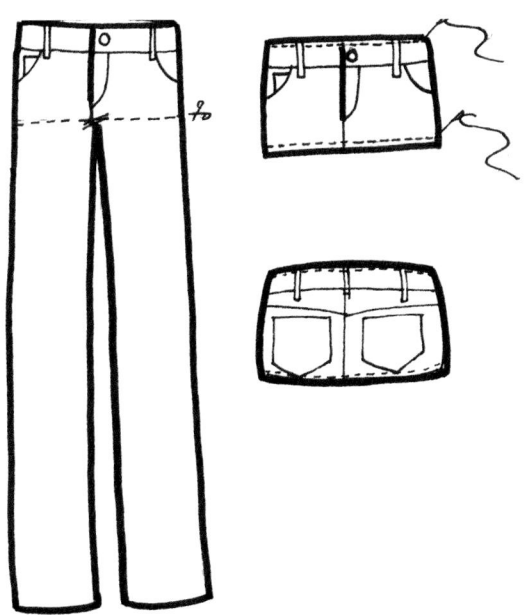

1. cut legs off at crotch
2. **clean finish sew** top and bottom closed (you may need to sew top by hand, due to thickness)
3. stuff the pillow through the zipper (and when it needs a wash, take out stuffing the same way)

#33

tylor

bikini top

You'll need
1 pair of jeans
1 thick elastic band 30 inches
   (76cm) long

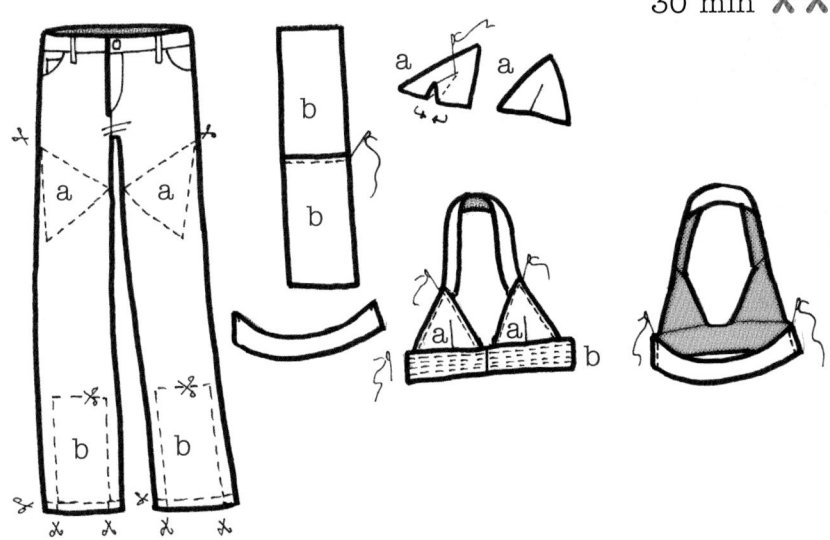

1. cut triangles (a) from front thighs of jeans
2. **make darts** on (a) pieces
3. cut off hems then cut rectangles (b) from front
4. **clean finish sew** (b) pieces together at 1 end (the length should be equal to half the circumference of your low bust)
5. **quilt** pieces (b) to make front band
6. **clean finish sew** (a) pieces onto (b) as indicated
7. cut elastic strip and sew 1 piece onto tips of (a) pieces to make "halter" neck
8. use other part of elastic strip for back piece, **clean finish sew** to each side of front band as shown

#34

sue

cd case for
the car

You'll need
1 pair of jeans
1 piece of cardboard
1 elastic band 6 inches (15 cm) long

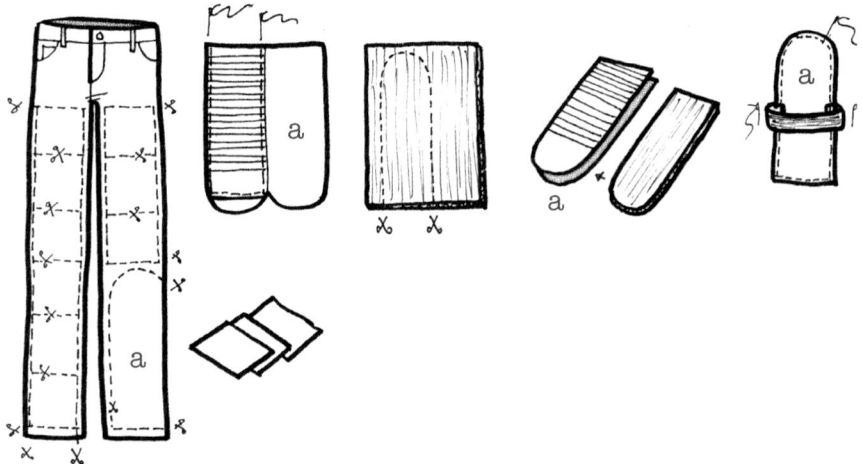

1. cut 9 squares (slightly larger than a normal CD) from front of jeans
2. cut out shape (a) from front and back of jeans width should be 7 inches (18cm), length 13 inches (33cm)
3. overlap squares onto one side of (a); pin and **hand stitch** to create pockets
4. cut out a piece of cardboard to the same shape as one side of (a) (but make it a wee bit smaller)
5. sandwich cardboard in between (a) as shown
6. **top stitch** (a) closed, fold in raw edges for clean look
7. pin elastic piece on center back and **hand stitch** to either side, as indicated
8. slip onto sun visor in your car for a handy CD holder!

#35

silvia

swing top

You'll need
1 pair of jeans
1 piece of jersey fabric 24 x 24 inches (61 x 61cm)

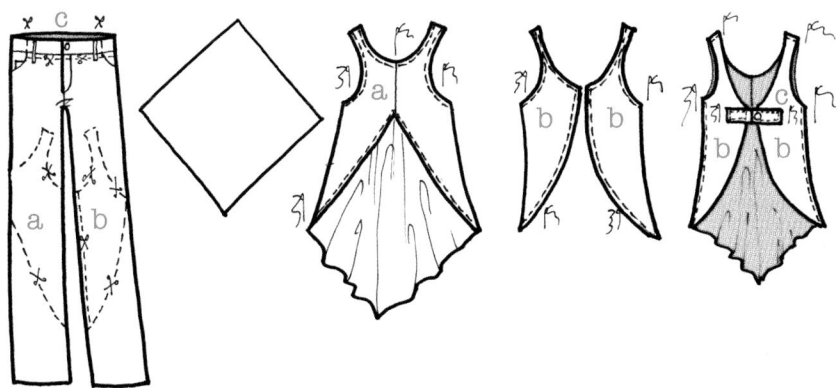

1. cut (a) and (b) out of front and back of jeans [ATTN: (a) and (b) are not the same]; try using the **pattern technique**
2. **flat hem** armholes and neckline
3. insert fabric square into slit of piece (a), pin and sew
4. **roll hem** pieces (b) on indicated edges
5. **clean finish sew** pieces (a) and (b) together on sides and shoulders
6. cut out the front part of waistband of jeans, eliminating belt loops (c)
7. **top stitch** piece (c) onto pieces (b) to use as closure

#36

sara

a-line skirt

You'll need
2 pairs of jeans in contrasting colors

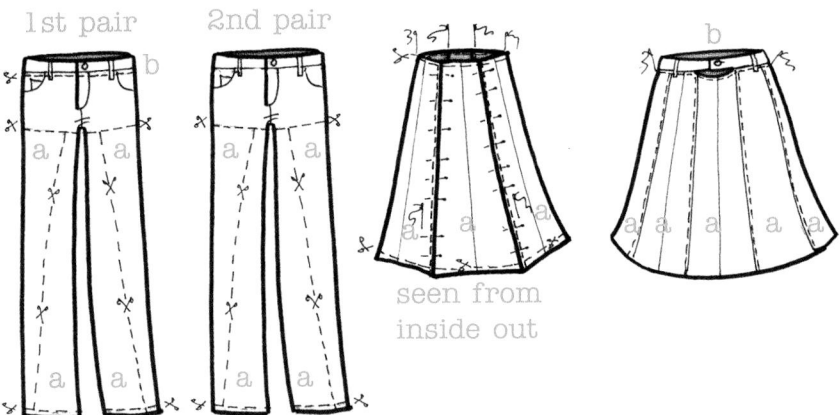

1st pair   2nd pair

seen from
inside out

1. cut legs off both pairs of jeans (a) and eliminate hems
2. cut waistband (b) off 1st pair, leaving seam allowance
3. cut each leg (a) in half on a diagonal, as shown
4. make sure all 8 pieces are the same length, trim if necessary
5. align and pin pieces (a) with thin sides facing upwards, alternating colors (make sure that the thin side of each piece forming the waist circumference corresponds with your measurements)
6. **clean finish sew** pieces (a) together, trim top and bottom evenly to create cone-shaped tube
7. **clean finish sew** waistband (b) onto waist of skirt, leave 2 inches (5cm) unsewn on either side of closure, and **flat hem** remaining raw edge of waist

#37

manuel

gym bag

You'll need
1 pair of jeans or 2 of contrasting colors
2 vintage buttons

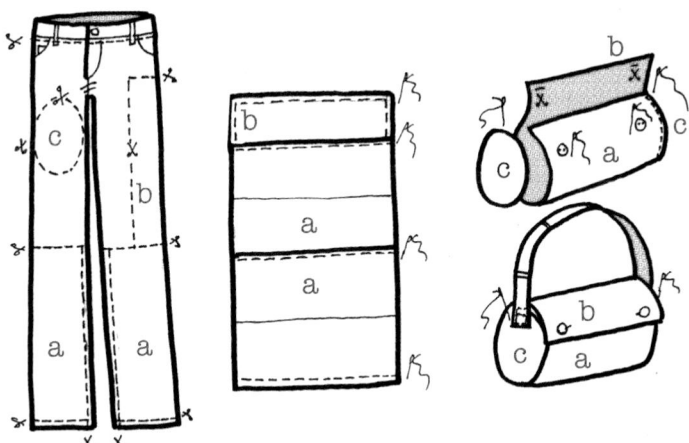

1. cut off jean legs at the knee (a), then cut off hems
2. cut open (a) pieces, eliminating inseams
3. cut out rectangle (b) [should be same length as (a) pieces and 3 1/2 inches (9cm) wide]
4. **clean finish sew** pieces (a) together with piece (b) and **flat hem** 2 short ends
5. cut 2 circles (c), 1 from front, 1 from back [the circumference should be slightly smaller than length of (a)]; add seam allowance
6. **clean finish sew** circular pieces (c) onto either side of (a) to form a closed tube
7. **sew buttons** onto (a), **make eyelets** on (b)
8. cut off waist of jeans (eliminate belt loops) and **top stitch** onto pieces (c) as strap

38

nadine

country vest

You'll need
1 pair of jeans

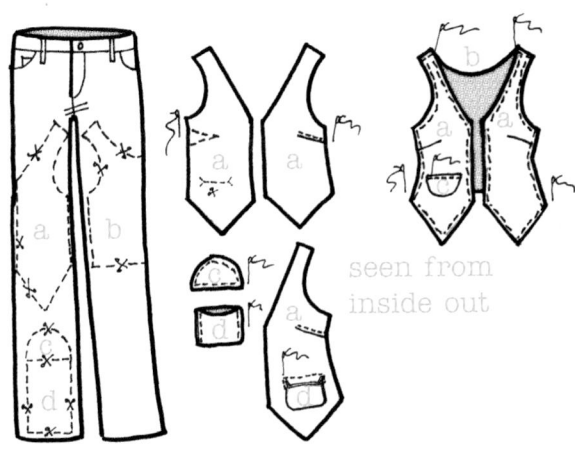

seen from
inside out

1. cut out pieces (a) and piece (b) from front and back, using **pattern** to ensure proper measurements [ATTN: (a) is 2 separate pieces and (b) is one piece]
2. cut out (c) and (d) while you're at it
3. cut and **sew darts** into pieces (a) at chest
4. cut slit in 1 piece (a) for pocket (ATTN: don't make slit too low or your pocket will hang out from bottom of vest—very un-chic!)
5. fold piece (d) in half, **clean finish sew** sides, insert (d) into slit piece (a) and **clean finish sew**
6. **flat hem** piece (c), **top stitch** onto piece (a) as flap for pocket
7. **clean finish sew** pieces (a) and piece (b) together on sides and shoulders, **roll hem** all raw edges

#39

carmen

checkbook

You'll need
1 pair of jeans
1 vintage button
1 piece of fabric 5 × 12 inches (13 × 30cm)

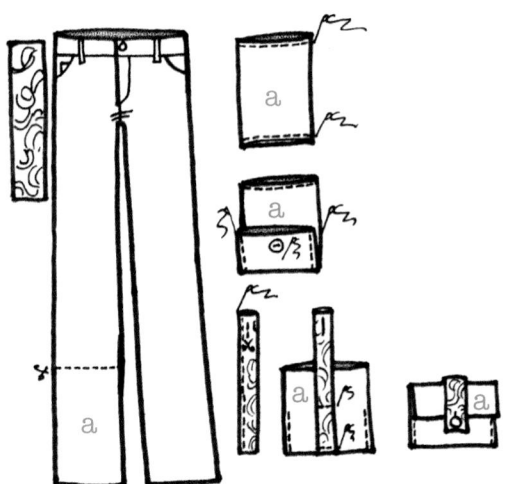

1. cut off bottom third of 1 jean leg (a)
2. **flat hem** around the top of (a) as indicated
3. fold up a third of (a) and sew sides closed (creating double pocket using **top stitch**)
4. fold fabric strip lengthwise and sew it into a tube, then stitch to center bottom and top on backside of piece (a)
5. **make eyelet** on fabric strip and **sew button** to center front of (a) (ATTN: button to be sewn only to outermost pocket)

#40

hiroko

kimono top

You'll need
2 pairs of jeans
1 piece of fabric 4 feet × 1 foot
(4 × 1m)

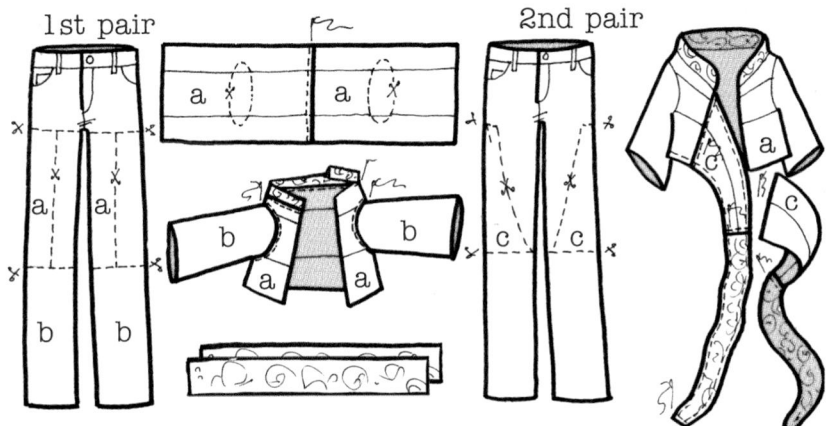

1st pair   2nd pair

1. cut legs off at knees and crotch to create pieces (a) and (b) on 1st pair of jeans
2. cut open pieces (a) in front center, as shown
3. sew pieces (a) together to form a long rectangle
4. cut holes in rectangle (a) for armholes
5. **clean finish sew** sleeves (b) onto holes (a)
6. cut fabric to apt length for collar, add seam allowance
7. fold fabric and sew collar onto edge of rectangle (a) where indicated, using **covered hem technique**
8. cut pieces (c) out of 2nd pair of jeans, front and back
9. **clean finish sew** (c) pieces onto (a) where indicated
10. cut remaining fabric strip into 2, then cut both pieces to the same width as ends of pieces (c)
11. **clean finish sew** each fabric strip onto the end of (c) and **roll hem** edges

#41

cookie

ragdoll

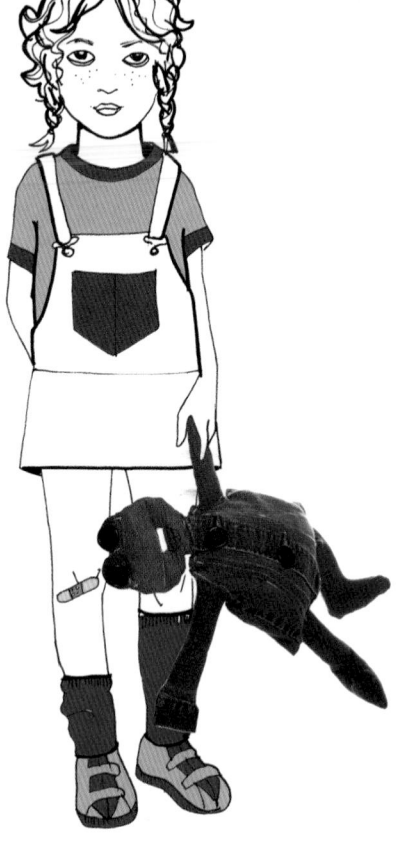

You'll need
1 pair of jeans
4 vintage buttons
1 piece of red fabric 2 × 2 inches (5 × 5 cm)

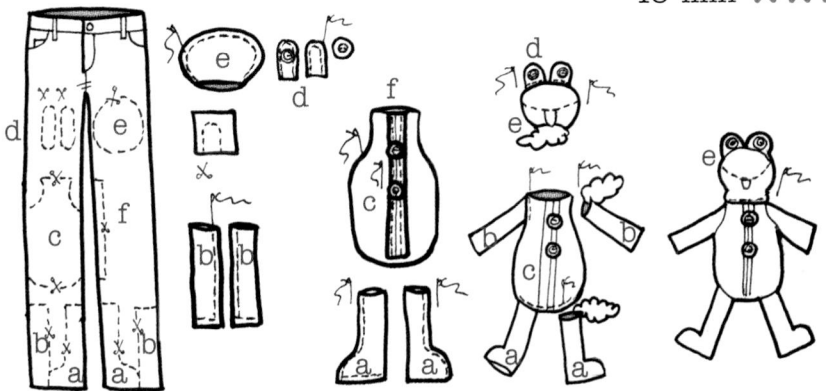

1. cut out pieces (a) through (f) from front and back of jeans as indicated [note that (a), (b), and (f) are connected in front and back]
2. **clean finish sew** (a) pieces closed to create legs and (b) pieces closed to create arms, (e) pieces for head, and (f) for tummy strip
3. **top stitch** strip (f) onto front center of body (c), then **sew 2 buttons** onto the strip
4. now **stuff** all the pieces except (f)
5. pin head, arms, and legs onto body (c) and stitch closed, securing limbs and head into seams
6. cut tongue shape from red fabric, **hand stitch** across head, creating smile while attaching tongue in place
7. fold pieces (d) in half, **hand stitch** closed, **sew buttons** onto them, and **hand stitch** both onto head for eyes, then give him a big hug and watch him come to life!

#42

lauren

head scarf

You'll need
1 pair of jeans or jean scraps

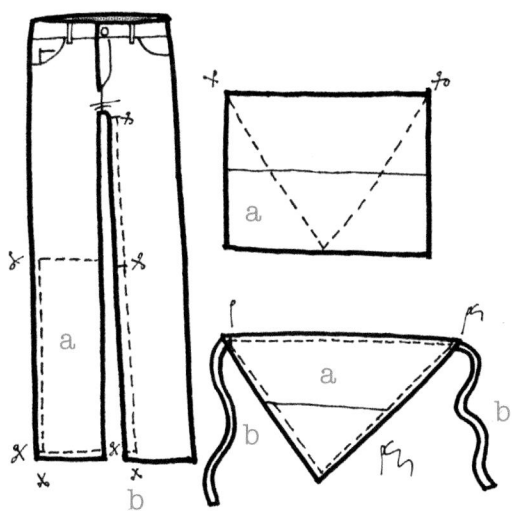

1. cut out rectangle (a) from front and back
2. cut out triangle from (a) as shown, then **roll hem**
3. cut out inseam from other leg, creating long strip (b)
4. cut strip (b) in half
5. **hand stitch** each strip (b) onto opposite corners of triangle (a)

#43

michael

seat cover

You'll need
1 pair of jeans
1 chair

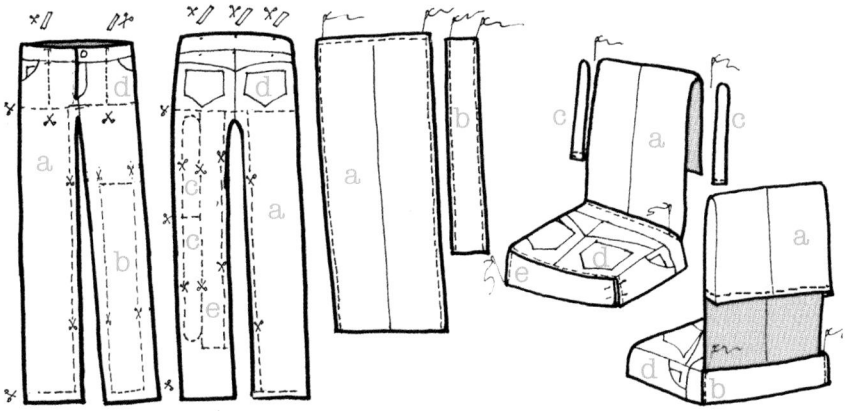

1. place backside of jeans over seat of chair to ensure that they are large enough for this project
2. cut off left leg at crotch (a), eliminating hem and inseam
3. cut strip (b) from front of right leg as shown
4. cut off 2 strips (c) from back of right leg, rounding 1 edge of each strip as shown
5. **flat hem** 1 short and 2 long sides of (a), 2 long sides of strip (b), and flat, short sides of strips (c)
6. cut out crotch from piece (d) and eliminate belt loops
7. **clean finish sew** piece (a) onto back of (d) as shown
8. pin and **clean finish sew** strip (e) to piece (d) as shown
9. fold piece (a) as shown, and sew strips (c) onto it with rounded end in fold
10. sew piece (b) onto sides of (e)

#44

zachary

ipod case

You'll need
1 pair of jeans with a 5th pocket
1 piece of velcro 2 inches (5 cm) long
1 ipod

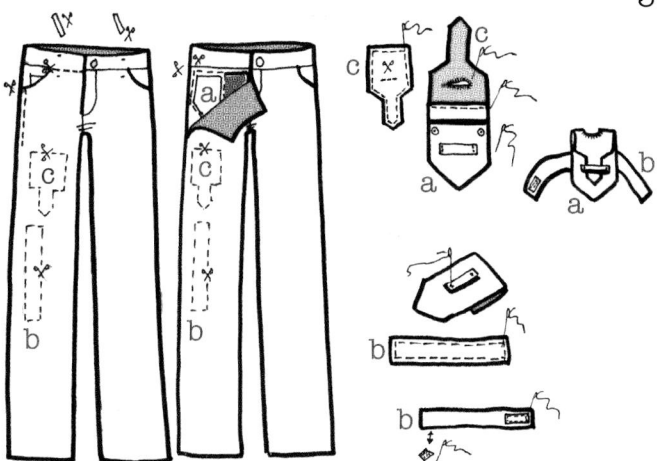

1. cut inner front pocket out in indicated shape (just under waistband) (a)
2. cut 1 strip (b) long enough to wrap around your arm, plus 2 inches (5cm) of margin
3. cut out shape (c) for flap, the width should be equal to the width of (a) plus seam allowance
4. **flat hem** piece (c) and **make eyelet** where indicated
5. sew flap (c) onto pocket (a) where indicated
6. unstitch 2 belt loops, **hand stitch** 1 onto front center of (a) and the other onto back of (a) (ATTN: don't sew pocket closed!)
7. **flat hem** strip (b), then sew velcro on front of 1 end and back of other as shown
8. thread strip (b) through back belt loop

#45

teresa

poncho

You'll need
1 pair of jeans
1 piece of fabric 3 feet × 1 foot
(1 x 3m)

1. **flat hem** 1 long side of fabric strip
2. eliminate hems of jeans, then cut off inseams, creating strips (a)
3. cut off legs at knee, then at crotch, creating pieces (b)
4. cut out strips (c) from front legs
5. cut off waistband (d) below belt loops
6. **clean finish sew** pieces (b) together on 1 long side
7. sew strips (c) onto short sides of piece (b) using **covered hem technique**, then **roll hem** bottom edge
8. sew waistband to top of piece (b) and (c)
9. **top stitch** strips (a) to poncho for closure
10. **top stitch** 3 sides of fabric strip to inside of (b) just below waistband for lining (fold in raw edges)
11. **hand stitch** 5 stitches onto bottom of fabric to keep in place

miriam

wraparound
skirt

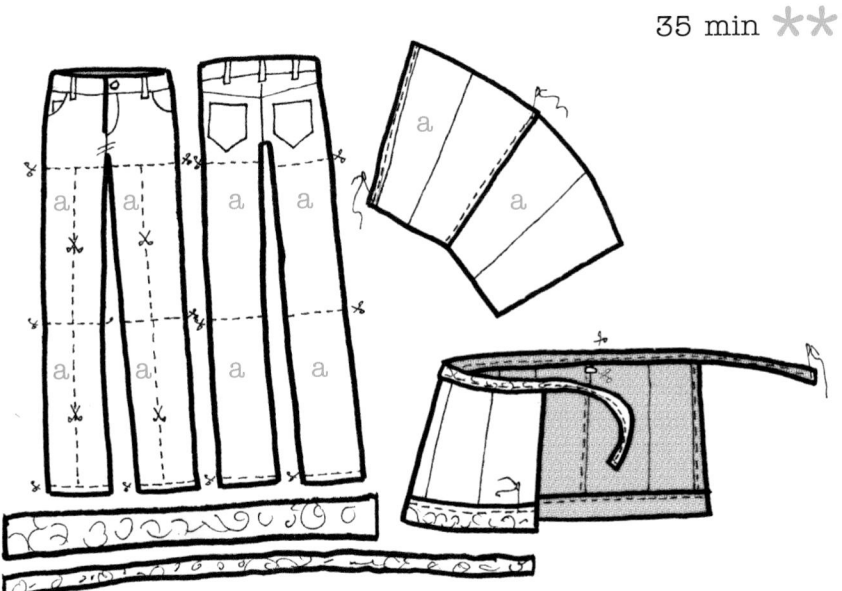

1. cut open center front on each leg and eliminate hems
2. cut legs in 2, creating 4 equally sized rectangles (a)
3. **clean finish sew** long edges of rectangles (a) together as shown, and **roll hem** both of the shorter sides
4. sew long, thin strip of fabric onto top edge of piece (a), using **covered hem technique**, finishing the ends with **rolled hem**
5. sew wider strip of fabric onto bottom edge of piece (a), using **covered hem technique**
6. **make an eyelet** where indicated to pass fabric strip for the tie

#47

arthur

reversible tie

You'll need
1 pair of jeans
1 strip of fabric
   30 × 12 inches (76 × 30cm)
1 tie of dimensions you like

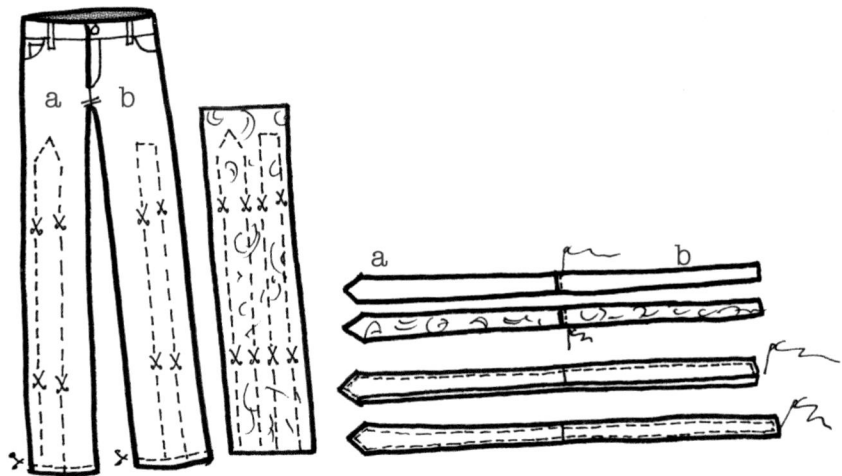

1. cut hems off jeans
2. cut tie form out of jeans—**use pattern technique** (pin original tie onto jeans and cut around, adding seam allowance)
3. use same technique to cut out same shape from fabric
4. **clean finish sew** (a) and (b) together
5. repeat step 4 with the fabric
6. place denim tie onto fabric tie inside out, and **clean finish sew** along 1 side as shown
7. turn right side out and **top stitch** around all edges, folding in raw edges

#48

diana

potholder

You'll need
1 pair of jeans

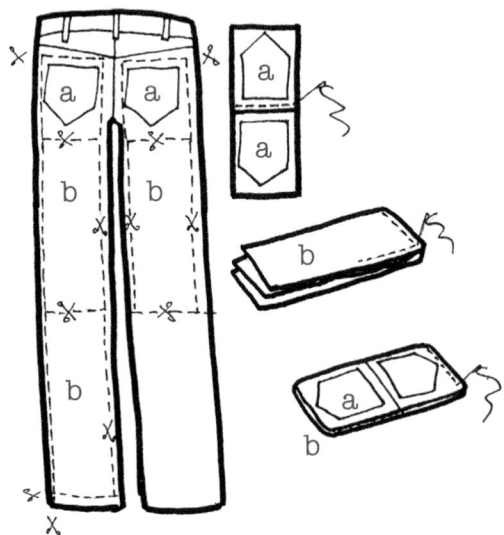

1. cut out square pieces (a) around back pockets as shown
2. **clean finish sew** pieces (a) together with pocket openings parallel (as indicated)
3. cut out 3 rectangles (b) with the same dimensions as the rectangle created with pieces (a)
4. place rectangles (b) 1 on top of the other and **top stitch** them together around the edge
5. stitch pockets onto pieces (b), folding in edges as you sew for a clean look

#49

noa

baby dress

You'll need
1 pair of jeans
2 fabric strips 3 × 7 inches
  (7.5 × 18 cm)
1 fabric strip 4 × 16 inches
  (10 × 41 cm)

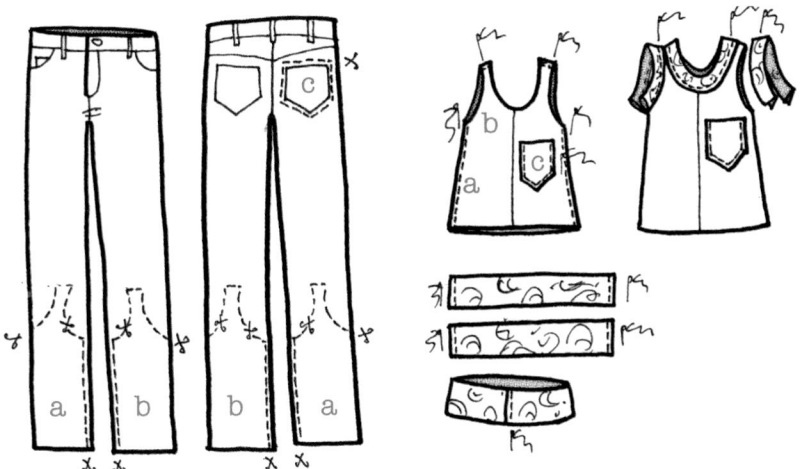

1. cut out pieces (a) and (b) in front and back, using **pattern technique** for precise measurements
2. fold 2 short strips lengthwise and **roll hem** them at each end
3. fold long strip lengthwise and sew into band as shown
4. cut out back pocket (c), leaving seam allowance
5. sew pocket onto (a) (ATTN: don't sew pocket closed!)
6. **clean finish sew** sides and shoulders of (a) and (b) together
7. sew band onto neckline and short strips onto armholes, using **covered hem technique**

#50

dagmar

hanger cover

You'll need
1 pair of jeans
4 wire coat hangers

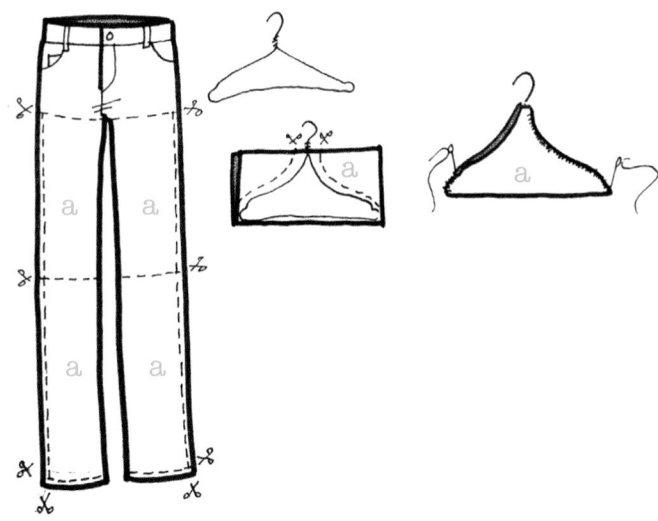

1. cut off hems and side seams
2. cut legs off at knee, then cut them off at crotch (each piece should have the same dimensions)
3. place a hanger onto (a), and, leaving (a) folded at the seam, cut out around hanger, adding seam allowance
4. place hanger into (a) and **blanket stitch** around the hanger as shown
5. with 1 pair of jeans, you can make 4 hanger sleeves!

51

janice

bracelet

You'll need
1 pair of jeans
1 quart water bottle
vintage buttons

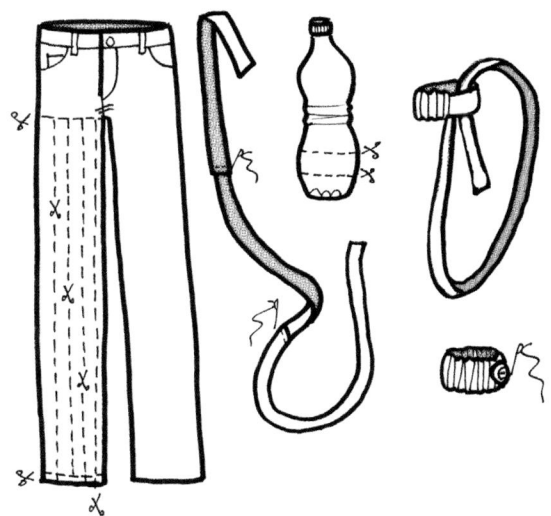

1. eliminate hem, then cut strips from jeans
2. **clean finish sew** strips together
3. cut ring out of water bottle all around as indicated
4. wrap superlong strip around piece of water bottle until it is entirely covered in jean fabric
5. **hand stitch** ends of jean strip in place and **sew on buttons** where desired
6. you can use the same water bottle and jeans to make bracelets for all your friends!

#52

gladys

shorts with tie waist

You'll need
1 pair of jeans
1 piece of jersey fabric 6 feet x 1 foot
(2 x .3m)

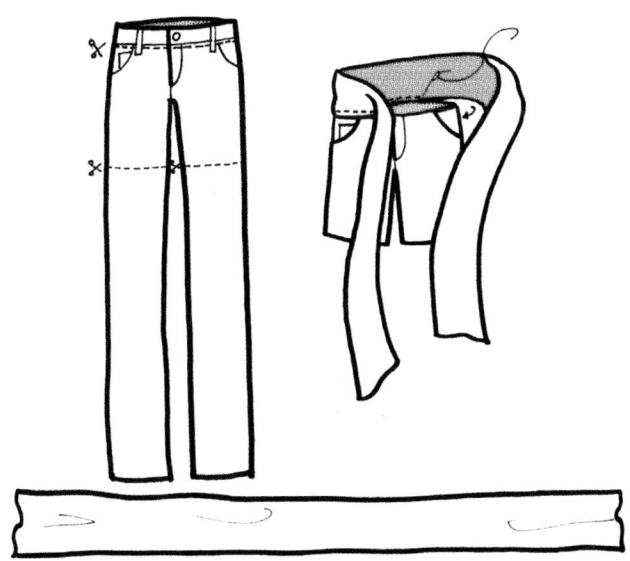

1. cut off legs at thighs (allow enough length to be able to roll up afterwards)
2. cut off waistband, including belt loops
3. **clean finish sew** fabric around waist as shown (ATTN: don't sew fly closed)
4. roll up legs of shorts, tie fabric into knot or bow, and hit the beach!

53

jackie

jumpsuit

You'll need
2 pairs of jeans

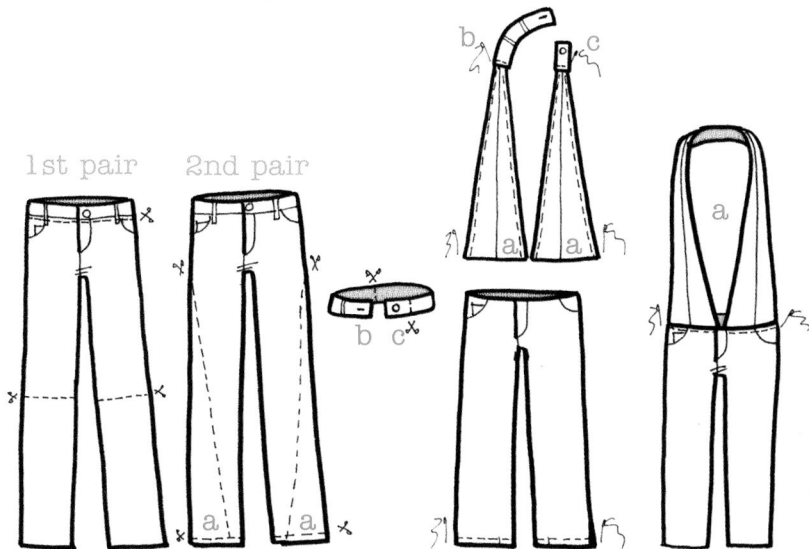

1. cut off legs at knee and waistband on 1st pair of jeans
2. cut off hems on 2nd pair
3. cut diagonal lines across jeans at thigh from side seam to 1 inch (2.5cm) from inseam at hem on front and back, creating 2 long thin triangles (a)
4. **flat hem** pieces (a) on long sides
5. cut off pieces (b) and (c) from waistband as shown
6. **clean finish sew** (b) onto 1 piece (a) and (c) onto the other piece (a) as closure for halter
7. **clean finish sew** pieces (a) onto waist of 1st pair
8. hem bottom using **rolled hem technique**

#54

vivian

bustier vest

You'll need
1 pair of jeans

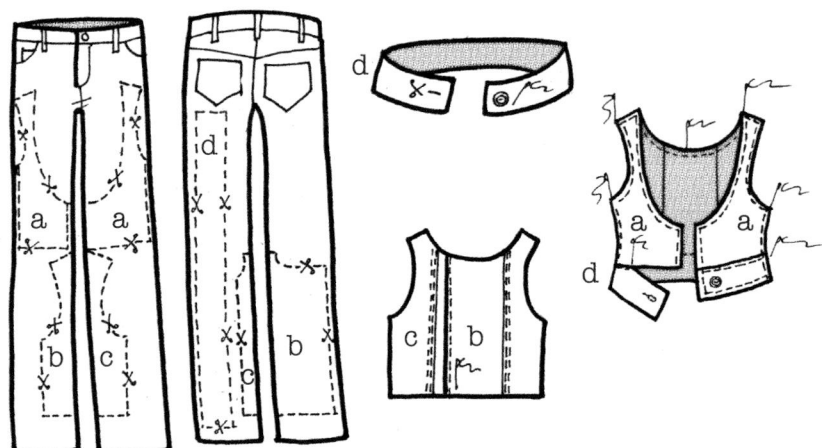

1. cut shapes (a) from front of jeans using **pattern technique**
2. cut out pieces (b) and (c) from front and back, making sure that the outer sides of (a), (b), and (c) are of equal length and that the height of the armholes are equal on all 4 pieces
3. **clean finish sew** piece (b) and piece (c) together as shown
4. cut out long strip (d) about 3 inches (7.5cm) wide
5. **clean finish sew** pieces (a) and (b) together on shoulders and sides
6. **roll hem** bottom edges of (d) and **clean finish sew** onto bottom of vest all around
7. **sew button** and **make eyelet** on strip (d)

#55

anka

hip bag

You'll need
1 pair of jeans

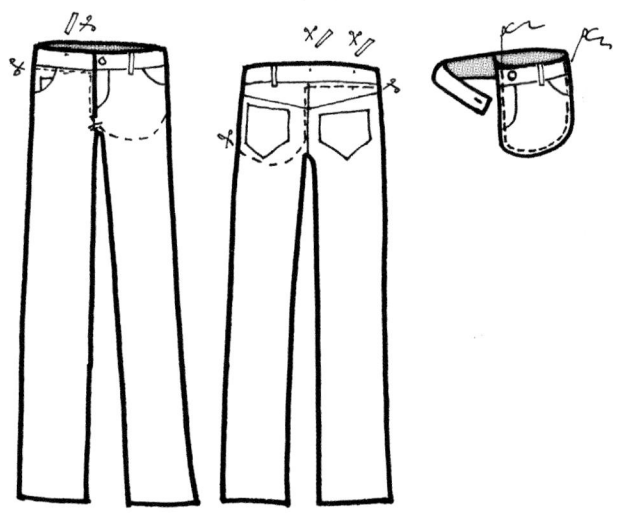

1. cut out half of waistband (the half with the button-hole)
2. cut down around button fly/zipper and cut rounded edge from crotch to outer seam in front and back (you should end up with 1 single piece resembling the finished product)
3. **clean finish sew** around all edges except, of course, the top

56

jordan

sundress

You'll need
2 pairs of jeans
elastic strip 5 feet × 1 inch (1.5 m × 2.5 cm)

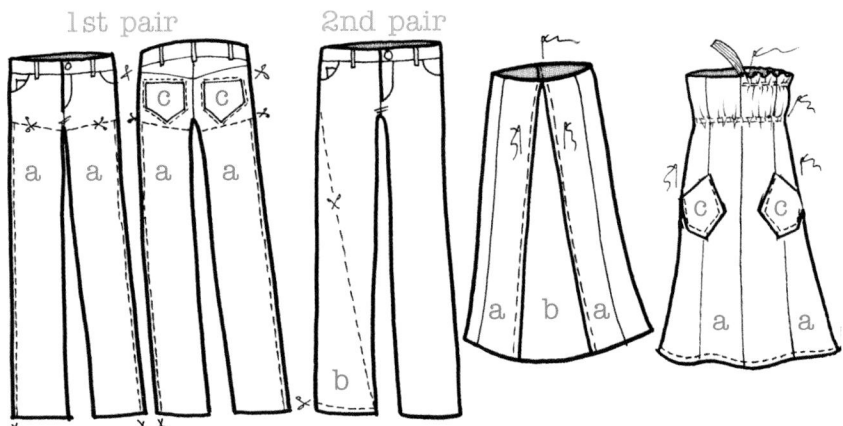

1. cut legs off of 1st pair of jeans below crotch in slightly diagonal line (a) as shown
2. cut out pockets (including seam allowance) from back of 1st pair (c)
3. cut off hem of left leg of 2nd pair of jeans, then cut a diagonal line from thigh at side seam to inseam on front and back of same jeans, creating a long thin triangle (b)
4. sew pieces (a) together with (b), making sure tip of triangle (b) and original hemmed edges are at the top
5. sew elastic onto top edge and under bust on the inside, using **gathering with elastic technique**
6. sew pockets (c) onto front where indicated
7. **roll hem** bottom of dress

#57

jan

apron

You'll need
1 pair of jeans

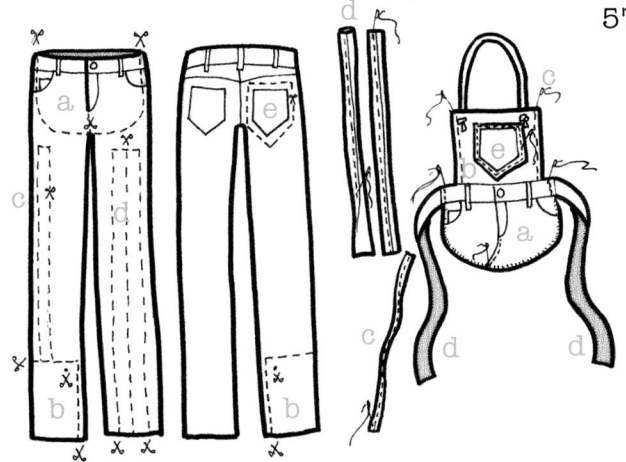

1. cut out piece (a) (ATTN: do not cut open pockets' lining), then cut and **flatten crotch**
2. cut rectangle from left leg front and back (b)
3. cut out strip from left leg (c) then **flat hem**
4. cut out 2 long strips from other leg (d) and **flat hem** strips
5. cut out back pocket (e), leaving seam allowance
6. **clean finish sew** (b) onto waistband in front and **roll hem**
7. **top stitch** pocket (e) onto (b) in center, folding in raw edges
8. **clean finish sew** strips (d) onto sides of waistband
9. hem raw edge of (a) using **blanket stitch**
10. pierce 2 holes in (b) in top corners as shown
11. thread strip (c) into holes of (a) and tie knots to keep in place

#58

liv

livin' large
pants

You'll need
2 pair of jeans
1 piece of fabric 36 x 8 inches (91 x 20cm)

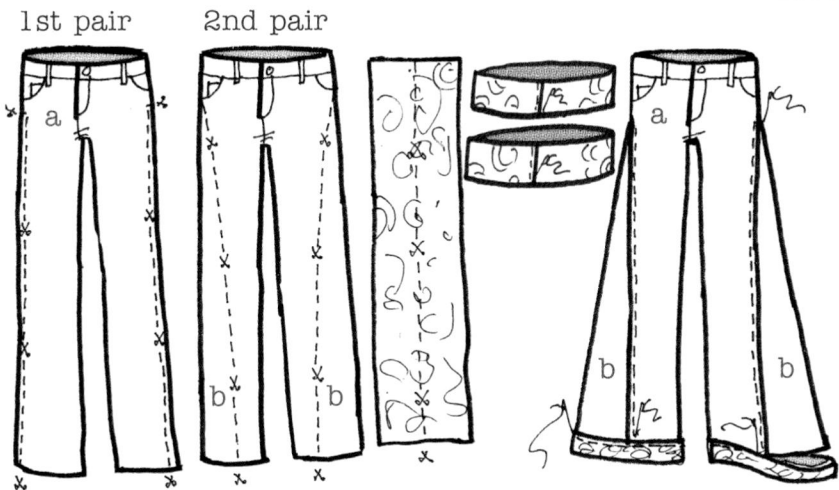

1st pair   2nd pair

1. cut off side seams of 1st pair of jeans from bottom to 2 inches (5cm) from front pockets (a)
2. cut diagonally from hip at side seam to center bottom in front and back of 2nd pair of jeans (b)
3. insert 2 long triangles (b) into long slits created on 1st pair (a), **pin and clean finish sew,** then refinish with **top stitch**
4. trim new jean bottom edge to even out (if necessary)
5. cut fabric strip in half lengthwise and **clean finish sew** into 2 bands, making sure circumference is equal to bottom of jean legs
6. sew fabric strip onto each leg at bottom using **covered hem technique**

#59

amy

a-line top

You'll need
1 pair of jeans

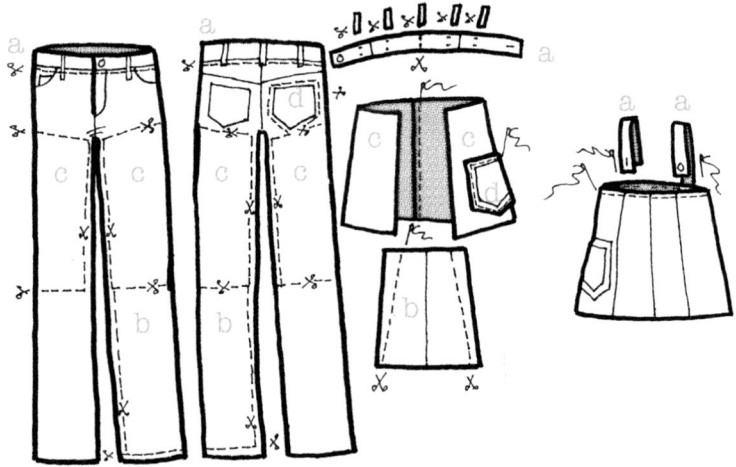

1. cut off waistband, eliminate belt loops, cut (a) in half
2. cut off both legs at knee, eliminate hem and inseam of 1 leg, creating piece (b)
3. cut legs off on a slight diagonal at crotch (eliminate inseams), creating pieces (c)
4. cut out back pocket (d), leaving seam allowance
5. **clean finish sew** pieces (c) together as shown
6. **top stitch** pocket (d) to piece (c), folding in raw edges
7. cut (b) as indicated (make it the right size for you, considering that this will be the width of your top)
8. **clean finish sew** piece (b) in between pieces (c) to create tube, **roll hem**
9. **top stitch** on pieces (a) as shoulder straps

#60

audrey

skirt with appliqués

You'll need
1 pair of jeans
we recommend using scraps from
other projects of contrasting colors
for flower appliqués

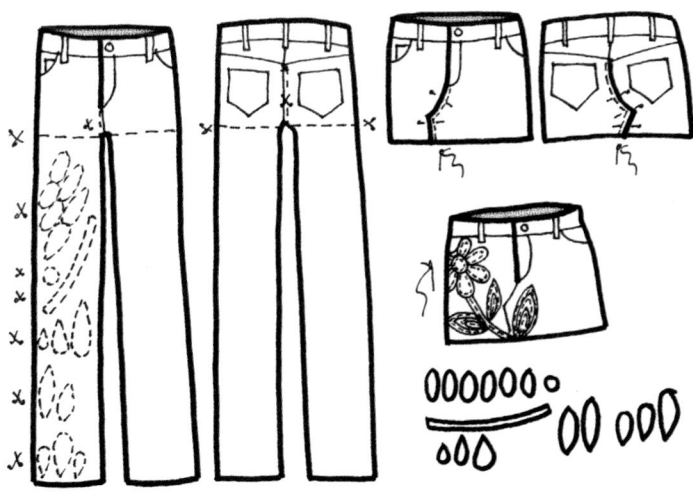

1. cut legs off at crotch and **flatten crotch**
2. cut out pieces indicated for petals, leaves, and stems of flower, making sure the dimensions are right for your miniskirt
3. pin down flower pieces in place and **hand stitch** onto skirt (ATTN: don't sew front pockets closed)

#61

natasha

bolero

You'll need
1 pair of jeans
1 piece of fabric 6 feet x 3 inches (2m x 7.5 cm)

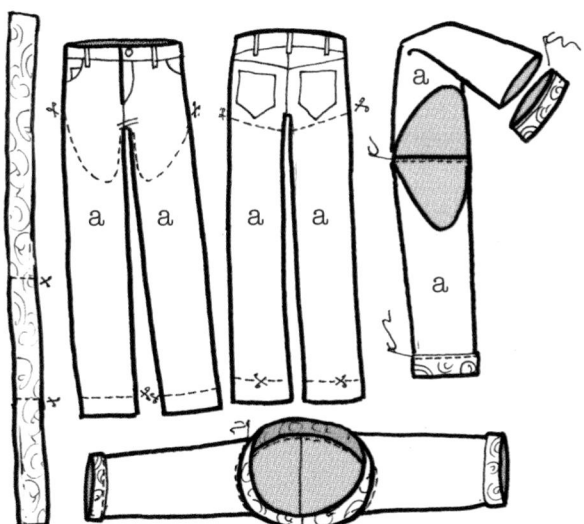

1. cut off legs of jeans at very bottom (how much depends on your arm length)
2. cut odd U shape in front of both legs, cut straight across both legs in back as shown to create piece (a)
3. **clean finish sew** both legs together at flat edges where shown
4. cut fabric into 3 strips, 1 for body opening and 2 for sleeve openings
5. sew strips onto their respective openings using **covered hem technique**

#62

venus

tennis dress

You'll need
1 pair of jeans
1 piece of fabric 4 feet x 4 inches (1.2m x 10cm)

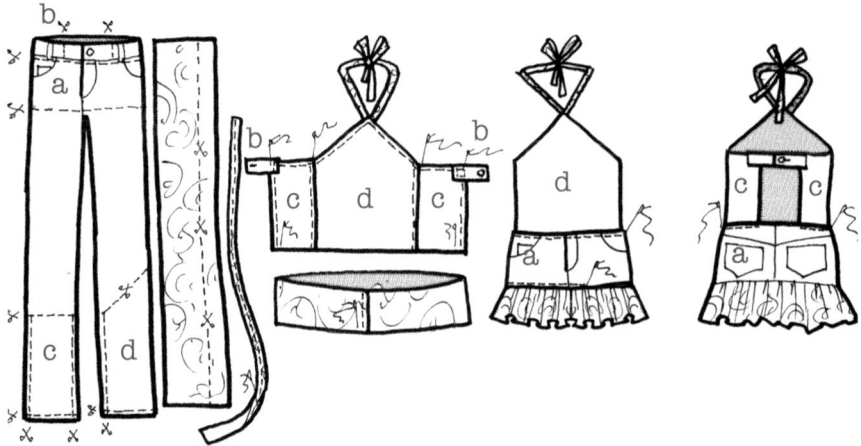

1. cut legs off above crotch (a) and eliminate waistband
2. cut out waistband pieces (b) where indicated
3. cut out 2 rectangles (c) from 1 leg in front and back
4. cut out shape (d) from other leg, front and back
5. cut thin strip—1 inch (2.5cm) wide—from fabric, **roll hem**
6. **hand stitch** strip to top corner of (d) to create halter
7. **clean finish sew** pieces (c) onto either side of (d), **flat hem** edges
8. **top stitch pieces** (b) onto pieces (c) on top corners as indicated (to create closure)
9. **clean finish sew** thick strip (a) into band and **gather**
10. **clean finish sew** pieces (c) and (d), onto (a)
11. sew gathered band onto bottom of (a)

#63

leah

sporty pants

You'll need
1 pair of large jeans
1 piece of jersey
3 x 3 1/2 (91 x 107 cm)

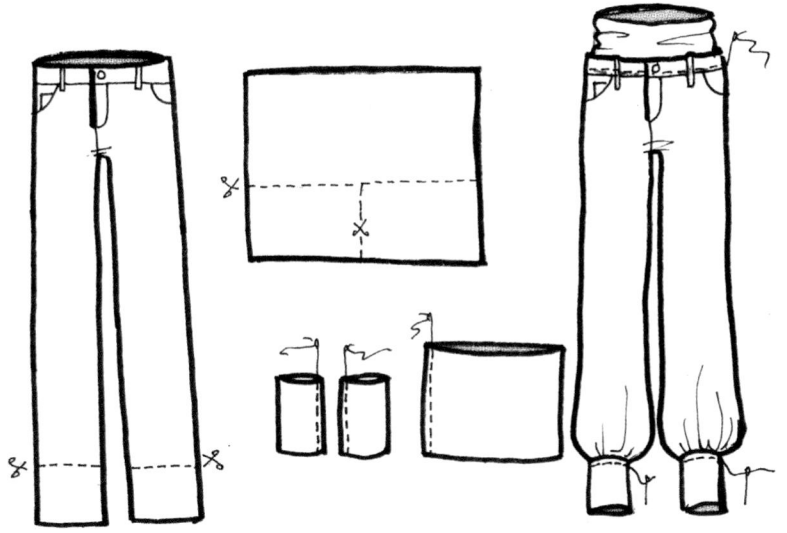

1. cut legs off just above ankles
2. cut fabric into 3 pieces as indicated, 2 pieces at 15 x 21 inches (38 x 53cm), and 1 piece at 17 x 42 inches (43 x 107cm)
3. **clean finish sew** each piece of fabric into a tube
4. sew big tube onto inside of jeans at waistband
5. **clean finish sew** smaller tubes onto bottom of jeans using **gathering techniques**

#64

gustav

banana bag

You'll need
1 pair of jeans

24 min ✹✹

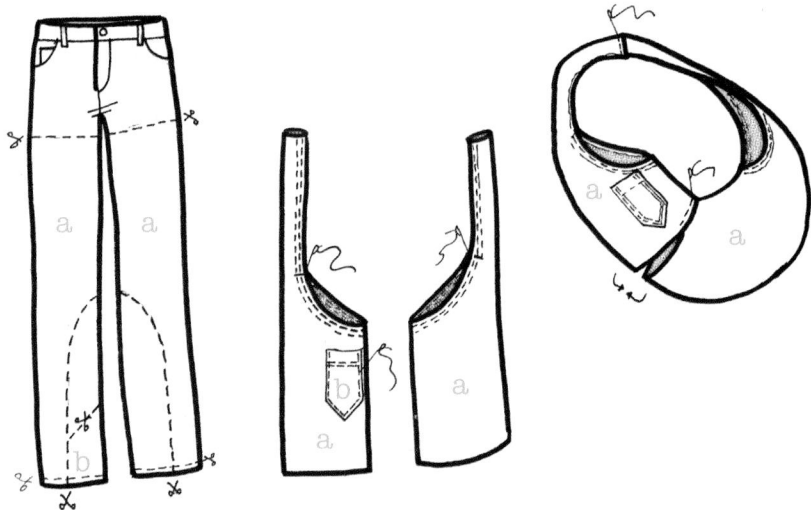

1. cut legs off below crotch
2. cut off hems and cut half U shape from inner seam to bottom of both legs in front and back to create pieces (a)
3. **flat hem** curved edges of pieces (a)
4. cut out piece (b) to create pocket
5. **top stitch** pocket (b) onto 1 of the (a) pieces where shown, folding in raw edges
6. connect pieces (a) by **clean finish sewing** bottom edges together
7. **clean finish sew** top of pieces (a) together, creating strap

#65
toby

sun hat

You'll need
1 pair of jeans
2¹/2 feet (76cm) of wire

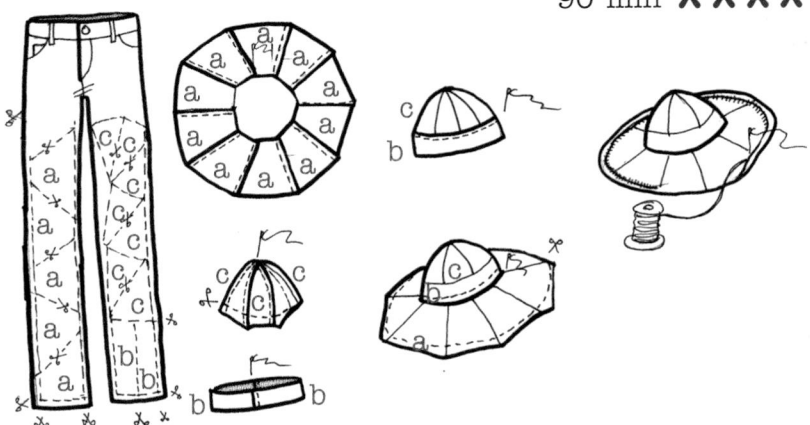

1. cut out 10 triangular shapes (a) from front and back of left leg, avoiding hem
2. cut 2 strips (b) from bottom of right leg (avoid hem)
3. cut out 7 triangular shapes (c) from front of right leg
4. **clean finish sew** triangles (a) together, creating a circle with a hole in the center
5. measure your head, and trim hole in (a) accordingly
6. pin pieces (c) together to form a bowl shape, try it on, modify if needed, **clean finish sew,** and even edge
7. **clean finish sew** pieces (b) into band; the circumference should equal width of hole in (a)
8. **clean finish sew** edge of (c) to band (b) and **clean finish sew** to hole in piece (a)
9. **roll hem** the brim, while inserting wire into hem, then fasten wire and **top stitch** closed

#66 matteo

jean masterpiece

You'll need
1 pair of jeans
1 canvas or wooden frame
hammer and pictureframe nails

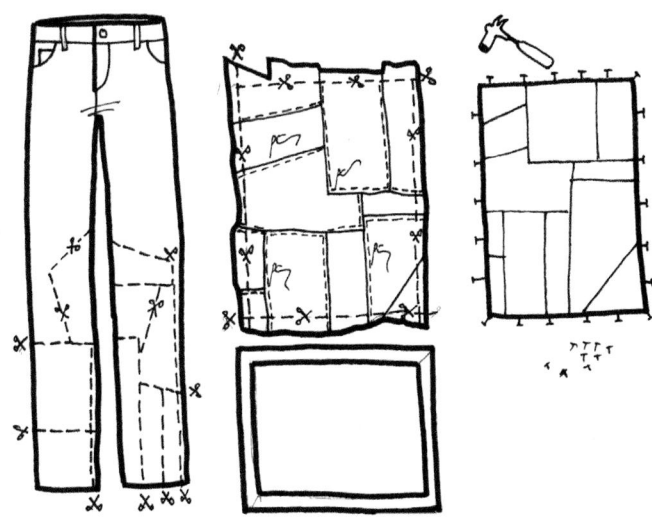

1. cut out jeans or jean scraps into desired shapes
2. **pin and sew** shapes together and make **patchwork** (ATTN: make sure the dimension is at least 1 inch [2.5cm] larger than your frame on each side)
3. fold edges over sides of frame and nail down as shown
4. hang it on the wall and marvel at your own artistic capacity!

#67

alison

midnight mask

You'll need
1 pair of jeans
cotton for stuffing
2 feet (61cm) of ribbon

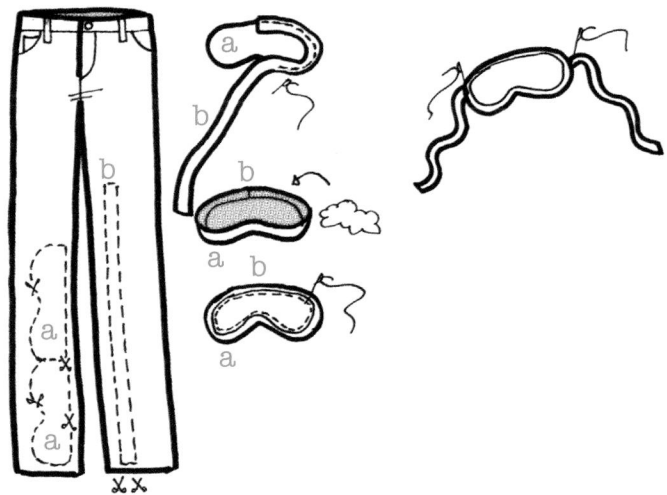

1. cut out indicated shapes from front of left leg (a)
2. cut out half-inch (1.3cm) wide strip (b) from other leg, avoiding hem
3. pin strip (b) around 1 piece (a), then **clean finish sew**
4. place a thin layer of cotton onto same (a) piece
5. **hand stitch** other piece (a) onto strip (b), folding in raw edges
6. stitch ribbons onto each side—and hit the sack!

#68

martina

bowbelt

You'll need
1 pair of jeans
1 vintage button

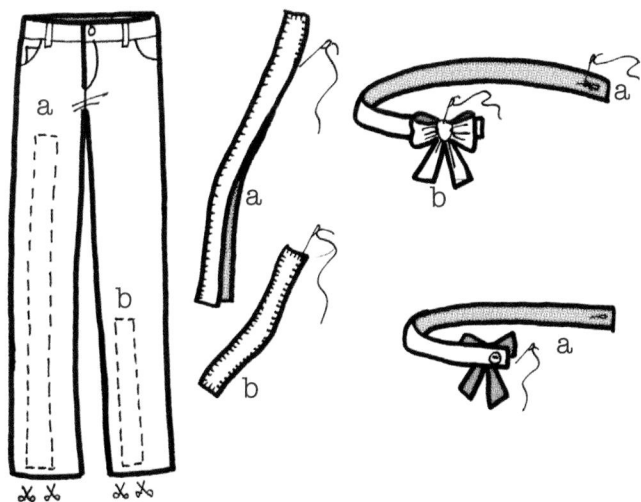

1. cut 2 strips 2 inches (5cm) wide, 1 in front and 1 in back (a), 2 inches (5cm) longer than the circumference of your waist
2. cut 2 strips (long enough to tie a bow) 2 inches wide (5cm), 1 in front and 1 in back (b)
3. **blanket stitch** 2 long strips (a) together around edges
4. **blanket stitch** 2 short strips (b) together around edges
5. make shorter strip into bow and **hand stitch** onto end of long strip
6. **sew button** on the inside of one end of (a) and **make eyelet** on opposite side

#69
shia

doggie bone

You'll need
1 pair of jeans
1 dog

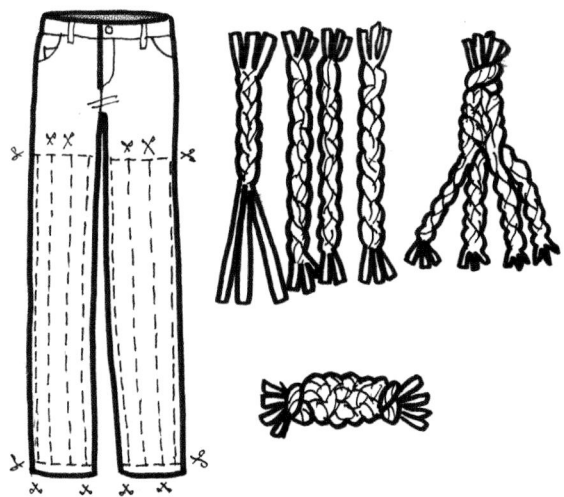

1. cut 3 strips into each leg on front and back (12 strips in all)
2. take 12 strips and make 4 braids
3. knot all 4 braids together and make into 1 thick braid
4. make a knot on the other end and call your dog!

70

duane

guitar case

You'll need
1 big pair of jeans
1 belt
1 guitar

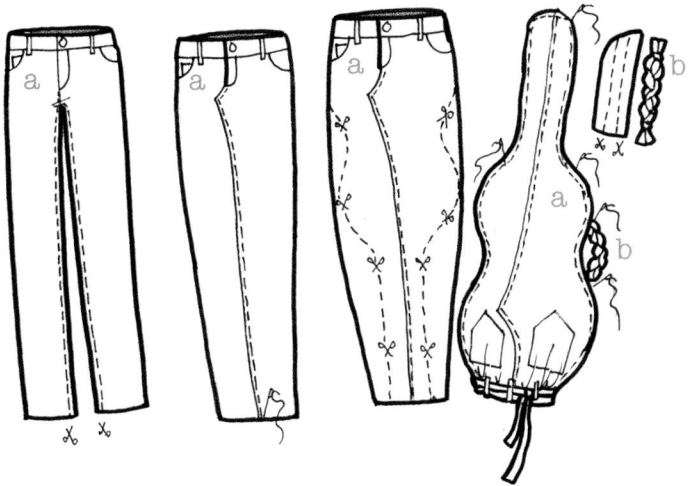

1. cut out inseams and **flatten crotch** (a) in front and back
2. cut shape indicated out of jeans (a) (place guitar into jeans and mark precise form—don't forget to add seam allowance)
3. use scraps to cut 3 strips, braid them, and **hand stitch** on as handle (b)
4. **clean finish sew** sides closed, tighten
5. take inseams and thread them through belt loops, tighten for closure

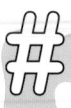

#71
andrew

stuffed visor

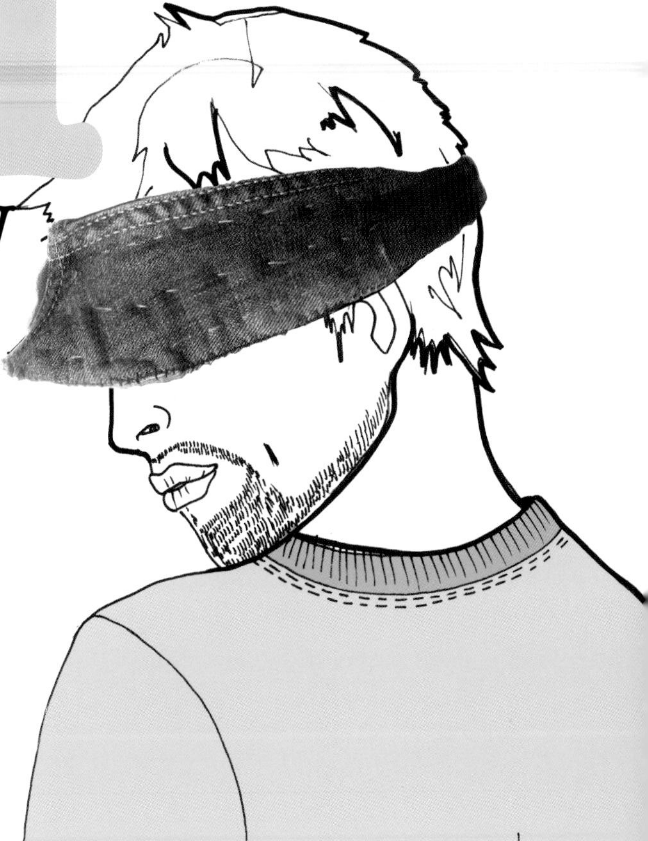

You'll need
1 pair of jeans
cotton stuffing

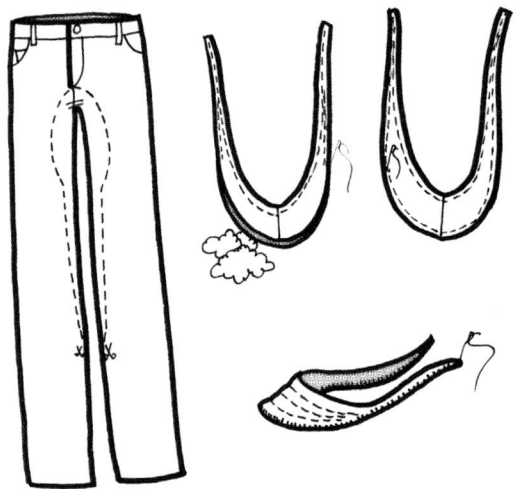

1. cut out shape from crotch as indicated, in front and back
2. place thin layer of stuffing in between flaps and **top stitch,** folding in raw edges
3. **top stitch** several lines in the bill of the visor to keep the cotton in place, using **stuff and quilt technique**
4. **blanket stitch** around edge of visor
5. tie in back

#72

ellie

pencil skirt

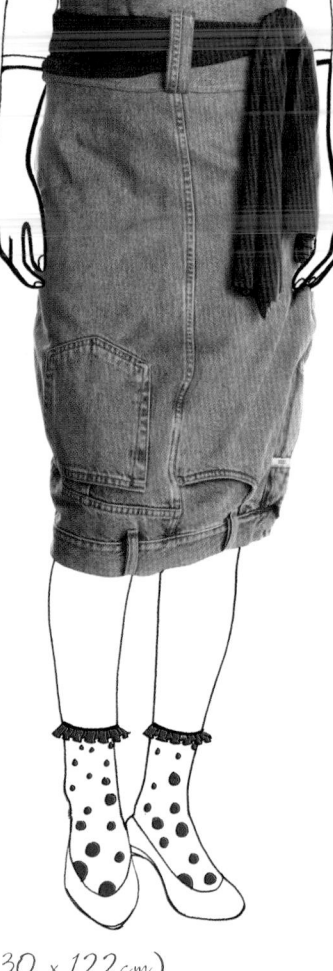

You'll need
1 pair of jeans
1 piece of jersey fabric 12 x 48 inches (30 x 122cm)

side view

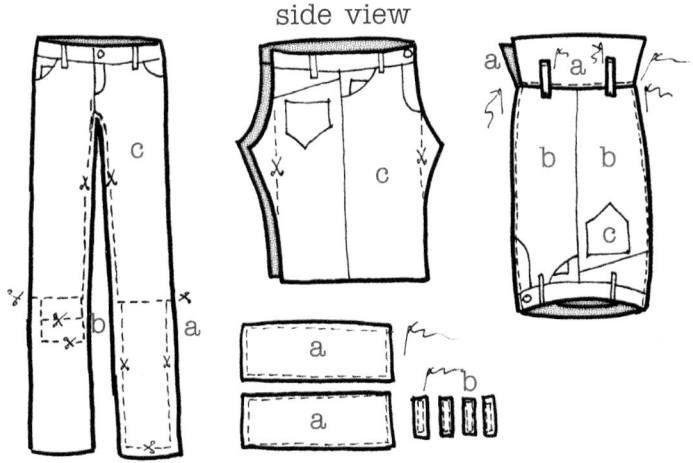

1. cut legs off at knees, cut out pieces (a), front and back
2. cut 4 small rectangles (b) from bottom of left leg, front and back, and **roll hem** each piece on all sides
3. eliminate inseams on (c) and cut open crotch as shown
4. fold piece (c) so that side seams are front and center as shown, and cut off protruding crotch pieces
5. **clean finish sew** piece (c) closed on both sides and flip upside down
6. **flat hem** all sides of both pieces (a)
7. **clean finish sew** (a) pieces onto (c) as shown
8. **top stitch** pieces (b), for belt loops where indicated, 2 on front and 2 on back
9. use fabric strip as belt, thread through belt loops, tie, and go!

#73

christina

shorts with
suspenders

You'll need
1 pair of jeans
1 piece of fabric 48 × 3 inches (122 × 7.5 cm)
2 vintage buttons
elastic 18 inches × 1 inch (46 × 2.5 cm)

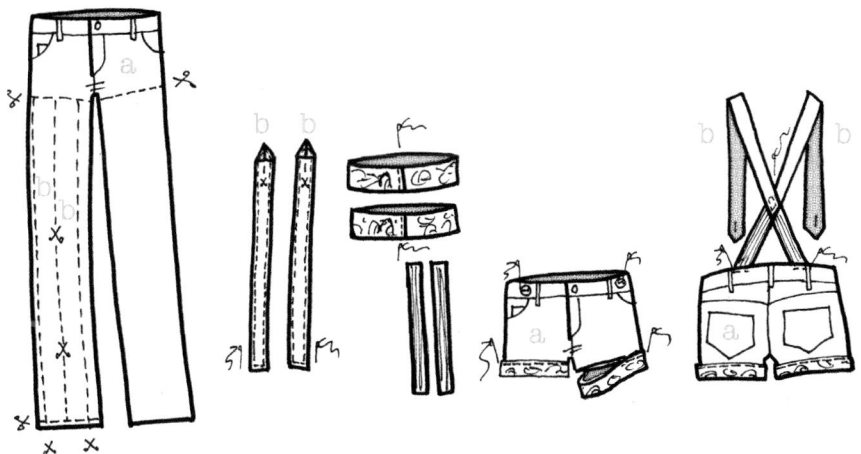

1. cut legs off below crotch (a)
2. eliminate hem on 1 leg, then cut out 2 long strips (b) 1.5 inches (4cm) wide
3. **flat hem** strips (b), then fold 1 end of each strip into triangle; **top stitch** in place
4. **make eyelets** on triangular edge of strips (b)
5. **clean finish sew** fabric into bands (the circumference should equal that of a leg)
6. **clean finish sew** fabric to shorts using **covered hem technique**
7. **top stitch** elastic onto inside of waistband and onto end of strips (b), crossing them as indicated
8. **sew buttons** onto waistband where indicated

#74

hattie

headband

You'll need
1 pair of jeans
   or jean scraps
1 headband
fabric or hot glue

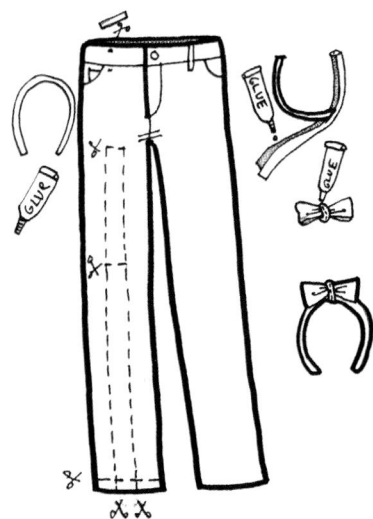

1. eliminate hem and cut 2 strips (1 long enough to completely cover your headband, and 1 long enough to make a bow)
2. fold long strip around edges of headband and glue in place
3. unstitch 1 belt loop
4. make a bow with short strip, using belt loop to cover the knot of bow, and glue belt loop in place
5. slip bow onto headband

#75

matt

bathroom mat

You'll need
1 pair of jeans
much much patience

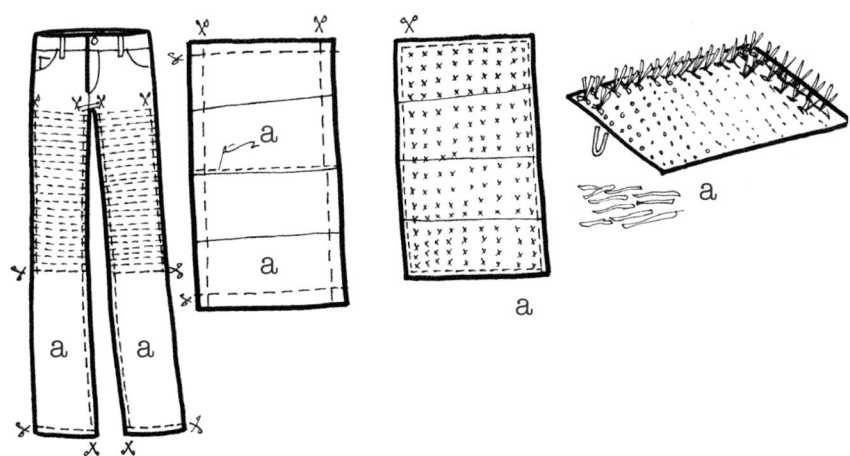

1. cut off legs at knee
2. eliminate inseams
3. **clean finish sew** pieces (a) together as shown
4. cut into proper square shape, **roll hem** all 4 sides
5. cut thin strips—6 inches long x .5 inch wide (15 x 1.3cm)—from remaining part of jeans in front and back
6. pierce piece (a) with holes where indicated by X, 1 inch (2.5cm) apart (remember: you need 2 holes per strip)
7. thread each strip into 1 hole and out the next, then tie a knot
8. repeat and repeat and repeat—you get the point!

76

jennifer

super tight jeans

You'll need
1 pair of jeans that you would like tighter in the legs

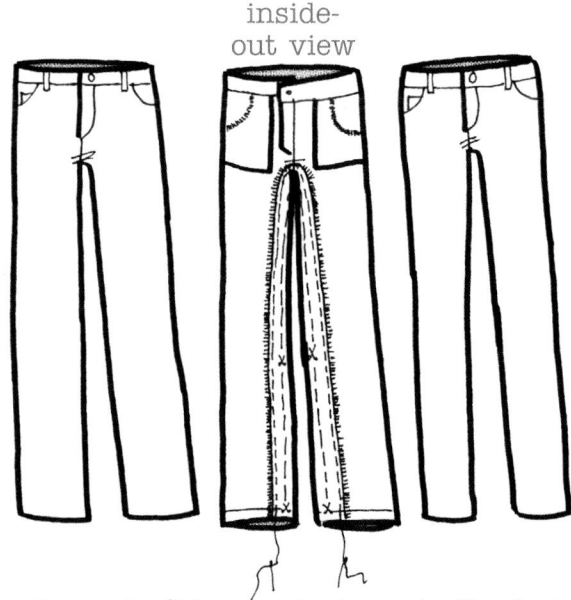

inside-
out view

1. try on jeans to figure out where in the legs they need to be tightened
2. turn jeans inside out and put them back on
3. pin jeans down the inside of each leg to the correct tightness (ATTN: don't poke yourself!)
4. take jeans off and sew the new inseam
5. cut off extra jean fabric and turn back right side out
6. put them back on and run to that rock concert!

77

rachel

quilted vest

You'll need
1 pair of jeans
cotton stuffing

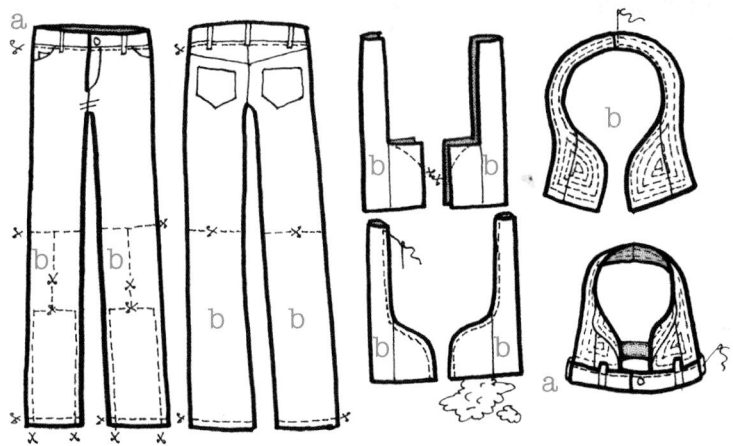

1. cut off hems, cut off waistband (a), leaving seam allowance
2. cut out rectangles in front, cut front center from rectangles to knees, and cut legs off at knees as shown to create pieces (b)
3. fold pieces (b) as shown and trim off indicated corners
4. **clean finish sew** pieces (b) closed on indicated sides, then **stuff** with thin layer of cotton
5. **clean finish sew** (b) pieces closed, then **top stitch** the top ends together (b) to create halter
6. **top stitch** on decorative pattern to hold cotton in place using **stuff and quilt** technique
7. **clean finish sew** waistband (a) onto bottom edge of (b)
8. **top stitch** the ends of detached belt loops onto the vest

#78

kira

cinch belt

You'll need
1 pair of jeans
1 piece of fabric 5 × 5 inches (12.5 × 12.5 cm)
3 pieces of elastic 24 × .5 inch (61 × 1.3 cm)
2 vintage buttons

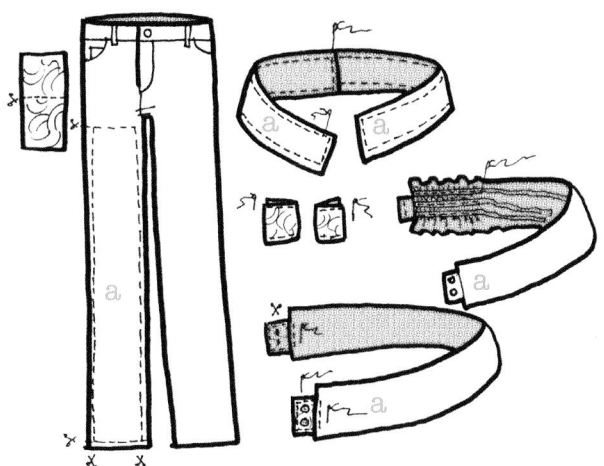

1. cut piece (a) out of front and back of jean leg, about 6 inches (15cm) wide
2. **clean finish sew** pieces (a) together, then **flat hem** edges (the length should be 2 times the circumference of your waist)
3. cut fabric in half widthwise, fold each piece as shown, and **clean finish sew** 2 sides closed
4. **top stitch** fabric pieces onto each side of piece (a), folding in raw edges
5. stitch 3 rows of elastic onto back side of (a) using **gathering with elastic technique**
6. **sew 2 buttons** on 1 piece of fabric, and **make 2 eyelets** on the other

#79

irene

shorts with ribbon

You'll need
1 pair of jeans
1 ribbon 9 feet (3m) long

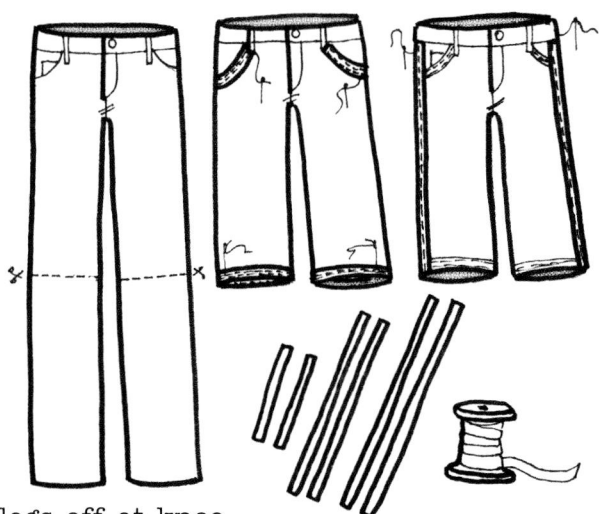

1. cut legs off at knee
2. measure pocket, cut 2 pieces of ribbon to same length, and **top stitch** onto pockets
3. measure circumference of bottom of leg, cut 2 pieces of ribbon to same length
4. **double top stitch** to bottom of leg
5. measure length of side seam, from top of waistband to bottom of leg, cut 2 pieces of ribbon accordingly
6. **double top stitch** to sides of jeans (ATTN: watch out for rivets and thick seams!) (HINT: if sewing gets tricky along the leg, open up button and fly to create more room)

80

astrid

open top

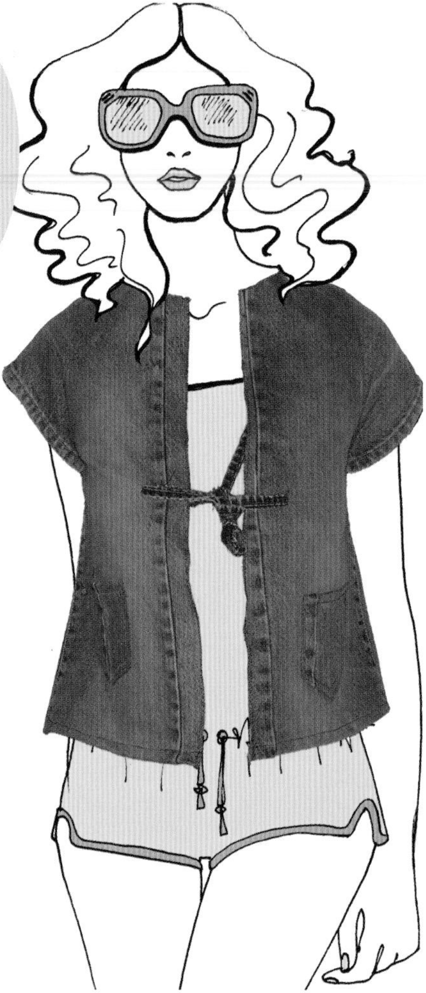

You'll need
1 pair of jeans

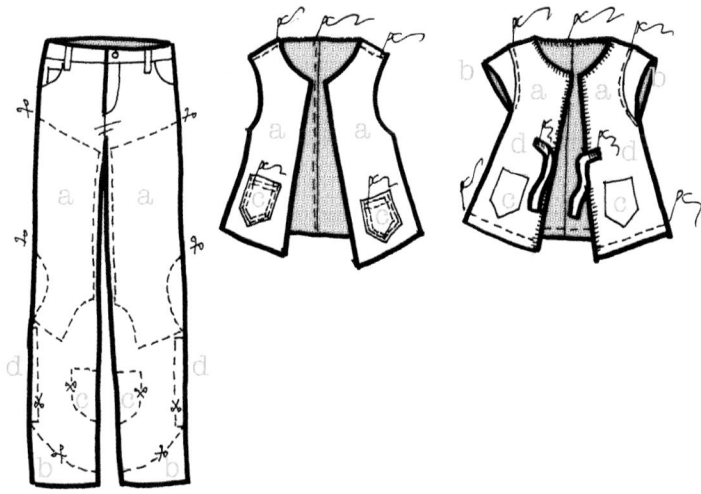

1. cut out indicated shapes (a) in front and back using **pattern technique**
2. cut out pieces (b) from bottom of jeans, on front and back for sleeves, using **pattern technique**
3. cut thin strips (d) from side seams of both legs
4. cut out shapes (c) for pockets, leaving seam allowance
5. sew shoulders and back seams of pieces (a) together
6. **double top stitch** pockets (c) to pieces (a)
7. **clean finish sew** sleeves (b) onto armholes
8. **top stitch** strips (d) to front center to create closure
9. **roll hem** bottom, then **zigzag stitch** around remaining edges

#81

ashley

peasant skirt

You'll need
1 pair of jeans
1 piece of fabric
1 elastic strip

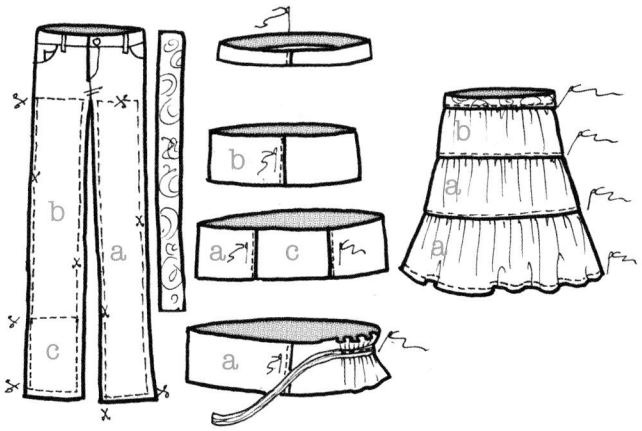

1. cut out right leg in front and back (eliminate seams), creating pieces (a)
2. cut out left leg in front, then cut off bottom rectangle where indicated, creating 2 pieces—longer piece (b), shorter piece (c)
3. fold fabric strip in half widthwise, then sew into band
4. **clean finish sew** (b) into band (make sure the circumference is the same as the band of fabric)
5. **clean finish sew** 1 (a) piece together with (c) piece to create band; **clean finish sew** other (a) piece into band
6. sew elastic to inside of each jean band as close as possible to edge, using **gather with elastic technique**
7. **clean finish sew** bands together from small to large
8. attach fabric band to (b) using **covered hem technique**
9. **roll hem** bottom of skirt

#82

82

eleanor

bloomers

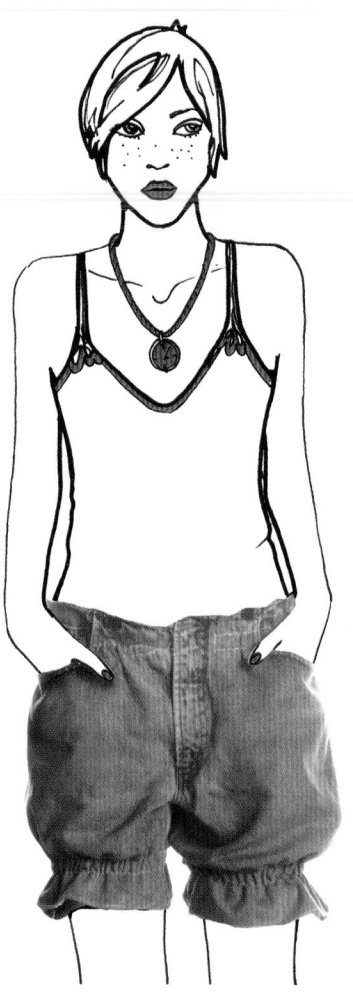

You'll need
1 pair of large jeans with button fly
1 piece of elastic 4 feet (1.2m) long

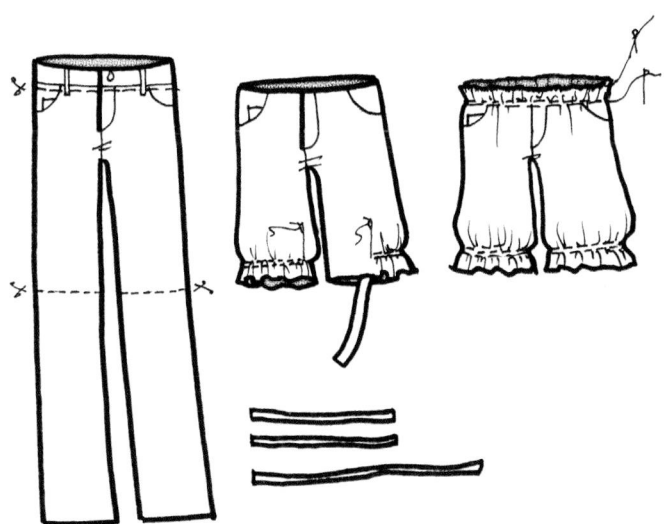

1. cut off legs just above knee
2. cut elastic piece into 3 strips—2 for legs, 1 for waist
3. hem bottoms using **rolled hem technique**
4. sew an elastic strip to the inside of each leg, about 2 inches (5cm) above hemmed edge, using **gathering with elastic technique**; simultaneously fix elastic to denim and hem edges of legs
5. **zigzag stitch** around waist
6. sew an elastic strip to the inside of the waist, using **gathering with elastic technique** about an inch (2.5cm) from the edge (ATTN: don't sew over fly)

#83

janine

overall dress

You'll need
1 pair of jeans
1 safety pin
2 vintage buttons
5 feet (1.5m) of string

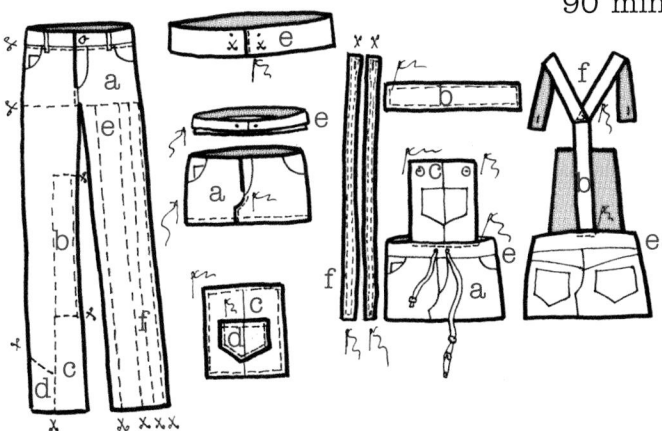

90 min ★★★★

1. cut off waistband and legs at crotch, creating (a)
2. **flatten crotch** (a)
3. cut strip (b) from front, then a rectangle (c) and
   piece (d) from front and back of left leg as shown
4. cut 3 strips, 1 thick (e) and 2 thin (f) from other leg
5. sew (e) into band, pierce 2 holes on each side of seam
6. fold band (e) in half lengthwise and sew it to skirt
   (a) using **covered hem technique**
7. **flat hem** rectangle (c) and piece (d) on all sides, then
   stitch pocket (d) to (c); **sew buttons** to sides of (c)
8. **make eyelets** on 1 end of strips (f), then **flat hem**
   strips (f) and (b)
9. **clean finish sew** rectangle (c) to (e), thread string
   through holes in (e) (use safety pin to help thread)
10. **hand stitch** strips (f) to strip (b) and to skirt in back

#84

victoria

victorian top

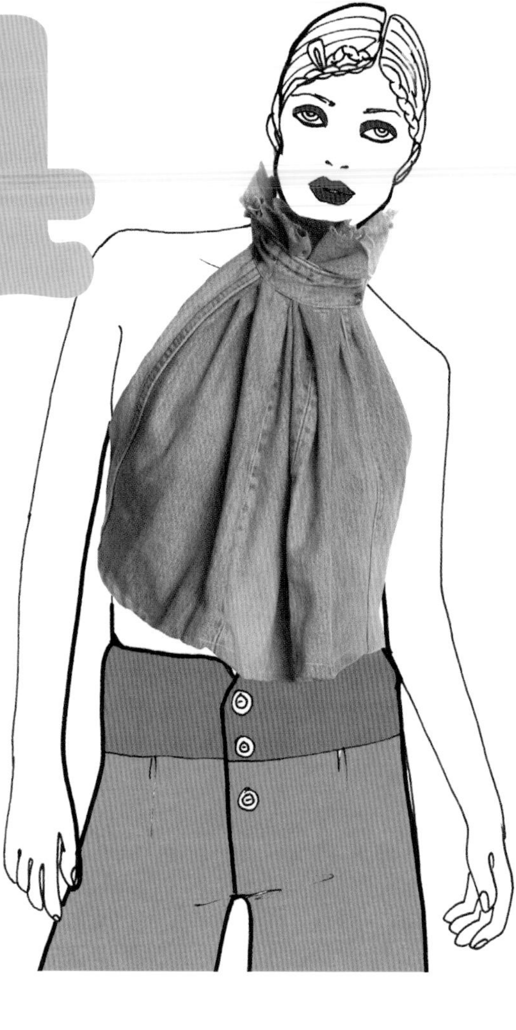

You'll need
1 pair of jeans

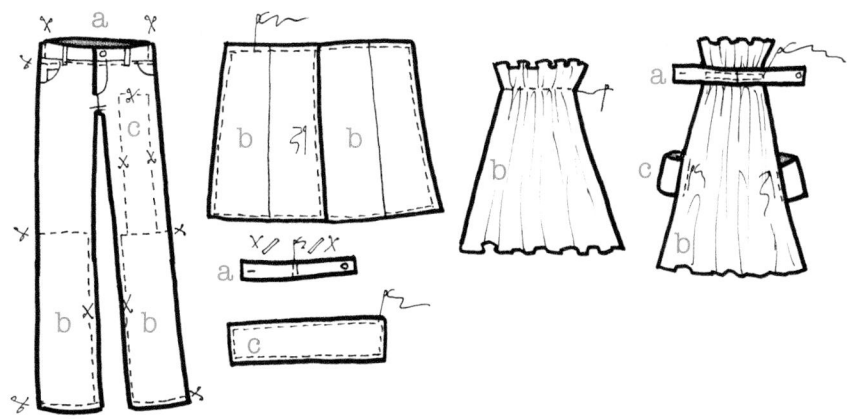

1. cut off waistband piece from front (a) and eliminate belt loops
2. cut off legs at knees, eliminating inseams and hems and creating rectangles (b)
3. cut out thick strip from front of right leg (c) as shown, then **flat hem** all sides
4. **clean finish sew** rectangles (b) together as shown
5. **hand stitch** ends of waistband (a) together
6. **gather** piece (b) 4 inches (10cm) from top to create collar
7. **top stitch** waistband (a) onto piece (b) at collar as shown
8. sew strip (c) to sides of piece (b)

#85

teva

stacked bracelet

You'll need
1 pair of jeans or jean scraps

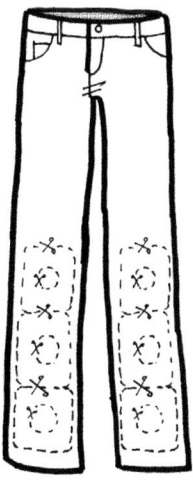 

1. cut out indicated shape from front and back 6 times (make sure center circle is the right size to slip onto your wrist)
2. place 1 on top of the other, stacking them as shown, then **blanket stitch** them all together by hand, leaving outer edges raw
3. repeat until bracelet is the desired thickness

#86

melissa

necklace

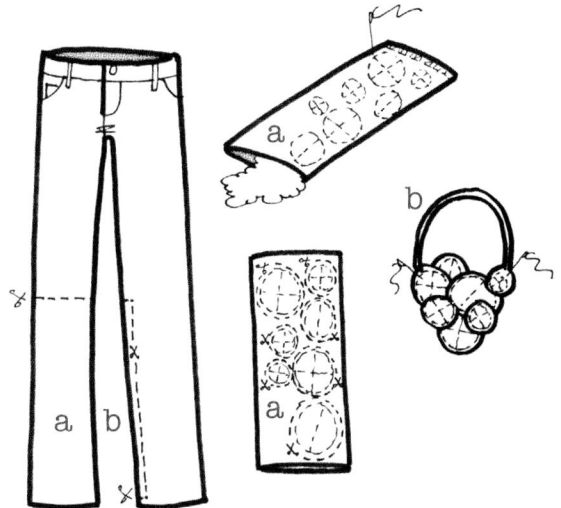

1. cut off left leg (a) at knee
2. cut out inseam (b) of right leg up to knee, about 1 foot (30cm)
3. **stuff** (a) with thin layer of cotton
4. stitch circles of different sizes onto (a) as shown
5. stitch an X into each circle, use **stuff and quilt technique** to keep cotton in place
6. cut circles out of (a) as close as possible to outer stitch
7. pin circles into desired form and **hand stitch** them together on back side
8. **hand stitch** (b) onto each side of (a) to complete your necklace

87

benedetta

a-line dress

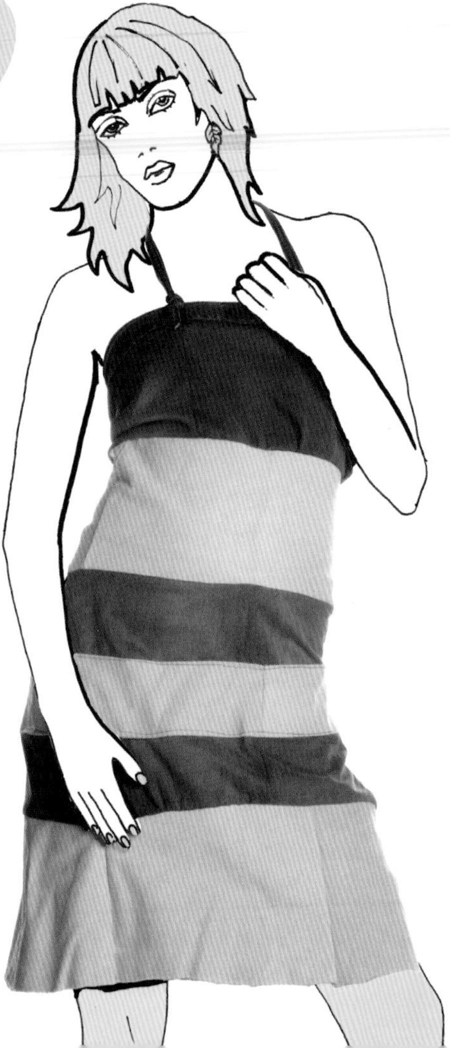

You'll need
2 pairs of jeans

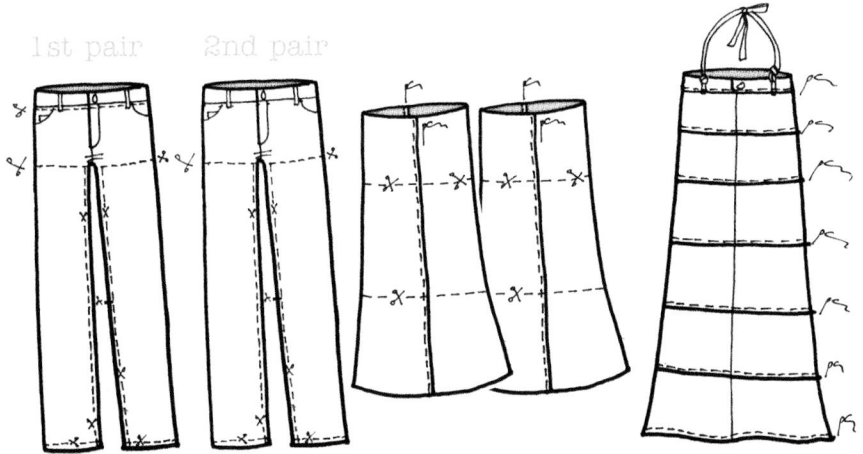

1. cut off legs on both pairs of jeans at crotch; cut out inseams and cut 1 in half
2. cut off waistband of 1st pair of jeans, leaving seam allowance
3. **clean finish sew** 4 legs into 2 tubes, making sure that the wider parts of the legs are sewn together as shown
4. cut each tube into 3 smaller tubes and pin them together, adjusting, trimming, and using **gathering technique** as necessary to fit your figure
5. **clean finish sew** all tube pieces together, starting with waistband, then smallest tubes, gradually sewing on the bigger ones; **flat hem** bottom
6. cut 1 strip from inseam in half and tie onto front 2 belt loops as halter neck; tie in back

#88
88

muriel

sporty shorts

You'll need
1 pair of jeans
2 cuffs and 1 waistband of an old sweatshirt

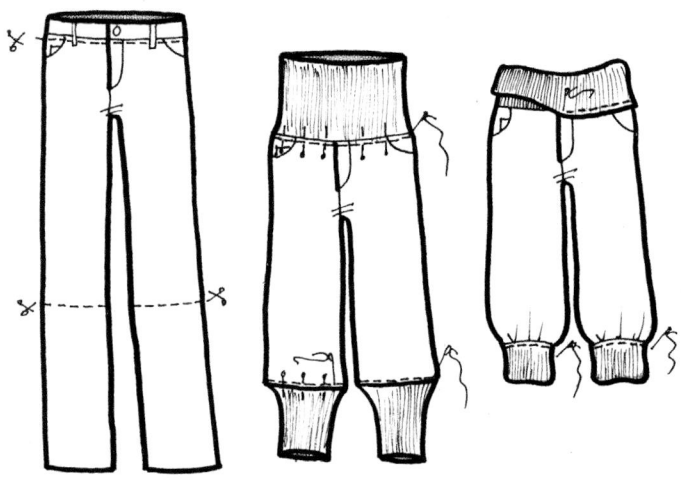

1. cut off waistband of jeans
2. cut off legs below the knee (or to desired length)
3. pin waistband and cuffs from sweatshirt onto legs and waist of jeans using **gathering technique**
4. sew using **covered hem technique**

#89

paige

strapless funky top

You'll need
5 pairs of jeans
or 9 back pockets and 1 waistband

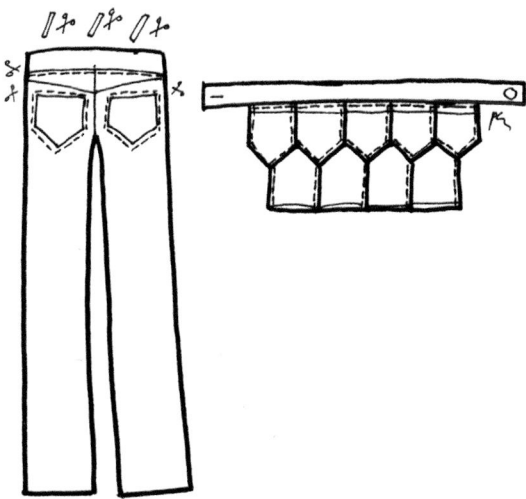

1. cut off waistband from 1 pair of jeans and eliminate belt loops
2. make sure waistband fits around your high bust
3. cut out 9 back pockets, leaving seam allowance
4. pin pockets together as indicated, then **clean finish sew** (ATTN: depending on your size, you may need more pockets)
5. sew waistband on pockets where indicated
6. trim remaining hem allowance off bottom and sides, you go girl!

90

shannon

shoulder bag

You'll need
1 pair of jeans
2 vintage buttons
1 piece of ribbon 3 feet (91cm) long

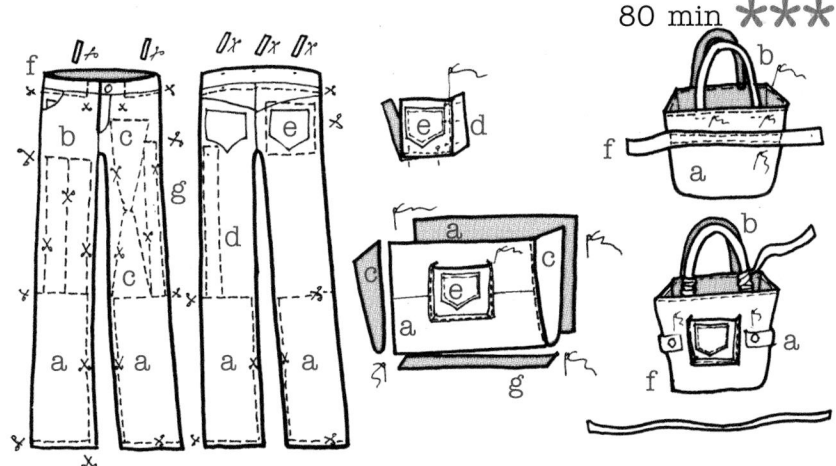

80 min ★★★

1. cut off legs at knee, eliminating inseams and hems (a)
2. cut 2 strips (b) from left leg on front, **roll hem**
3. cut 2 triangular shapes (c) from front of right leg
4. cut strip (d) from front and (g) from back of right leg
5. cut out 1 back pocket (e), leaving seam allowance
6. pin and sew strip (d) around (e), **roll hem** ends of (d)
7. **top stitch** pocket to front center of an (a) piece, then **sew buttons** to each side
8. **clean finish sew** pieces (c) onto pieces (a) as sides, then **clean finish sew** strip (g) to (a) and (c)
9. cut off waistband piece (f), eliminating belt loops
10. **top stitch** waistband (f), centered, onto back of bag, and **make eyelets** on either side
11. **hand stitch** strips (b) onto bag as handles and wrap ribbon around each end of handles, **top stitch** to secure

#91

91

laura

bustier

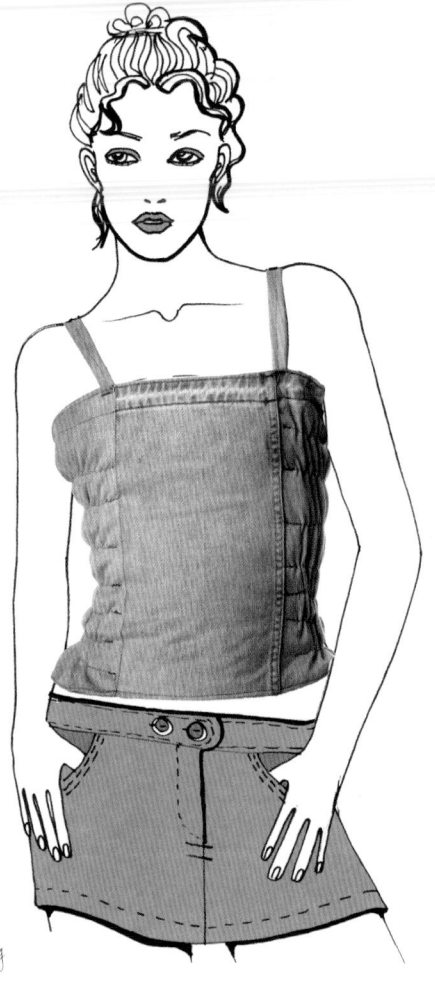

You'll need
1 pair of jeans
1 thin elastic strip 9 feet (3m) long

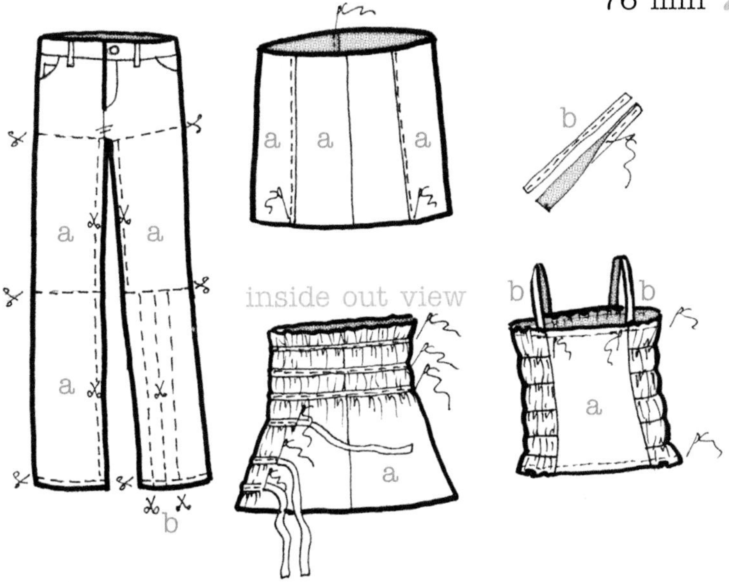

1. cut legs at knee and crotch, eliminating inseam and hems, creating pieces (a)
2. cut 4 strips (b) from right leg, 2 in front, 2 in back
3. **clean finish sew** 3 (a) pieces into tube as shown
4. cut elastic into 6 equal pieces
5. sew elastic strips 2/3 of the way around inside of tube (a) then **gather with elastic**
6. **roll hem** 4 strips (b) and stitch them onto top as shoulder straps

penelope

flower pin

You'll need
1 pair of jeans
1 large saftey pin or pin backing

1. take a pen and draw a flower design directly on the jeans, then draw the same design 2 more times, getting progressively smaller; draw several leaves and a circle slightly bigger than your biggest flower
2. cut out all the shapes
3. place pieces in order of size, 1 on top of the other, from biggest to smallest, leaving out the leaves
4. fold pile of pieces, pinching the bottom, and **hand stitch** them together in center
5. **hand stitch** on leaves where desired
6. attach safety pin on center back then pin it onto your favorite jacket, or your favorite friend!

#93

olga

hood

You'll need
1 pair of jeans
1 vintage button
1 piece of fabric 24 × 2 inches (61 × 5 cm)

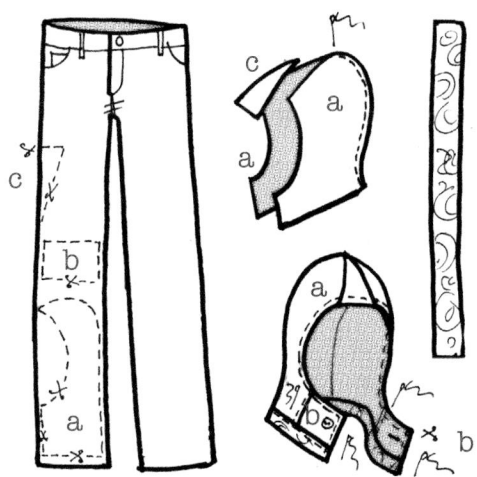

1. cut out funny hood shape from leg, using **pattern technique** in front and back (a)
2. cut out rectangle from same leg in front and back (b)
3. cut triangle from side seam as shown (c)
4. **clean finish sew** pieces (a) together where indicated
5. insert triangle (c) and sew between pieces (a) where shown
6. **clean finish sew** pieces (b) onto flaps of pieces (a)
7. sew fabric onto bottom edge of hood using **covered hem technique**
8. **roll hem** around hood
9. **sew on button** and **make eyelet** where indicated

94

esperanza

bag with braids

You'll need
1 pair of jeans
1 elastic strip 18 inches (46cm) long
1 piece of fabric 3 x 4 inches (7.5 x 10cm)

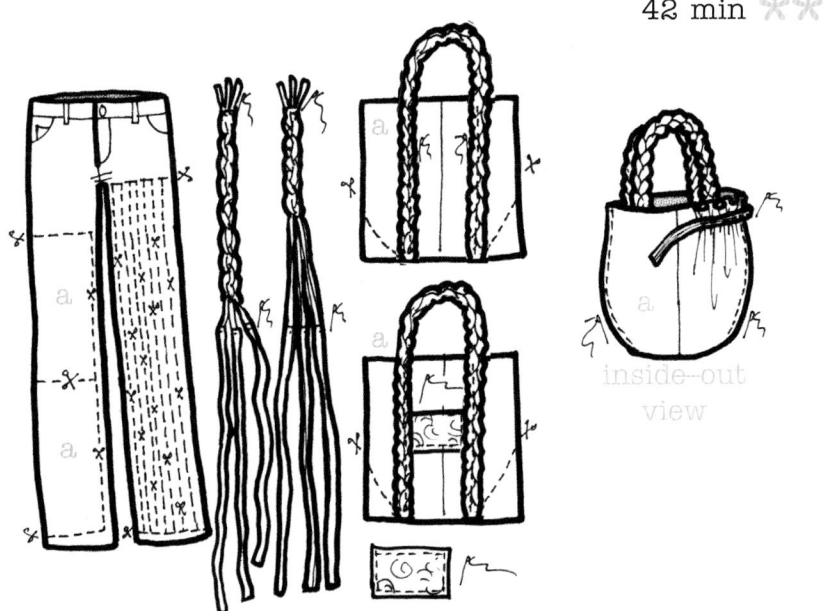

inside--out
view

1. cut off left leg at knee and then 3 inches (7.5cm) below crotch, eliminating inseam and hem, creating pieces (a)
2. cut right leg into 12 long, thin strips in front and back
3. sew 12 long, thin strips into 6 superlong thin strips, braid them, and stitch ends to secure
4. round bottom corners of pieces (a)
5. **hand stitch** braids onto pieces (a) as shown
6. **flat hem** sides of fabric, then stitch to (a) as pocket
7. flip bag inside-out, **clean finish sew** sides closed, and **gather with elastic**

#95

95

linnea

mermaid skirt

You'll need
1 pair of jeans
1 elastic strip 12 inches (30cm) long

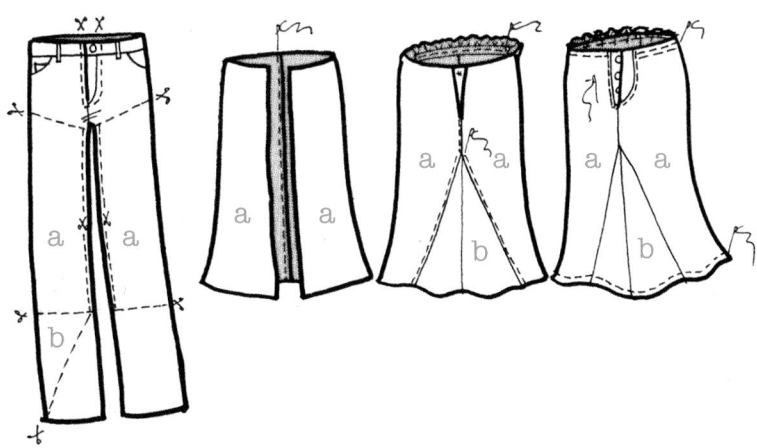

1. cut legs to capri length
2. cut legs off at crotch on slight diagonal, eliminating inseam and creating pieces (a)
3. cut out button fly (zipper)
4. cut bottom left piece in half on diagonal, creating (b)
5. flip pieces (a) upside down and sew together on 1 side with the diagonal edge on bottom
6. **clean finish sew** (a) pieces together, inserting triangle (b) on bottom and zipper/fly on top, **pin before sewing**
7. **flat hem** top of waistband, then sew elastic strip using **gather with elastic technique** onto back inside of skirt

#96

paula

baby doll halter
top

You'll need
1 pair of jeans
2 elastic bands 15 inches (38 cm) long

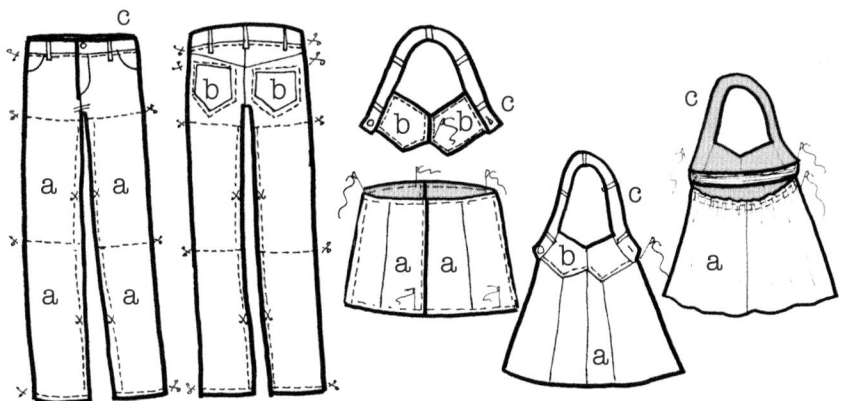

1. eliminate hems and inseams, then cut each leg off at knee and crotch, creating 4 pieces (a)
2. cut off waistband (c) and back pockets (b), leaving seam allowance
3. **clean finish sew** back pockets (b) together as indicated, then **flat hem** edges
4. **top stitch** waistband (c) onto pocket piece (b)
5. **clean finish sew** pieces (a) together, creating a tube, and **roll hem** bottom
6. **top stitch** pocket piece (b) onto top of piece (a), cutting off excess material from inside
7. sew elastic strip onto piece (c) at sides
8. **gather** top edge of piece (a) **with elastic**

#97

isa

shorts with appliqués

You'll need
1 pair of jeans
1 piece of fabric 8 inches x 1 inch (20 x 2.5 cm)

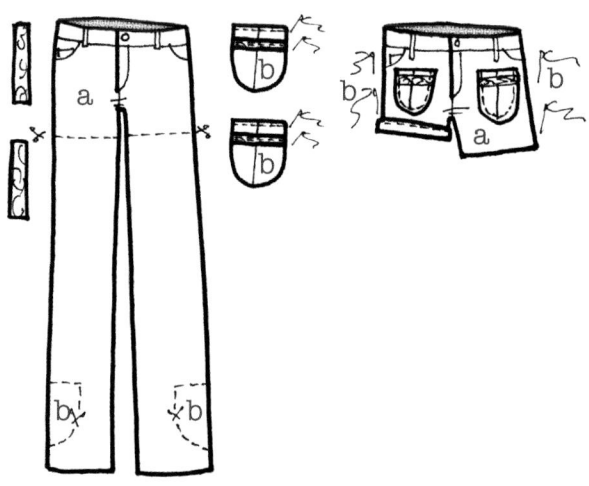

1. cut jeans off several inches below crotch (a)
2. cut out pieces (b) from legs on side seam as shown
3. **flat hem** both long sides of (b) and sew fabric strips onto pieces (b) close to edge
4. **top stitch** pockets (b) onto shorts (a) where indicated
5. roll up cuffs on legs of shorts (a) and stitch in place

#98

lily

handbag

You'll need
1 pair of jeans
cotton for quilting

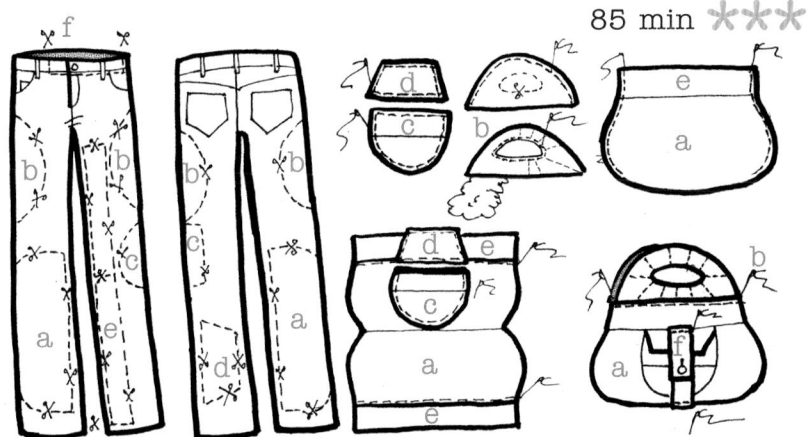

85 min ★★★

1. cut out shape (a) in front and back of left leg
2. cut out semicircles (b) on both sides, leaving seams intact
3. cut oval hole in folded (b) pieces, then **stuff and quilt**; **top stitch** all edges closed
4. cut out (c) from front and back for pocket (ATTN: front and back are different shapes), **flat hem** all sides
5. cut (d) from back of right leg, make sure length of long edge of (d) equals flat side of (c), **flat hem** sides
6. cut out long strip (e) from front of right leg, cut in half
7. **clean finish sew** strips (e) to both straight edges of (a)
8. **top stitch** pocket (c) and flap (d) to center of (a)
9. fold piece (a) in half and **clean finish sew** sides closed
10. cut out front piece of waistband (f) as shown and **top stitch** it onto (a) above and below pocket for closure
11. sew handles (b) to pieces (e) using **top stitch**

#99

nia

fancy top

You'll need
1 pair of jeans or jean scraps
1 piece of jersey 1 foot × 4 feet (30 × 122cm)

1. cut off waistband (a)
2. eliminate hem on 1 leg, cut out long strip, 2 inches (5cm) wide, from front and back of same leg (b)
3. place fabric around your neck so it hangs in front, equally on each side
4. gather fabric over bust, put the waistband (a) on top of the fabric just underneath the bust (with the button/eyelet in front center), pin, and **gather** (you may need to adjust waistband to smaller size to fit snugly under bust)
5. **clean finish sew** strips (b) together on both ends to form big band
6. **pin and sew** (b) onto bottom of fabric using **covered hem technique**

glossary techniques

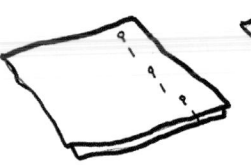
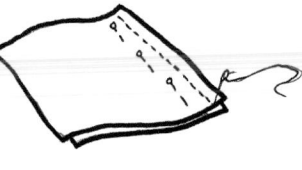

pin before sewing

Pin fabric down **before sewing** to help keep fabric in place.

iron seams and hems

Iron fabric before sewing to help keep fabric in place for hems, and iron fabric after sewing for flat seams.

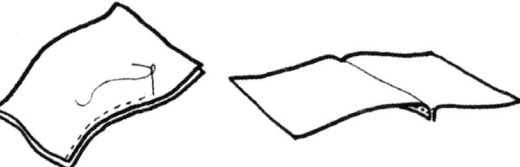

clean finish sewing

Sew the jeans inside-out (putting the "right" sides face to face). After sewing, turn right side out so that raw edges remain inside and unseen.

glossary techniques

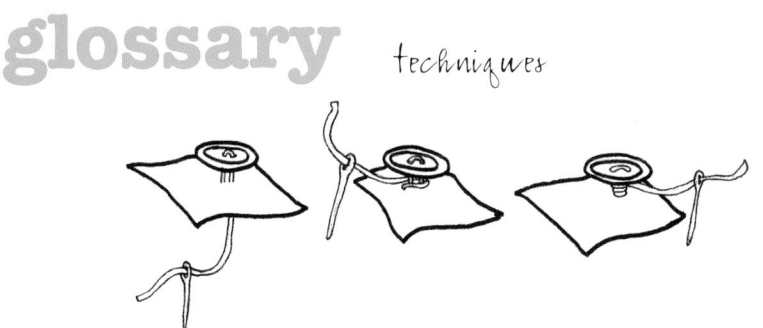

sewing on buttons by hand

Tie a knot in your thread. Push needle through fabric and button. Repeat a few times. Bring needle back up through fabric and wrap thread around the thread that is in between fabric and **button**. Fasten with knot underneath fabric.

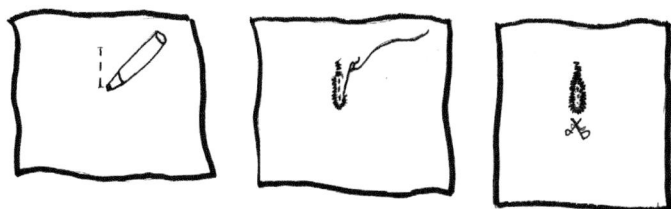

making eyelets

Draw a dotted line slightly larger than the diameter of the button that is to be used. Zigzag stitch around that dotted line (don't stitch over the line), making an opening with sharp scissors between the stitches.

glossary techniques

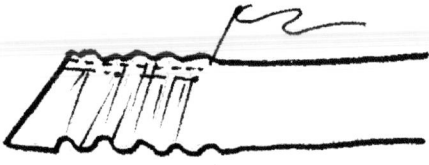

gathering

Fabric is **gathered** by making tiny folds in the fabric and sewing over the folds with small stitches. Unless otherwise indicated, gather fabric before sewing it onto desired location.

gathering with elastic

The piece of elastic should be about half the length of the fabric that will be **gathered** (when possible, try to measure the amount of **elastic** needed on your body). Pin the tip of the elastic onto the fabric, and stretch the elastic with your hand while sewing (using the zigzag stitch) over the elastic and fabric.

glossary *techniques*

closed darts

To create **closed darts,** pinch a triangle of fabric and sew the edges of the triangle together, then iron flat in a downwards direction.

open darts

To create an **open dart**, cut a triangle into the fabric and sew edges of the triangle together. Then iron remaining raw edges flat.

flattening crotch

To turn pants into a skirt, the **crotch** must be **flattened** by cutting the legs open on the inseams. Cut along the crotch seam until the beginning of the "fly," then overlap fork and top stitch closed, cutting off excess material on the inside. Repeat process in back.

glossary techniques

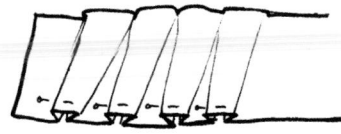

inverted pleats

Fold fabric into **pleats** (ironing folded edges can facilitate pleat making). Pin the folds into place.

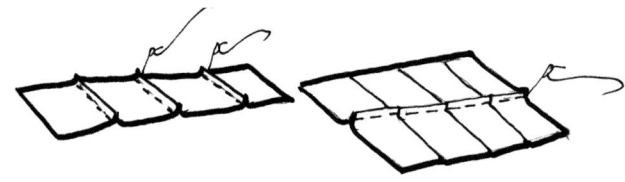

patchwork

To create **patchwork**, sew precut squares into strips, sew strips together, and iron seams open.

stuff and quilt

Evenly place soft filling on fabric, lay second piece of fabric on top, and sew all edges closed. If needed, sew small stitches over cotton for **quilted** effect.

glossary techniques (embellishing)

Take creative liberties! Embellish your creations with embroidery, beading, and appliqués.

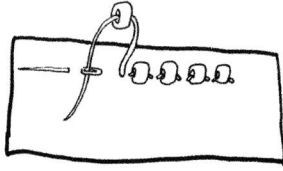

stitching on beads

Stitch beads to garment by stitching normally but adding a small bead to every stitch.

embroidery stitch

Hand stitch using embroidery floss or thread over a design of your choice to create **embroidery stitch.**

sewing on patches

Iron edge of **patch** inwards so the raw edges remain on the inside, then stitch patch on top of desired surface.

glossary

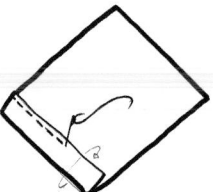

flat hem

To make a **flat hem,** fold edge upwards and stitch flat.

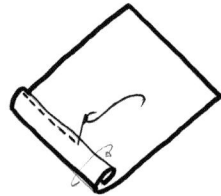

rolled hem

To make a **rolled hem,** fold edge 2 times. Raw edge should remain on the inside, then sew on top with **top stitch**.

covered hem

To make a **covered hem,** sew fabric strip onto raw edge ("right" side out), then fold edge of strip upwards, folding under raw edge of fabric. Iron flat, then **top stitch** onto the edge of fold.

glossary

stitches and hems

top stitch and double top stitch

For **top stitch**, place fabric on top of other piece of fabric and stitch on top. For **double top stitch,** sew 2 parallel seams on the clean side of fabric.

hand stitch and blanket stitch

For **hand stitch**, sew by hand with doubled thread through the needle. Use stitch for thick layers or delicate sewing. To make **blanket stitch**, sew a loop around the edge of the fabric, then thread the needle through the loop that was just created. Blanket stitch is usually employed to finish edges.

zigzag

To make **zigzag stitch**, sew around edges with the zigzag stitch on your sewing machine. This stitch is useful for stretch fabrics and elastic.

glossary

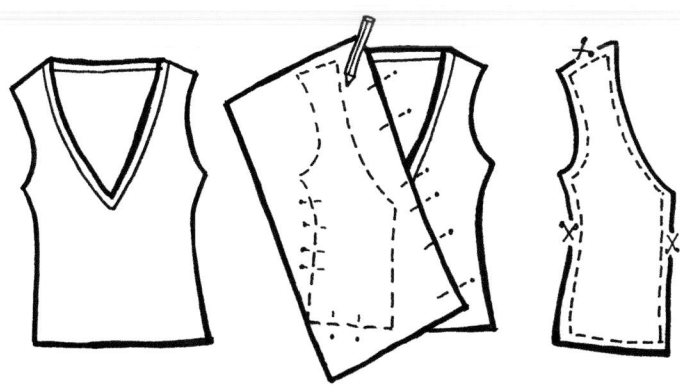

pattern technique example for armhole and V-neck on a tank top.

1. Find an item in your wardrobe that fits you well (that is not stretch fabric).
2. Pin a piece of paper over the area of the garment you wish to create a pattern from. (NOTE: It is sufficient to trace one armhole and half the neckline). Trace the garment's edges and seams with a pencil on the paper.
3. Cut out the paper pattern, adding half an inch (1.3cm) for seam allowance.

4. Pin the pattern down onto the denim and cut the pattern out. Once again, do not forget to add half an inch (1.3cm) for seam allowance. To make the opposite sleeve, simply flip the pattern over.

HINT: Try on your paper pattern before using to ensure a good fit!

pattern technique example for sleeve of a short-sleeved shirt

glossary

pattern-making technique 2

front torso

back torso

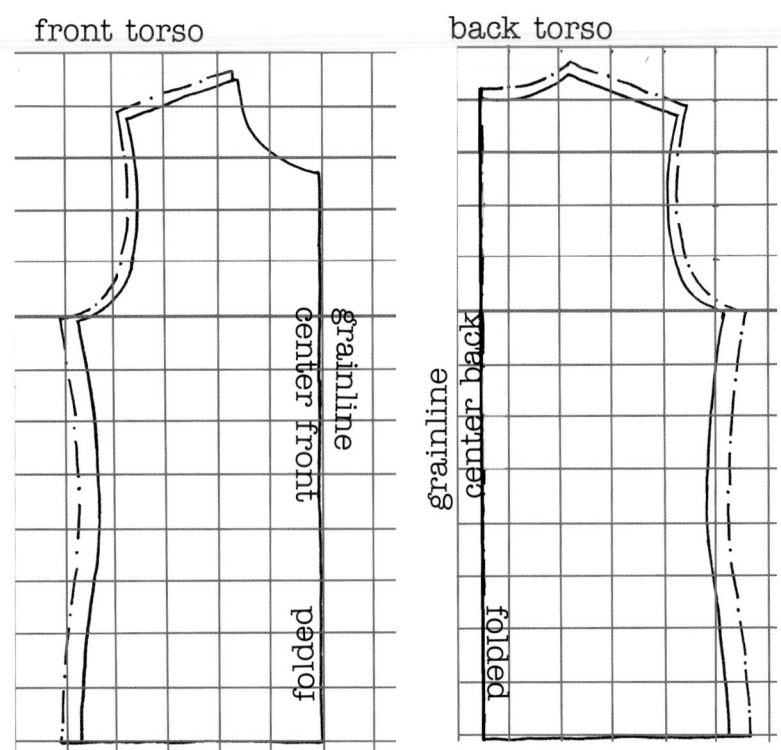

grainline
center front
folded

grainline
center back
folded

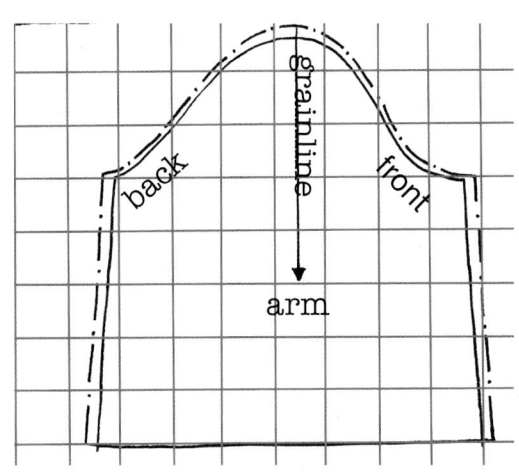

grainline

back

front

arm

*Enlarge this pattern so that each square in the graph is equal to 2 inches x 2 inches (5 x 5cm).

Use these patterns for necklines, sides, shoulders, arm-holes, and sleeves. Adjust the sleeve holes and necklines for desired shapes. The innermost lines in the patterns are for a size small, the outermost lines are for a size large. For a size medium, draw lines in between the innermost and outermost lines. Then create the full pattern, including left and right sides, and pin sides and shoulders together. Then try on paper pattern to ensure a good fit. Then pin it to fabric or denim and cut out pieces.

terminology

fifth pocket: the "fifth pocket" indicates a small change pocket often found on jeans above the right-hand pocket

stitch: unless otherwise indicated, for the purpose of this book, when we say stitch, we mean a row of stitches that is sewn on top of the garment

inseam: unless otherwise indicated, for the purpose of this book, when we say inseam, we are referring to the existing seam in between the legs of jeans

seam allowance: unless otherwise indicated, when we say seam allowance, we are referring to the area of fabric that is between the seam stitching and the cut edge

raw edges: unless otherwise indicated, for the purpose of this book, when we say raw edges, we are referring to an unhemmed seam on the denim or fabric

terminology

original seams: unless otherwise indicated, for the purpose of this book, when we say original seam, we are referring to the seams that are on the jean before altering begins

tube, band: in this book, we often use the term tube or band. They come in a number of shapes:

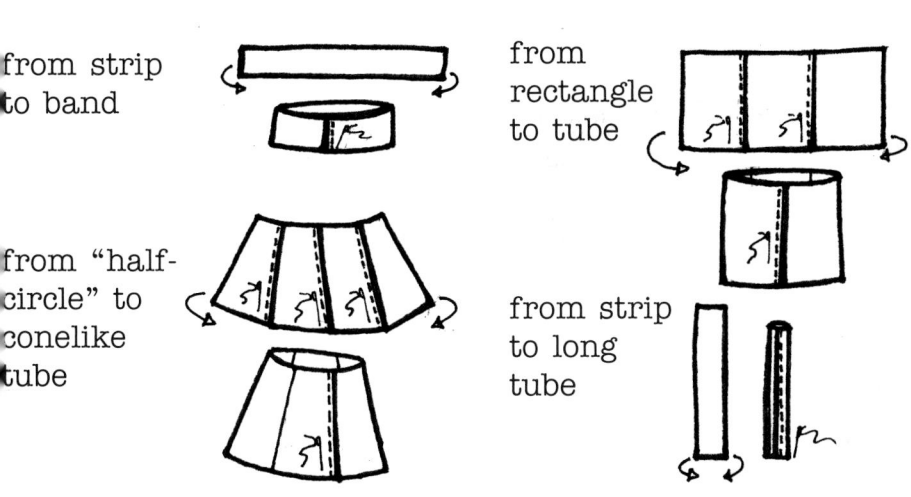

from strip to band

from rectangle to tube

from "half-circle" to conelike tube

from strip to long tube

measurements

how to take your measurements:

bust
measure around the fullest part of your chest
waist
measure around belly at navel for men, midway between bottom of ribs and top of hip bone for women
sleeve length
with arm slightly bent, measure from armpit to wrist
head
place tape measure across forehead, and measure around the fullest circumference of the head

When specific measurements are not indicated, consider it a test of your sewing savvy, think about it, and if all else fails, guess!

Seam allowance = half an inch (1.3cm), unless otherwise noted

*Remember measurements will vary according to your size.

acknowledgments

compai would like to thank and praise:
our parents and grandparents, bros and sis's—for support,
baby-sitting, and encouragement. our friends and grand-
friends—for distractions and the most out there denim ideas.
melissa flashman—for being our kickass agent with mad
style, and for getting it. kira lillie—friend and photograher
extraordinaire. you made this book happen. agnes schultz—
for oandligt talamod, var alskade topmodell andrew tailor
mosher—for the meticulous editing. benedetta and chris—for
the MAC and the love. lilith—for the sewing. anka—for the
support and the friendship PATATUSH!!! noa, mammina, and
rein—for being so BRAVI. flavio and katarina—per l'amicizia
e l'aiuto. caits, duane, sarit, and the NY crew—for the hospi-
tality, inspiration, and for always being there. lise—for the
time and passion. barbara—per i jeans e per la presenza.
the confortis—for always hookin' it up rosy ngo—for the
trust and faith in our creativity. lauren monchik—for the
patience and the ideas. isa lounden—for always having the
answers. paige alexander—for getting us out there. amy sly,
mona michael, and the whole potter craft crew—for all the
jeans, all the hours, all the quark lessons, all the quick
responses, all the fun . . . and for making our dreams
come true. AND A BIG THANK YOU TO pam kraus, lily kosner,
benjamine nugent, caitlin henderson, mark mccauslin,
linnea knollmueller, rachel ingram, and jenny frost.

index

shorts with tie waist, 52 gladys
skirt with appliqués, 60 audrey
skirt with gathered bottom, 11
   sofia
sporty pants, 63 leah
sporty shorts, 88 muriel
super tight jeans, 76 jennifer
wraparound skirt, 46 miriam

clothing—one-piece

a-line dress, 87 benedetta
baby dress, 49 noa
jumpsuit, 53 jackie
overall dress, 83 janine
sundress, 56 jordan
tennis dress, 62 venus

clothing—tops

a-line top, 59 amy
baby doll halter top, 96 paula
backless top, 1 caitlin
bikini top, 33 yylor
blazer, 4 piper
bolero, 61 natasha
bustier, 91 laura
bustier vest, 54 vivian
country vest, 38 nadine
fancy top, 99 nia
funky top, 16 kathy
kimono top, 40 hiroko

minijacket, 23 chelsea
open top, 80 astrid
poncho, 45 teresa
quilted vest, 77 rachel
strapless funky top, 89 paige
strapless top, 18 carla
swing top, 35 silvia
tiny top, 14 tessa
top with appliqués, 27 dawn
vest, 17 miki
vest with hood, 31 lena
victorian top, 84 victoria

home—accessories

apron, 57 jan
bathroom mat, 75 matt
hanger cover, 50 dagmar
heating pad, 10 benjamine
jean masterpiece, 66 matteo
laundry bag, 28 lilith
midnight mask, 67 alison
pillow, 32 mark
potholder, 48 diana
sseat cover, 43 michael

home—pets

dog collar and leash, 22 charlie
dog jacket, 5 mammina
doggie bone, 69 shia

about the authors

Officially **Compai** is a band of young hearts and minds who share ideas, philosophies, space, and resources to promote innovation in design and environmental awareness. Unofficially, we are a group of 3 girls who love style, people, and this planet.

Justina Blakeney and **Faith Blakeney** were raised in Berkeley, California. **Ellen Schultz** is from Stockholm, Sweden. Apart from making these cute little books, we are also fashion designers, illustrators, writers, and best friends.

In this book series we aim to fuse our passions by sharing our fashion and recycling know-how with fresh, curious people like yourselves. Our goal is to leave you drunk on your own creative juices, dizzy and longing for more. Strap on your seat belts: This is **Compai** the revenge. If you just can't get enough, visit us at:

www.compai.com

To

W9-BYO-518

_____

From

_____

May these reflections from Our Daily Bread enrich your soul and draw your heart closer to God throughout the year. May they bring you strength for each day and "bright hope for tomorrow."

Discovery House Publishers is affiliated with RBC Ministries, Grand Rapids, Michigan.

Contributing Writers: Henry G. Bosch (HGB); Dave Branon (DB); Anne Cetas (AC); Bill Crowder (BC); Dennis J. DeHaan (DJD); Mart DeHaan (MD); M. R. DeHaan (MRD); Richard DeHaan (RDH); David C. Egner (DCE); Dennis Fisher (DF); Vernon C. Grounds (VCG); C. P. Hia (CPH); Cindy Hess Kasper (CHK); Albert Lee (AL); Julie Ackerman Link (JAL); David C. McCasland (DCM); RBC Ministries (RBC); Haddon W. Robinson (HWR); David H. Roper (DHR); Joe Stowell (JS); Herbert Vander Lugt (HVL); Paul Van Gorder (PVG); Marvin Williams (MW); Joanie Yoder (JY).

Scripture quotations are from *The Holy Bible, New King James Version*, © 1979, 1980, 1982 by Thomas Nelson, Inc. Used by permission.

Requests for permission to quote from this calendar should be directed to: Permissions Department, Discovery House Publishers, P.O. Box 3566, Grand Rapids, MI 49501.

Design by Stan Myers

ISBN 978-1-57293-545-7

Printed in China

JANUARY 1

We have redemption through His blood, the forgiveness of sins.
Colossians 1:14

It was New Year's Day 1929. The University of California at Berkeley was playing Georgia Tech in college football's Rose Bowl. Roy Riegels, a California defender, recovered a Georgia Tech fumble, then turned and scampered sixty-five yards in the wrong direction! One of Riegels' own teammates tackled him just before he reached the wrong goal line. On the next play, Georgia Tech scored and went on to win. From that day on, Riegels was saddled with the nickname "Wrong-way Riegels."

Our failures may not be as conspicuous, but we've all gone the wrong way, and we have memories that haunt us. If only we could begin again! We can. When we confess our sins and repent before God, He forgives our past and puts it away. It's never too late to begin again. —DHR

God's forgiveness is the door to a new beginning.

JANUARY 2

I can do all things through Christ who strengthens me.
Philippians 4:13

Most people own a calendar or an appointment book in which they record details of future commitments. A friend of mine uses one in the opposite way. He doesn't record key activities until after they've taken place. For example, he may write, "Today God enabled me to overcome my fear through faith." Or, "Today I was enabled to help and encourage a troubled person."

My friend uses the word *enabled* because he knows he couldn't do these things without God's help. As you enter each new day, ask God to strengthen and use you. You can be sure that as you look back on your day, you'll praise and glorify the Lord as you realize what He has enabled you to do. —JY

God always gives enough strength for the next step.

JANUARY 3

Trust in the Lord, and do good; dwell in the land, and feed on His faithfulness.
Psalm 37:3

Our grandson Cameron was born six weeks prematurely. Undersized and in danger, he was in the neonatal unit for about two weeks until he gained enough weight to go home. His biggest challenge was that, in the physical exercise of eating, he burned more calories than he was taking in. No medicine or treatment could solve the problem; he just needed the strength-giving fortification of nourishment.

We are constantly finding our emotional and spiritual reserves drained by the challenges of life in a fallen world. We need nourishment to strengthen us and feed our souls. God's faithful care is the nourishment we need, giving us, as the hymn "Great Is Thy Faithfulness" says, "strength for today, and bright hope for tomorrow." —BC

Feed on God's faithfulness to find the strength you need.

JANUARY 4

He gives power to the weak.
Isaiah 40:29

I was watching an eagle in flight when for no apparent reason it began spiraling upward. With its powerful wings, the great bird soared ever higher, dissolved into a tiny dot, and then disappeared. Its flight reminded me of Isaiah's uplifting words: "Those who wait on the Lord shall renew their strength; they shall mount up with wings like eagles" (40:31).

Life's heartbreaks and tragedies can put an end to our resilience, our endurance, our nerve, and bring us to our knees. But if we put our hope in the Lord and rely on Him, He renews our strength. The key to our endurance lies in the exchange of our limited resources for God's limitless strength. —DHR

God gives strength in proportion to the strain.

JANUARY 5

*My God shall supply all your need according
to His riches in glory by Christ Jesus.*
Philippians 4:19

Do you ever get the blues when the press of day-to-day life gets you
down? Where you have too much to do? Too many problems? No
matter the cause, the result is the same: Your strength is zapped, your
joy is crushed, and your hope needs to be rejuvenated. Whenever
the blues threaten your day, try some of these blues-chasers:

Problem: Things seem impossible. *Answer*: All things are possible with God.
Problem: You are afraid. *Answer*: God will strengthen and help you. *Problem*:
You feel alone in this world. *Answer*: The Lord promises never to leave nor
forsake you. Trust God's answers. They'll help to chase the blues away. —DB

No burden is too heavy for God's almighty arms.

JANUARY 6

A merry heart does good, like medicine.
Proverbs 17:22

In his article "Laugh Your Way to Good Health," Nick Gallo made an observation that echoes what Solomon wrote thousands of years ago in Proverbs 17:22. Gallo said, "Humor is good medicine—sand can actually help keep you in good health." Comparing laughter to exercise, Gallo pointed out that when a person laughs heartily several physical benefits occur. "An enduring sense of humor, especially combined with other inner resources such as faith and optimism, appears to be a potent force for better health."

Christians, above all others, should benefit from laughter because we have the greatest reason to be joyful. Our faith is firmly rooted in God, and our optimism is based on the assurance that our lives are under His wise control. —RDH

He who laughs, lasts.

JANUARY 7

Forgetting those things which are behind . . . , I press toward the goal.
Philippians 3:13–14

Some people have trouble looking ahead with hope because they keep looking back and moping over the mistakes of the past. Their outlook for the future is dimmed, and their enthusiasm is dampened. But nothing is gained by continually grieving over the past.

On this day early in the new year, begin by confessing your sins to the Lord and accepting the gracious forgiveness He offers. Make right what needs correcting, and then, "forgetting those things which are behind," press onward with confidence and trust in your heavenly Father. Stop looking back and brooding over past failures. Rather, with a forward look, move ahead with hope and joy. —RDH

Walk in the light of today and the hope of tomorrow.

JANUARY 8

*He who dwells in the secret place of the Most High
shall abide under the shadow of the Almighty.*
Psalm 91:1

Dialing the numbers 9-1-1 in the United States will get you in touch
with emergency help. It's so simple that even preschoolers have
saved the lives of family members by using it. In an emergency,
help is as close as three pushes on the phone keypad.

Often, though, the situations we face cannot be remedied by human rescuers.
When that happens, we can call a different kind of 9-1-1—Psalm 91:1. There
we find the help and protection of our almighty God. God's protection
and the comfort of His presence are available for the asking. —DB

*We need not fear life's dark shadows when we
abide under the shadow of God's wings.*

Blessed be the God and Father of our Lord Jesus Christ, the Father of mercies and God of all comfort. 2 Corinthians 1:3

One day in 1932, pianist, singer, and songwriter Thomas A. Dorsey left his pregnant wife, Nettie, at home in Chicago while he drove to St. Louis to sing at a revival meeting. All went well, and the crowd responded enthusiastically. At the end of Dorsey's performance, he received a telegram with the tragic news that his wife had died in childbirth. Within hours, their baby boy also died. Filled with grief, Dorsey sought answers. A few days after Nettie's death, Dorsey sat down at the piano and began to play. Finally sensing God's peace and closeness, he began to sing some new words and play a new song: "Precious Lord, take my hand, lead me on, let me stand."

Is there a problem or a grief too big for you to handle alone? Put your hand in the Lord's. Let the "God of all comfort" lead you home. —DB

When God permits trials, He also provides comfort.

JANUARY 10

I am persuaded that neither death nor life ... shall be able to separate us from the love of God. Romans 8:38–39

Oswald Chambers loved the poetry of Robert Browning and often quoted a phrase from the poem *Rabbi Ben Ezra*: "The best is yet to be, the last of life for which the first was made. Our times are in His hand." As principal of the Bible Training College in London from 1911 to 1915, Chambers often said that the school's initials, B.T.C., also stood for "Better To Come." He believed that the future was always bright with possibility because of Christ. In a letter to former students written during the dark days of World War I, Chambers said, "Whatever transpires, it is ever 'the best is yet to be.'"

No matter what difficulties come our way, in Christ, "the best is yet to be." —DCM

You can be confident about tomorrow if you walk with God today.

JANUARY 11

*Whom have I in heaven but You? And there is
none upon earth that I desire besides You.*
Psalm 73:25

A cynic asked an elderly believer who had endured great physical
pain for twenty years, "What do you think of your God now?"
The godly sufferer replied, "I think of Him more than ever."

Sorrow and pain can be the means of bringing us heart-to-heart
with God. When repeated strokes of adversity have robbed us
of health, friends, money, or favorable circumstances, God then
becomes the only thing in life for us. We come to love Him for
who He is and not merely for what He has to give. —DHR

When we have nothing left but God, we find that God is enough.

JANUARY 12

Christ Jesus came into the world to save sinners, of whom I am chief.
1 Timothy 1:15

A thoughtful pastor friend of mine was slowly dying after fifty years of faithful ministry. He often talked with me about the nature of God and the eternity he would soon enter. As we talked, we both realized that we had only a superficial grasp of these mysteries, but we were not distressed. We knew that God had rescued us from our sin and guilt, and we rejoiced in our salvation. We had all we needed to obey the Lord gladly, live confidently, and serve Him gratefully, no matter how many days we had left on this earth.

Even when we are distressed by our inability to answer life's most vexing questions, let us trust Him and make obeying Him our highest goal. This is the path to a grateful, joyous, and hope-filled life. The answers can wait. —HVL

Christ came not to satisfy our curiosity but to save our souls.

JANUARY 13

You have put gladness in my heart.
Psalm 4:7

Did you know that the act of smiling can promote good feelings? Researchers have found that saying the word *cheese* causes a person to smile, which in turn creates pleasant feelings. On the other hand, saying the word *few* creates a different facial expression, which results in negative emotions. Interesting as such a study may be, there's a better way to have peace and gladness. It works from the inside out, not from the outside in.

The psalmist David rested in the assurance of God's peace and safety. He was confident that he would receive gladness in his heart as a gift from God. —MRD

The heart touched by God's grace brings joy to the face.

JANUARY 14

He restores my soul; He leads me in the paths of righteousness for His name's sake. Psalm 23:3

Studies show that a week's holiday each year can dramatically reduce stress and the risk of heart attack. A vacation can be good for body and soul. But what if we don't have the luxury of taking time away from work and daily responsibilities? What can we do when we must remain in demanding circumstances?

Psalm 23 paints a beautiful word picture of a caring shepherd, secure sheep, and a tranquil scene of quiet meadows and still waters. But it is the Lord, our shepherd, who gives rest, not the green grass or the flowing stream. Through prayer and meditation on His Word, we can commune with Him. In the Lord's presence we can experience the rest and renewal we so desperately need. —DCM

Spending quiet time with God will bring quiet rest from God.

JANUARY 15

*One thing I have desired of the Lord . . . that I may
dwell in the house of the Lord all the days of my life.*

Psalm 27:4

Most of the time I can take on as much work as anyone can give
me. But some days there just seems to be too much to do. The
schedule may be so full of meetings, appointments, and deadlines
that there's no room to breathe. Too much work, parenting, home
improvement, and other responsibilities for one person to handle.

When that happens, I need to get my perspective realigned by
reminding myself what Jesus said to Martha (Luke 10:38–42). Martha
got so wrapped up in her service that she forgot the most important
thing—fellowship with her Lord. Spend time with the Lord. He
will lift your load and give you the right perspective. —DB

To keep your life in balance, lean on the Lord.

JANUARY 16

Unto the upright there arises light in the darkness.
Psalm 112:4

A missionary in Peru went to visit a group of believers one evening. The house where they were meeting was located on a cliff and the path was treacherous. As she began the hazardous ascent to the house on foot, the night was dark and the way was difficult. Suddenly, as she rounded a bend, she came upon several people carrying lanterns. They had come out to light her way. Her fears were relieved, and she ascended the path easily.

In a similar way, when Jesus, the Light of the World, enters our lives, He removes the darkness of our sin and despair. This light continues to comfort us and brighten our way through times of sorrow, in the midst of sadness, trouble, illness, or disappointment. Jesus gives light in the darkest night! —DCE

God sometimes puts us in the dark to show us that Jesus is the light.

JANUARY 17

The eternal God is your refuge, and underneath are the everlasting arms.
Deuteronomy 33:27

A mother eagle builds a comfortable and secure nest for her young, padding it with feathers from her own breast. But one day the mother eagle will disturb the twigs of the nest, making it an uncomfortable place to stay. Then she will pick up a perplexed eaglet, soar into the sky, and drop it. The little bird will begin to free-fall. But Mama is not far away. Quickly she will swoop under and catch the fledgling on one strong wing. She will repeat this exercise until each eaglet is capable of flying on its own.

Are you afraid of free-falling, unsure of where or how hard you will land? Remember, God will spread His everlasting arms beneath you. He will also teach you something new and wonderful through it. Falling into God's arms is nothing to be afraid of. —JY

God's love does not keep us from trials but sees us through them.

JANUARY 18

Has God forgotten to be gracious? Has He in anger shut up His tender mercies?
Psalm 77:9

While visiting a World War I military cemetery in France, I was struck by the number of grave markers bearing only these words: A SOLDIER OF THE GREAT WAR: KNOWN UNTO GOD. Imagining the loneliness of men dying in war was overpowering.

Sometimes in life we may feel forgotten and alone. In our darkest moments, we can remember the words of Jesus: "Are not five sparrows sold for two copper coins? And not one of them is forgotten before God. But the very hairs of your head are all numbered. Do not fear therefore; you are of more value than many sparrows" (Luke 12:6–7). We are never forgotten by God. —DCM

In every desert of trial, God has an oasis of comfort.

JANUARY 19

The women said to Naomi, "Blessed be the Lord, who has not left you this day without a close relative."
Ruth 4:14

The name *Naomi* means "my delight." But when bad things happened to her, Naomi wanted to change her name to match her circumstances. She said, "Call me Mara, for the Almighty has dealt very bitterly with me" (Ruth 1:20).

Naomi judged God in light of her circumstances, and she judged wrongly. The hand of the Lord had not gone out against her. In fact, Naomi had a God-given treasure she had not yet discovered. Although Naomi lost her husband and two sons, she was given something totally unexpected—a devoted daughter-in-law and a grandchild who would be in the lineage of the Messiah. As Naomi's life shows us, sometimes the worst thing that happens to us can open the door for the best that God has to give us. —JAL

God's purpose for today's events may not be seen till tomorrow.

JANUARY 20

Yet I will rejoice in the Lord . . . . The Lord God is my strength. Habakkuk 3:18–19

What do you fear would test your faith in God the most? When I was a single woman in my twenties, my answer to that was "I don't know if I could stand the pain of losing my parents." I faced that test when I learned that my dad had heart disease and didn't have long to live. He didn't know Jesus as his Savior, so I begged God not to let him die without coming to know Him. Not only did he die that year, so did Mom, who was a believer. I didn't know if my prayer for Dad was answered.

As I wrestled with Him about my questions, I experienced the Lord as my "refuge and strength, a very present help in trouble" (Psalm 46:1). I rejoiced in the truth that God, "the Judge of all the earth," would do what was right by everyone (Genesis 18:25). —AC

God tries our faith so that we may try His faithfulness.

Two are better than one.
Ecclesiastes 4:9

When Leo and Amy opened a new restaurant, Leo admitted he was "scared of everything." Amy equates their leap of faith in starting their business to holding hands while jumping off a mountain. But if you're going to do something scary, "you want to do it with someone you know and trust," says Leo.

Solomon, the wisest man who ever lived, knew how crucial it is to have companions in life: "Two are better than one." When one falls during a difficult time, another provides comfort and support. We need others to help us through the scary times and to provide emotional support and encouragement. Because two *really are* better than one. —AC

Those who trust God can help others to do the same.

How long, O Lord? Will You forget me forever? How long will You hide Your face from me? Psalm 13:1

My friends Bob and Delores understand what it means to wait for answers that never seem to come. When their son and future daughter-in-law were murdered, a national manhunt was undertaken to find the killer and bring him to justice. After two years of prayer and pursuit, there were still no answers to the painful questions the two hurting families wrestled with. There was only silence.

David, too, wrestled with the problem of unanswered prayer. Yet, in the end, his doubts and fears and frustration turned to trust (13:5). Why? Because the circumstances of our struggles cannot diminish the character of God and His care for His children. In the pain and struggle of living without answers, we can always find comfort in our heavenly Father. —BC

When we pray, God wraps us in His loving arms.

Walk circumspectly, not as fools but as wise, redeeming the time.
Ephesians 5:15–16

A man was sitting on a park bench with his hands folded, staring into the distance. When asked what he was doing, he replied, "Oh, just killing time." What a cruel thing to do to something as valuable as time! Time should never be wasted but used to the best advantage.

Of course, there are times when we must relax and rest. That is not "killing time"; it is using time for restoration. But if a fraction of the time that we do waste could be used to pray, read the Bible, witness to others, visit a friend in distress, or comfort someone who is grieving, what a difference it would make! It is not true that we can "make up lost time." It is gone forever! —MRD

Time — use it or lose it!

JANUARY 24

Rejoice with those who rejoice, and weep with those who weep. Romans 12:15

After having his job terminated, Marty spent months fruitlessly searching for a new job. Finally his frustration got to him. Angrily, he screamed at God, "Why did you do this to me? Don't you care?" He continued his tirade until he noticed his dog Mandy cowering by a chair. Composing himself, he said, "Come here, pup. You should be glad you're a dog. At least you can't get fired from being man's best friend." As he poured out his woes and talked to Mandy, his bitterness disappeared.

David Biebel, who told the story, wrote: "Marty's relief came from all the things he said to God. But Mandy also played a part. She didn't argue or offer advice. She just listened." Sometimes our listening ear may be just what someone needs, so they can hear what God is saying to them. —DJD

Listening may be the most important thing you do today.

Let them praise the name of the Lord, for His name alone is exalted.
Psalm 148:13

A friend who experienced a total solar eclipse in England described the incredible sensation of being engulfed by the rushing shadow of darkness, then being awed by the rapidly approaching dawn. Some observers saw it as merely a coincidence that the moon was in the exact position to shut out the sun's light from reaching the earth at that particular time and place. My friend, though, called it an amazing show put on by God. She saw it as evidence of God's design, order, and precise control in the universe that He created.

God's creation sings His praise and reminds us of His sovereign purposes and control of all things in our lives. These truths can be comforting when the sunlight of our lives is eclipsed by a time of darkness and difficulty. —DCM

Because God is in control, we have nothing to fear.

JANUARY 26

Let him who glories glory in this, that he understands and knows Me, that I am the Lord.
Jeremiah 9:24

It's one thing to know about God, but it's quite another to know Him personally. The thought that God is present everywhere is staggering. But to be aware of His presence in times of need brings comfort and hope. The thought that God knows everything is mind-boggling. But to have the confidence that no detail of our lives escapes His attention is to enjoy a peace that endures through every trial. The thought that God is love is wonderful to contemplate. But to know Him as a loving Redeemer through personal faith in His Son, Jesus Christ, brings the joy of sins forgiven. —RDH

Knowing about God is fascinating; knowing God personally is life-changing.

JANUARY 27

The effective, fervent prayer of a righteous man avails much. James 5:16

While crossing the Atlantic on a ship, Bible teacher F. B. Meyer was asked to speak to the passengers. An agnostic listened to Meyer's message about answered prayer and told a friend, "I didn't believe a word of it." Later, the agnostic passed a woman fast asleep in her deck chair, her arms outstretched and her hands wide open. As a joke he put two oranges in her palms.

Later, when he saw the woman happily eating one of the pieces of fruit, he said, "You seem to be enjoying that orange." She replied, "Yes. I have been seasick for days, and I asked God somehow to send me an orange. I fell asleep while I was praying. When I awoke, I found He had sent me not only one but two oranges!" The agnostic was amazed by the unexpected confirmation of Meyer's talk on answered prayer. Later, he put his trust in Christ. —HGB

God always gives us what we ask — or something better.

JANUARY 28

Where are your gods that you have made for yourselves? Let them arise, if they can save you in the time of your trouble. Jeremiah 2:28

Accounts of plane crashes, floods, tornadoes, or hurricanes often reveal that when tragedy strikes, even the nonreligious try to get the attention of God. It would be nice to think that the heavenly Father is just waiting for such times of panic so He can send all the emergency equipment of heaven to the rescue. But the Bible indicates otherwise. Through Jeremiah, the Lord challenged His people who were in trouble to get help in the hour of death from the idols they had worshiped. He wanted them to see the futility of trusting false gods.

God doesn't want us to think we can go on trusting false gods and still expect Him to protect us from trouble. He offers hope and help to those who have learned to depend on Him all the time. —MRD

Those who walk with God always find Him close at hand.

JANUARY 29

When you do good and suffer, if you take it patiently,
this is commendable before God.
1 Peter 2:20

It's natural to want to defend ourselves against injustice and to strike back. But if we're quiet and peaceful when others mistreat and persecute us, we are responding in a Christlike way. Fenelon, a seventeenth-century theologian, put it this way: "Don't be so upset when evil men and women defraud you. Let them do as they please; just seek to do the will of God . . . . Silent peace and sweet fellowship with God will repay you for every evil thing done against you. Fix your eyes on God."

As we respond to injustice in a Christlike way, our anxiety, insecurity, and pessimism will be transformed into tranquility, stability, and hope. —DHR

The best way to respond to wrong is to do what's right.

JANUARY 30

They departed . . . rejoicing that they were counted worthy to suffer shame for His name. Acts 5:41

Imagine for a moment that you are driving through the desert in Southern California and you see the magnificent Golden Gate Bridge spanning the dried-up bed of "Three Frogs Creek" on the outskirts of "Turtle Soup Junction." What a ridiculous sight that would be!

So, too, the Lord never displays His power and grace at an inappropriate time or place, but He always provides according to the difficulty of the hour. He does not impart strength until it is needed.

As servants of Christ, we can take one step at a time and be confident that whether we come to a dried-up gulch or a surging river, the Lord's bridges of grace will be just right to allow us safe passage to the other side. —MRD

God gives enough grace for each trial we face.

JANUARY 31

Count it all joy when you fall into various trials.
James 1:2

On the back of a wedding anniversary card we received were some wiggly lines drawn by our three-year-old grandson. Alongside was a note from our daughter explaining that Trevor told her what he had written: "I'm writing a letter for your love and happy adversity."

Trevor's "mistake" has become our watchword, because it embodies the biblical principle of facing difficulties with joy. Affliction does not come as a thief to steal our happiness, but as a friend bringing the gift of staying power. Through it all, God promises us His wisdom and strength. So don't be offended if I wish you "Happy Adversity" today. —DCM

Life's burdens are designed not to break
us but to bend us toward God.

FEBRUARY 1

*He gives power to the weak, and to those
who have no might He increases strength.*
Isaiah 40:29

Researchers have found that most people perceive a hill to be steeper than it really is, especially if they're tired or carrying a heavy load. When asked to estimate the slope of a hill, test participants consistently misjudged it, thinking a ten-degree slant was about thirty degrees, and rating a five-degree slope as nearly twenty degrees.

When we're burdened and exhausted, we're tempted to sit down at the base of that difficult hill and stay there, convinced that the grade is too steep for us. That is why we need the encouragement of God's Word. It draws our attention to our untiring God, who knows our need. In His strength, we can conquer any difficult hill. —DCM

God always gives enough strength for the next step.

FEBRUARY 2

Do you not know that those who run in a race all run, but one receives the prize? Run in such a way that you may obtain it.
1 Corinthians 9:24

A computer study of 5,000 race horses has revealed a way to predict whether or not a young horse will develop into a good runner. A professor used computers and high-speed cameras to find out how a good horse runs. He discovered that the legs of a fast horse operate much like the spokes of a wheel. Each leg touches down only as the leg before it pushes off. The effect is peak efficiency of effort and speed.

In the New Testament, the Christian life is likened to a race. The apostle Paul indicated that those who run well are characterized by self-control and self-discipline. Wait on the Lord. Practice self-control. Lay aside sinful burdens. These are the secrets of running well. —MRD

Those who wait on the Lord run without the weight of sin.

FEBRUARY 3

I can do all things through Christ who strengthens me.
Philippians 4:13

I received a letter from a woman who was challenged as she read about the way I had learned to live a life dependent on God, particularly when I started a Bible study while recovering from a nervous condition. She read about my trembling hands, and how my neighbors were encouraged to admit their own weaknesses and to depend on Christ as they saw me learning to do. She wrote, "I laughed and cried as I read your story. I feel deeply encouraged that God can use me, even though I feel weak."

When we admit that we experience Christ's strength in our weakness, we proclaim this hope: "The strength Christ gives to me, He can give to you!" Whose strength will you proclaim today—your own, or God's? —JY

To experience God's strength, we must first admit our weakness.

FEBRUARY 4

He gives more grace.
James 4:6

Pastor and author F. B. Meyer once confided to a friend that he felt welcome in any home in England except his own. His loveless marriage was a source of deep heartache. Yet Meyer believed that he, by his aching soul, was being prepared to give love and strength to others, especially to his wife at the end of her days.

When you know and experience God's unconditional love, you can then give yourself to others—even to those who have caused you great pain. Allow God by His grace to work through your heartache, to control your intentions and desires, and to mold you to His perfect design. There is no greater love! —DHR

No one is beyond the reach of God's love.

FEBRUARY 5

Your way was in the sea, Your path in the great waters, and Your footsteps were not known.
Psalm 77:19

I don't wade in swift streams anymore. The bottom is too slippery, the current is too strong, and my old legs aren't what they used to be. So many challenges that I once took on readily are now too difficult for me. Like the psalmist, I lose sleep sometimes, wondering how I can negotiate them (Psalm 77:1–4). Then I remember the "works of the Lord," His "wonders of old" (v. 11). His "way was in the sea, [His] path in the great waters," though He left no footprints behind (v. 19).

That's the way it is with God. Although you can't see Him, He is surely there. Unseen, He leads His people "like a flock" (v. 20). He does not fear the currents and storms of life, for His strength and courage are infinite. —DHR

God tells us to burden Him with what burdens us.

Do not be afraid nor dismayed because of this great multitude, for the battle is not yours, but God's.

2 Chronicles 20:15

A wise Bible teacher once said, "Sooner or later God will bring self-sufficient people to the place where they have no resource but Him—no strength, no answers, nothing but Him. Without God's help, they're sunk."

He then told of a despairing man who confessed to his pastor, "My life is really in bad shape." "How bad?" the pastor inquired. Burying his head in his hands, he moaned, "I'll tell you how bad—all I've got left is God." The pastor's face lit up. "I'm happy to assure you that a person with nothing left but God has more than enough for great victory!" —JY

When all you have is God, you have all you need.

He said to them, "Come aside by yourselves
to a deserted place and rest a while."
Mark 6:31

God writes the music for our lives. Our role is to follow His lead—
humming, harmonizing, blending, and singing in tune.

Serving the Lord, like singing, can be stirring and rewarding. But when we
are set aside by illness, or replacement, or retirement, the interludes can be
frustrating and unfulfilling. It is then that we need to remind ourselves that the
Lord may be using our time of rest to make our music better. The quiet times
are opportunities to quiet our souls and compose ourselves for the measures
that lie ahead. The rest is not a mistake, but a necessary part of the symphony
God wrote in the beginning and is conducting for us every day. —DHR

God uses life's stops to prepare us for the next start.

You show lovingkindness to thousands . . . .
You are great in counsel and mighty in work.
Jeremiah 32:18–19

Christians are often asked whether their faith is strong enough to withstand *bad* times. I'm wondering, though, if a better question is this: "Is my faith strong enough to survive *good* times?" I keep hearing about people who drift away from the Lord not when life is bad but when it's good. That's when God seems unnecessary. We assume we deserve everything pleasant that happens, and we fail to appreciate what He is telling us about himself through the good gifts He lets us enjoy.

In *The Problem of Pain*, C. S. Lewis wrote, "God whispers to us in our pleasures . . . but shouts in our pains." If we refuse to listen when He whispers to us, He may use shouts to get our attention. —JAL

The goodness of God speaks volumes about His character.

FEBRUARY 9

Look among the nations and watch—be utterly astounded.
Habakkuk 1:5

During World War II, Prime Minister Winston Churchill and President Franklin Roosevelt led Great Britain and the United States to defeat Nazism and Fascism. Yet both men nearly lost their lives before the war began. In December 1931, Churchill was struck by a car as he crossed Fifth Avenue in New York City. In Miami in December 1933, an assassin's bullet barely missed Roosevelt and killed the man standing beside him. Both leaders could have died, but they survived. Why? I believe God wanted these two men alive to lead their respective nations to victory over the enemy.

The Bible teaches that God causes nations and their leaders to rise and fall. No matter what may happen in this world, God still rules! —DCE

God's sovereignty overrules any calamity.

We are His workmanship, created in Christ Jesus for good works. Ephesians 2:10

A church organist was practicing a piece by Felix Mendelssohn and not doing well. Frustrated, he gathered up his music. As he turned to leave, a stranger who had been sitting in a rear pew came forward and asked if he could play the piece. "I never let anyone touch this organ!" was the blunt reply. Finally, after two more polite requests, the grumpy musician reluctantly gave him permission. The stranger sat down and filled the sanctuary with beautiful, flawless music. When he finished, the organist asked, "Who are you?" The man replied, "I am Felix Mendelssohn." The organist had almost prevented the song's creator from playing his own music!

Sometimes we too try to play the chords of our lives, and, like that stubborn organist, we only reluctantly take our hands off the keys. But our lives won't produce beautiful music unless we let Him work through us. —DCE

God's ability is not limited by our inability.

Daniel purposed in his heart that he would not defile himself.
Daniel 1:8

Except for some man-made waterways, all rivers have one thing in common—they all are crooked. The reason is simple—they follow the path of least resistance. Rivers find their way around anything that blocks their flow because they take the easy way.

The same can be said for some people. They yield to temptation and deviate from the path God would have them follow. Unlike Daniel, who "purposed in his heart that he would not defile himself," they bend to worldly pressures and compromise what they know is right. Nothing should deter us from the course God wants us to travel. We don't have to follow the path of least resistance. The Holy Spirit will strengthen us so that we can remain steadfast. —RDH

You won't go astray on the straight and narrow way.

She called the name of the Lord who spoke to her, You-Are-the-God-Who-Sees.
Genesis 16:13

Hagar, Sarah's handmaid, was being treated unkindly by Sarah, so she fled into the wilderness. As Hagar stood alone in that desolate place, the Angel of the Lord visited her. He assured her that God was aware of her situation. Hagar responded, "You-Are-the-God-Who-Sees." She found great comfort in knowing that the Lord God saw her and knew about her distress.

Whatever your troubling circumstances are, whether you're afflicted by illness or injury, brokenhearted over the loss of a loved one, depressed, lonely, discouraged, or disillusioned, God knows and cares. Like Hagar, you can know that God sees you. —RDH

We need not fear the perils around us because the eye of the Lord is always upon us.

FEBRUARY 13

*He said to me, "My grace is sufficient for you,
for My strength is made perfect in weakness."*
2 Corinthians 12:9

One day my old college friend Tom said to me, "I can't believe how many years it has taken me to learn my latest lesson—and I'm a Bible teacher!" He went on to list some of the trials and testings he and his family had been facing and how unworthy he felt teaching an adult Sunday school class. "Week after week I felt I was a total failure and kept wondering if this might be my last Sunday before announcing my resignation." Then one Sunday, after class, a young woman said to him, "Tom, I hope you won't take this the wrong way, but you're a much better teacher when you're going through tough times."

When we recognize how much we need God, He will strengthen us. That's the advantage of weakness. —JY

In tough times, God teaches us to trust.

FEBRUARY 14

Why are you cast down, O my soul? . . . Hope in God, for I shall yet praise Him for the help of His countenance. Psalm 42:5

Looking at the western shores of Sri Lanka, I found it hard to imagine that a tsunami had struck just a few months earlier. The sea was calm and beautiful; people were going about their business in the bright sunshine. The impact of the disaster was still there, but it had gone underground into the hearts and minds of the survivors. The trauma itself would not be easily forgotten.

It was catastrophic grief that prompted the psalmist to cry out in anguish. While the rest of the world went on with business as usual, he carried in his heart the need for deep and complete healing. He submitted his brokenness to the good and great Shepherd and found the peace that allowed him to respond to life. Hope in God— it's the only solution for the deep traumas of the heart. —BC

No one is hopeless whose hope is in God.

FEBRUARY 15

Your hands shall be strengthened to go down against the camp.
Judges 7:11

The Midianites and their allies had invaded Israel. Gideon could muster only 32,000 men against an army "as numerous as locusts" (Judges 7:12). Then God cut the army down to three hundred. Gideon was afraid, but God gave him an encouraging sign that Israel would win the battle. After worshiping God, Gideon organized his three hundred men and routed the superior Midianite forces.

As Christ's followers we're not battling armies, but we are at war. Spiritual foes attack us, undermine our confidence, and sap our strength. But our God is the great Encourager. When our resolve weakens, by His power He will give us the strength we need (Ephesians 3:16). —DCE

To trust is to triumph, for the battle is the Lord's.

FEBRUARY 16

Your faithfulness endures to all generations.
Psalm 119:90

Jim and Carol Cymbala prayed and praised and preached their way through a personal two-year nightmare. Their teenage daughter Chrissy had turned her back on the God they loved and served so faithfully. Although their hearts were breaking, Jim and Carol continued ministering to the people of the Brooklyn Tabernacle in New York City. Some people think that Carol wrote the song "He's Been Faithful" after her daughter's dramatic return to God, but she didn't. She wrote it before. Carol refers to it as "a song of hope born in the midst of my pain." The words she wrote during that time helped her to move forward. Although her daughter had not yet come back to the Lord, Carol could praise Him for His loving faithfulness in her own life. —JAL

When we have nothing left but God, we find that God is enough.

Whenever I am afraid, I will trust in You.

Psalm 56:3

Few of us are traveling to heaven in a state of freedom from all fear. We do trust in God, and yet we may be troubled at times by gnawing worries. Even the apostle Paul, who wrote many of the New Testament letters, had some anxieties. He confessed to the Corinthians, "I was with you in weakness, in fear, and in much trembling" (1 Corinthians 2:3).

So don't worry that you have worries. Admit them to yourself. Share them with a trusted friend. Above all, talk to the all-compassionate Friend, Jesus Christ, who knows your every thought and emotion. Ask Him for the grace to help you overcome your fears and worries. On your journey through life, whenever you're afraid, trust in the Lord. —VCG

Trusting God's faithfulness dispels our fearfulness.

*I have come that they may have life, and that they
may have it more abundantly.* John 10:10

A veteran mountain climber who had conquered most of the world's most difficult peaks was sharing his experiences with a group of novices preparing for their first major climb. "Remember this," he said, "your goal is to experience the exhilaration of the climb and the joy of reaching the peak. Each step draws you closer to the top. If your purpose for climbing is just to avoid death, your experience will be minimal."

I see an application here to the Christian's experience. Jesus did not call us to live the Christian life just to escape hell. If that's our primary motivation, we are missing the wonders and joys and victories of climbing higher and higher with Jesus. When we walk by faith, we will see each day of the Christian life as a challenge to be met, and as one more upward step to glory! —DCE

We get the most out of life when we live for Christ.

He who has begun a good work in you will complete it.
Philippians 1:6

In his book *Laugh Again*, Charles Swindoll writes of three common "joy stealers"—worry, stress, and fear. He defines worry as "an inordinate anxiety about something that may or may not occur." (And it usually doesn't.) Stress is "intense strain over a situation we can't change or control." (But God can.) And fear is a "dreadful uneasiness over danger, evil, or pain." (And it magnifies our problems.)

Whatever causes you worry, stress, and fear cannot ultimately keep God from continuing His good work in you. With this confidence we can begin each day knowing that He is in control. You can resist those "joy stealers" by renewing your confidence in God each morning. Then relax and rejoice. —JY

Happiness depends on happenings; joy depends on Jesus.

Ask, and it will be given to you.
Luke 11:9

In Luke 11, a man who needed food for a guest went to a friend's house at midnight and asked for three loaves of bread. It was the middle of the night, yet the friend got up and provided the requested food. I don't think the man gave his friend what he wanted just because he wouldn't go away. Rather, he got up because he realized that this friend would not have had the boldness to wake him if he hadn't been desperate.

If an earthly friend will graciously meet your need, will not your heavenly Father do far more than that? He never sleeps, and He wants the very best for you. Therefore, do not hesitate to ask, seek, and knock. He will always be there for you. —HVL

God is never inconvenienced by our prayers.

Jesus stood and cried out, saying, "If anyone thirsts,
let him come to Me and drink." John 7:37

Lee Atwater was a well-known figure in U.S. politics. He engineered the successful 1988 presidential campaign of George H. W. Bush and was the head of the Republican National Committee (1988–1991). But in the midst of all his successful activities he developed an inoperable brain tumor and died at the age of forty. During his illness, Atwater came to realize that wealth, honor, and power are not life's supreme values. Admitting to a deep emptiness within himself, he confessed, "My illness helped me to see that what was missing in society is what is missing in me—a little heart, a lot of brotherhood."

What about your own life? Is it spiritually dried up? Ask Jesus, the fountain of living water, to fill you with His presence. Then joy and peace will begin to bubble up and even overflow. —VCG

The only real thirst quencher is Jesus — the living water.

[God] is able to do exceedingly abundantly above all that we ask or think.
Ephesians 3:20

A missionary wrote a newsletter to thank his supporters for being "prayer warriors." Because of a typing error, though, he called them "prayer *worriers*." For some of us, that might be a good description. During an anxious time in my life, I became a "prayer worrier." I would beg, "Lord, please keep my neighbor from causing me problems tomorrow." Or, "Father, don't let that ornery person spread gossip about me."

But then the Lord taught me to pray *for* people, rather than *against* them. I began to say, "Lord, bless and encourage my neighbor, and help him to sense your love." Then I watched to see what God would do. The Lord's amazing answers not only helped others but also helped to cure my own anxiety! —JY

Fervent prayer dispels anxious care.

Those who wait on the Lord . . . shall mount up with wings like eagles.
Isaiah 40:31

One of the pitfalls of living in our troublesome world is that we can become problem-centered rather than God-centered. When this happens, we lose the proper perspective. Our problems begin to look huge and the strength of almighty God seems small. Instead of moving mountains by faith, we become constant worriers, creating mountains of needless pressure for ourselves and others.

In Isaiah 40 God offers us a new perspective. If we will depend on Him instead of brooding over our problems, He will renew our strength, and wings of faith will lift our hearts above our difficulties. Some of them may be huge, but we can see them as smaller than our great God. And that makes all the difference. —JY

Worry ends where faith begins.

The Lord is in His holy temple. Let all the earth keep silence before Him.
Habakkuk 2:20

In 1861, during the U.S. Civil War, author and lecturer Julia Ward Howe visited Washington, D.C. One day she went outside the city and saw a large number of soldiers marching. Early the next morning she awoke with words for a song in her mind. She was aware of all the ugliness of the war, but her faith led her to write: "Mine eyes have seen the glory of the coming of the Lord." She saw, I believe, that in spite of all the ugliness, God was "marching on" toward the day when He will right the wrongs of the ages.

The prophet Habakkuk came to a similar conclusion. God assured His servant that through all the ugliness and wrongs of history, He is "marching on" toward the day when "the earth will be filled with the knowledge of the glory of the Lord." —HVL

Someday the scales of justice will be perfectly balanced.

*Why are you cast down, O my soul? . . . Hope in God, for I shall
yet praise Him for the help of His countenance.* Psalm 42:5

I love settling down with a good book by a crackling fire when it's snowing,
although my love grows a little dim when the long gray days of winter drone
on into February. Yet regardless of the weather, there is always something
special about winter: Christmas! Thankfully, long after the decorations are
down, the reality of Christmas still lifts my spirits no matter what's happening.

If it weren't for the reality of Christ's birth, not only would winter be
dark and dreary, but our hearts would be bleak and have nothing to
hope for. In the winter of a troubled life, the psalmist declared, "Hope in
God, for I shall yet praise Him for the help of His countenance." —JS

*For those who know the God who made the seasons,
it is always Christmas in our hearts!*

FEBRUARY 26

Let us therefore come boldly to the throne of grace, that we
may obtain mercy and find grace to help in time of need.
Hebrews 4:16

I sometimes ask people, "Where does it say in the Bible, 'God helps those who help themselves'?" Most say they're not sure, but the concept is so familiar that they think it must be somewhere in God's Word. Actually, the Bible doesn't say that at all. It tells us just the opposite: God helps the helpless.

Are you feeling helpless today? God's grace is available for those who recognize that they cannot help themselves. "Come boldly to the throne of grace" to find help in your time of need. —DHR

God helps those who know they are helpless.

Are [angels] not all ministering spirits sent forth to minister? Hebrews 1:14

At one point in Martin Luther's life, he received some discouraging news. He responded by saying, "Recently I have been looking up at the night sky, spangled and studded with stars, and I found no pillars to hold them up. Yet they did not fall." Luther was encouraged knowing that the same unseen God who was upholding the universe was caring for him.

There is another unseen source of help for God's children when facing a physical or spiritual crisis—angels! Those heavenly hosts are called "ministering spirits," and they are instantly responsive to God's command. Just knowing that these unseen helpers are on our side strengthens our trust in God, whom they faithfully serve. —DJD

*The angels of God assist the people of
God as they do the work of God.*

FEBRUARY 28

You have been my defense and refuge in the day of my trouble.
Psalm 59:16

In a world where violence and terrorism may strike anytime, anyplace, where can we find security? Where can we be safe? The Bible says that our security is not in human protection but in God himself. The book of Psalms contains more than forty references to taking refuge in the Lord, many of them from David's experience of being pursued by his enemies. In his prayers for help, he centered his hope in the Lord: "You have been my defense and refuge in the day of my trouble . . . God is my defense, my God of mercy."

God doesn't guarantee to protect us from difficulty and physical harm, but He does promise to be our refuge in every situation. In Him we find real security. —DCM

No one is more secure than the one who rests in God's hands.

In God I have put my trust; I will not be afraid. What can man do to me?
Psalm 56:11

Was David paranoid? Did he think the whole world was out to get him? You might get that impression as you read through some of his psalms. Of course, for a period of time David was hotly pursued by Saul and his men, and later he had to deal with other enemies, so it's easy to see why he felt as he did.

David's observations about people may echo the way we feel when others criticize or oppose us. Perhaps it's those with whom we work, or family members who apparently enjoy irritating us. Or people at church who seem to be critical and faultfinding. We feel as if everyone is against us. If this describes your situation, it's time to do what David did. He declared, "In God I have put my trust; I will not be afraid. What can man do to me?" —DB

God is stronger than our strongest foe.

MARCH 1

He is my refuge and my fortress; my God, in Him I will trust. Psalm 91:2

In his book *The Fisherman and His Friends*, Louis Albert Banks tells of two men who were assigned to stand watch on a ship out at sea. During the night the waves from a raging storm washed one of them overboard. The sailor who drowned had been in the most sheltered place, while the one who survived was more exposed to the elements. What made the difference? The man who was lost had nothing to hold on to.

When life is peaceful, many people are self-sufficient, but when the going gets rough they are swept off their feet. Because they have refused God's help and have nothing to hold on to, they are easily overwhelmed. People who cling to the Lord, though, can weather the fiercest storms of adversity. —RDH

God has not promised to keep us from life's storms, but to keep us through them.

Go, and I will be with your mouth and teach you what you shall say.
Exodus 4:12

When God called Moses to serve, Moses replied, "I am slow of speech and slow of tongue" (Exodus 4:10). The language in this verse suggests that Moses may have had a speech impediment. Whatever his problem might have been, Moses is an example of how our impairments, disabilities, and handicaps can be used by God for His glory. He may not remove them, but He will endow us with strength and use our limitations for good.

If our weaknesses cause us to seek God and rely on Him, they actually help us instead of hinder us. In fact, they become the best thing that could happen to us, because our growth in courage, power, and happiness depends on our relationship with the Lord and how much we are relying on Him. —DHR

God's strength is best seen in our weakness.

MARCH 3

*Though the labor of the olive may fail, and the fields
yield no food . . . yet I will rejoice in the Lord.*
Habakkuk 3:17–18

In the book *450 Stories for Life*, Gust Anderson tells about visiting a church in a farming community of eastern Alberta, Canada, where there had been eight years of drought. The farmers' economic situation looked hopeless. But in spite of their poverty, many of them continued to meet together to worship and praise God. Anderson was especially impressed by the testimony of a farmer who stood up and quoted Habakkuk 3:17–18. Anderson thought, *That dear saint has found the secret of real joy!*

It's not wrong to find pleasure in the good things money can buy, but we should never rely on them for happiness. If our joy is found in the Lord, however, nothing can disrupt it, not even economic distress. —RDH

Happiness depends on happenings; joy depends on Jesus!

Command Joshua, and encourage him and strengthen him.
Deuteronomy 3:28

When a corporate accountant committed suicide, an effort was made to find out why. The company's books were examined, but no shortage was found. Nothing could be uncovered that gave any clue as to why he took his life—that is, until a note was discovered. It simply said: "In thirty years I have never had one word of encouragement. I'm fed up!"

All of us need words of encouragement, appreciation, and commendation as we carry out our daily responsibilities, whether at home or at work. Every day let's determine to encourage (not flatter) at least one person. Let's do our part to help those around us who are dying for encouragement. —RDH

A word of encouragement can make the difference between giving up or going on.

MARCH 5

God is faithful, who will not allow you to be tempted beyond what you are able.
1 Corinthians 10:13

We've all seen load-limit signs on highways, bridges, and elevators. Knowing that too much strain can cause severe damage or complete collapse, engineers determine the exact amount of stress that various materials can safely endure.

Human beings also have their load limits, which vary from person to person. But the Lord knows our limitations and never allows any difficulties to enter our lives that exceed our strength and ability to endure. So when trials and temptations press down on you, take courage. Draw on His strength; no temptation will ever be greater than that! —RDH

God knows the limits of our ability to stand up under life's pressures.

MARCH 6

The things which are seen are temporary, but the things which are not seen are eternal. 2 Corinthians 4:18

I have a friend who was denied a doctorate from a prestigious West Coast university because of his Christian worldview. As he was approaching the conclusion of his studies, his advisor invited him to come into his office and informed him that his dissertation had been rejected. My friend's first thought was of thousands of dollars and five years of his life taking flight, and his heart sank. But then he thought of the words of the hymn by Rhea Miller: "I'd rather have Jesus than silver or gold, I'd rather be His than have riches untold; I'd rather have Jesus than anything this world affords today." And then my friend laughed—for he realized that nothing of eternal value had been lost. —RDH

Living only for temporary gain leads to eternal loss.

MARCH 7

"The Lord is my portion," says my soul, "therefore I hope in Him!"
Lamentations 3:24

A mother was told that her son had been killed in an accident on the job. In that moment, her life was flooded with tears. In another family, a sudden heart attack snatched away a husband, leaving a wife to face life alone. More tears! We live in a weeping world.

The book of Lamentations was written by Jeremiah, who is called the weeping prophet. Yet Jeremiah still affirmed the mercies, the compassions, and the faithfulness of God. Weeping and lamentations do not necessarily reflect a weak faith or a lack of trust in God. Tears are a natural part of a Christian's life. But thank God, one day our blessed Savior will wipe them all away. —DJD

The soul would have no rainbow if the eyes had no tears.

Rejoice in the Lord always. Again I will say, rejoice!
Philippians 4:4

Fanny Crosby lost her sight when she was only six weeks old. She lived into her nineties, composing thousands of beloved hymns. On her 92nd birthday she cheerfully said, "If in all the world you can find a happier person than I am, do bring him to me. I should like to shake his hand."

What enabled Fanny Crosby to experience such joy in the face of what many would term a "tragedy"? At an early age she chose to "rejoice in the Lord always." In fact, Fanny carried out a resolution she made when she was only eight years old: "How many blessings I enjoy that other people don't. To weep and sigh because I'm blind, I cannot and I won't." —VCG

*Rather than complain about the thorns on roses,
be thankful for roses among the thorns.*

MARCH 9

His compassions fail not. They are new every morning;
great is Your faithfulness. Lamentations 3:22–23

The prophet Jeremiah witnessed unimaginable horrors when the Babylonians invaded Jerusalem in 586 BC. Solomon's temple was reduced to ruins, and with it went not only the center of worship but also the heart of the community. The people were left with no food, no rest, no peace, no leader. But in the midst of suffering and grief, one of their prophets found a reason for hope. "Through the Lord's mercies we are not consumed," wrote Jeremiah, "because His compassions fail not. They are new every morning; great is Your faithfulness."

Jeremiah's hope came from his personal experience of the Lord's faithfulness and from his knowledge of God's promises in the past. Without these, he would have been unable to comfort his people. —JAL

The best reason for hope is God's faithfulness.

MARCH 10

*Be clothed with humility, for "God resists the proud,
but gives grace to the humble."* 1 Peter 5:5

Kevin Rogers, pastor of a church in Canada, has likened the grace of
God to an imaginary secretary who compels him to treat other people
as God does. "Grace is my secretary. She lets the strangest people into
my workspace to interrupt me. Somehow she lets calls get through that
I would prefer to leave for a more convenient time. Doesn't Grace know
that I have an agenda? Some days I wish that Grace weren't here. But
Grace has an amazing way of covering my mistakes and turning the
office into a holy place. Grace finds good in everything, even failures."

When "the God of all grace" (5:10) controls our lives, He can
transform interruptions into opportunities, mistakes into successes,
pride into humility, and suffering into strength. —DCM

When you know God's grace, you'll want to show God's grace.

MARCH 13

They tempted the Lord, saying, "Is the Lord among us or not?"
Exodus 17:7

The people of ancient Israel had just been delivered from slavery, and they ought to have been thankful. Instead, they started to complain to Moses and Aaron, "Oh, that we had died by the hand of the Lord in the land of Egypt!" (Exodus 16:3). In reality, their complaint was with God, but they picked a fight with Moses because he was the leader. They even began questioning if God was really with them (v. 7). Yet He always met their needs.

If we're honest, we have to admit that we sometimes complain when God isn't coming through for us the way we want. We accuse Him of being absent or disinterested. But when our heart is concerned with God's purposes rather than our own, we will be patient and trust Him to provide all that we need. —AL

To conquer the habit of complaining, count your blessings.

MARCH 14

In our spiritual walk with the Lord, we have a hard time seeing while we're on the go. We need to stop between steps—to pause and refocus on the Word and the will of God. That's not to say we have to pray and meditate about every little decision in life. But certainly our walk with the Lord needs to have built into it a pattern of stops that enable us to see more clearly before moving on.

Daniel's practice of praying three times a day was an essential part of his walk with God. He knew there's a certain kind of spiritual refocusing that we can't do without stopping. His stops gave him a very different kind of walk—one that was obvious to those around him. —MRD

Time in Christ's service requires time out for renewal.

Rejoice with those who rejoice, and weep with those who weep.
Romans 12:15

Following the death of our seventeen-year-old daughter in a car accident in June 2002, each member of our family handled the loss differently. For my wife, among the most helpful sources of comfort were visits from moms who had also lost a child in an accident. Sue found strength in their stories, and she wanted them to tell her how God had been faithful in their lives, despite the deep sorrow that comes with losing a precious child. Soon Sue became part of a circle of compassion, a small group of moms who could weep, pray, and seek God's help together as they faced their daily sorrow.

Each person grieves uniquely, yet we all need to share our hearts, our burdens, our questions, and our sadness with someone else. That's why it's vital that we find others with whom to discuss our pain and sorrow. —DB

We must learn to weep before we can dry another's tears.

Your Father knows the things you have need of before you ask Him.
Matthew 6:8

A man had transformed an overgrown plot of ground into a beautiful garden and was showing a friend what he had accomplished. Pointing to a bed of flowers, he said, "Look at what I did here." His companion corrected him, "You mean, 'Look at what God and I did here.'" The gardener replied, "I guess you're right. But you should have seen the shape this plot was in when He was taking care of it by himself."

We chuckle at the man's reply, but it expresses a wonderful spiritual truth—we are co-workers with God. God has graciously chosen to give us the privilege of being His partners in both the physical and spiritual areas of life. Through prayer we work with Him in defeating the powers of evil and in bringing about the fulfillment of His loving purposes in the world. —HVL

God's work is done by those who pray.

MARCH 17

Set your mind on things above, not on things on the earth. Colossians 3:2

A young boy was sailing his toy boat on a pond. While he was playing with it along the water's edge, the boat floated out beyond his reach. In his distress he asked an older boy to help him. The older child picked up some stones and started to throw them toward the boat. The little boy became upset, thinking that the one he had turned to for help was being mean. Soon, though, he noticed that instead of hitting the boat, each stone was directed beyond it, making a small ripple that moved the vessel a little nearer to the shore. Every throw of the stone was planned, and at last the treasured toy was brought back safely to his waiting hands. —HGB

God uses the waves of trial to draw us closer to Him.

MARCH 18

O Lord of hosts, blessed is the man who trusts in You!
Psalm 84:12

I was sitting in my chair by the window, staring out through fir and spruce trees to the mountains beyond, lost in thought. I looked down and saw a young fox, staring up at my face. She was as still as a stone. Days before, I had seen her at the edge of the woods, looking nervously over her shoulder at me. I went to the kitchen for an egg, and rolled it toward the place I had last seen her. Each day I put another egg on the lawn, and each day she ventured out of the trees just long enough to pick it up. Then she would dart back into the woods. Now she had come on her own to my door to get an egg, convinced, I suppose, that I meant her no harm.

You may at times distrust God, as the fox was wary of me at first. But give Him a chance to prove His love. Taste and see that He is good! —DHR

No one is beyond the reach of God's love.

MARCH 19

You heard the voice of my supplications when I cried out to You.
Psalm 31:22

During Antarctica's nine-month winter, the continent is engulfed in darkness and the temperature sinks to -115° F (-82° C). Flights are halted from late February to November, leaving workers at scattered research stations isolated and virtually cut off from outside help. Yet, during 2001, two daring rescue missions penetrated the polar winter and airlifted people with serious medical conditions to safety.

We all feel helpless and cut off at times. It may seem that not even God can hear or answer our cries for help. But in Jesus Christ, God has pierced the dark winter of our world in a daring rescue through His redeeming love. He is able to reach us and calm our fears in the most desperate circumstances. —DCM

God's help is only a prayer away.

MARCH 20

You, O Lord, are a shield for me, my glory and the One who lifts up my head.
Psalm 3:3

Some people measure their worth by beauty, intelligence, money, power, or prestige. But David, who wrote Psalm 3, found his security and worth in God. He said that many stood against him. He heard their cruel voices and was tempted to believe them. Nevertheless, he comforted and strengthened his heart with these words: "You, O Lord, are . . . my glory and the One who lifts up my head." The word *glory* is the translation of a Hebrew word meaning "weight" or "significance." What a change that realization made! David had God, and his enemies did not. So he could hold up his head with confidence.

Tell God all about your troubles. Let Him be your glory. You don't have to defend yourself. Ask Him to be your shield—to protect your heart with His overshadowing love and care. —DHR

No one is more secure than the one who is held in God's hands.

MARCH 21

For this child I prayed, and the Lord has granted me my petition.
1 Samuel 1:27

Nine months can seem like forever for a mother-to-be. Then, suddenly, the endless waiting is over. The nine long months become insignificant, a faint memory—overcome by joy. Ask the new mom if she regrets enduring her pregnancy. Never!

Hannah's wait began even more slowly. For years she was unable to have a child. She felt so unfulfilled, so dishonored. But the Lord remembered her, and she conceived. Her joy was complete. Hannah waited patiently and saw the Lord turn her sorrow into overflowing joy. —MRD

God's gift of joy is worth the wait.

MARCH 22

I will not leave you orphans; I will come to you. John 14:18

Even though Jesus doesn't move among us physically, by the Holy Spirit He is here—a continuous, living presence—outside of us and inside of us.

That may be a terrifying thought for some. Insecurity and sin can create a sense of fear, awkwardness, and clumsiness in Jesus' presence. But think of what you know about Him. Despite what you are or what you may have done, He loves you (Romans 5:8; 1 John 4:7–11). He will never leave you nor forsake you (John 14:18; Hebrews 13:5). Others may not like the way you look, but He looks at your heart (1 Samuel 16:7; Luke 24:38). Jesus loves you in spite of all the conditions that cause others to turn away. He wants to change you to be like Him, but He loves you as you are and will never abandon you. —DHR

If you know Jesus, you'll never walk alone.

Everyone who asks receives, and he who seeks finds. Matthew 7:8

A twelve-year-old Cambodian boy began to question his family's religious beliefs. He asked his uncle, a temple priest, if he had ever had a prayer answered. The man was shocked by the brashness of his nephew's question, but he admitted that he couldn't remember a single time one of his prayers had been answered. Later, the boy asked a Christian if God had ever answered his prayers. The man recounted several instances. The boy was so impressed that he accepted Jesus as his Savior that day. Since then, prayer has become a vital part of his life.

Jesus said, "Ask, and it will be given to you; seek, and you will find; knock, and it will be opened to you" (Matthew 7:7). The true and living God hears and answers according to His will. And His will is always good. —VCG

Through prayer, finite man draws upon the power of the infinite God.

When he brings out his own sheep, he goes before them; and the sheep follow him, for they know his voice. John 10:4

After a hijacked plane slammed into the Pentagon on September 11, 2001, many people inside the building were trapped by a cloud of thick, blinding smoke. Police officer Isaac Hoopi ran into the blackness, searching for survivors, and heard people calling for help. He began shouting back: "Head toward my voice!" Six people, who had lost all sense of direction in a smoke-filled hallway, heard his shouts and followed Hoopi's voice to safety.

"Head toward My voice!" That's also the invitation of Jesus to each of us when we are in danger or when we have lost our way. Whatever our need for guidance or protection, He calls us to heed His voice and follow Him. —DCM

You don't need to know where you're going if you're following the Shepherd.

MARCH 25

In all things we commend ourselves as ministers of God:
in much patience, in tribulations, in needs, in distresses.
2 Corinthians 6:4

An online publication called the *Journal of Mundane Behavior* says that ordinary, routine events fill most of our time. The managing editor, a sociologist, says everyday life is valuable, since we spend nearly 60 percent of our lives doing things like commuting to work and shopping for groceries.

Oswald Chambers said that we tend to lose our enthusiasm "when there is . . . just the common round, the trivial task. The thing that tells in the long run for God and for men is the steady persevering work in the unseen, and the only way to keep the life uncrushed is to live looking to God" (*My Utmost for His Highest*, March 6). So let's live today to the fullest for the Lord, because it's such an important, ordinary day. —DCM

To get the most out of life, make every moment count for Christ.

MARCH 26

I will never leave you nor forsake you. Hebrews 13:5

Robinson Crusoe, the chief character in a novel by Daniel Defoe, was shipwrecked and stranded on an uninhabited island. Life was hard, but he found hope and comfort in the Word of God. Crusoe said, "One morning, being very sad, I opened the Bible upon these words, 'I will never, never leave thee, nor forsake thee.' Immediately it occurred that these words were to *me;* why else should they be directed in such a manner, just at the moment when I was mourning over my condition, as one forsaken of God and man?

"From this moment I began to conclude in my mind that it was possible for me to be more happy in this forsaken, solitary condition than it was probable that I should ever have been [elsewhere] . . . and with this thought I was going to give thanks to God for bringing me to this place." —DHR

Fear will leave us when we remember that God is always with us.

If God is for us, who can be against us? Romans 8:31

Naomi, her husband, and their two sons left Israel and moved to Moab because of a famine. Eventually Naomi's husband and sons died, so she decided to return to Israel. But she felt that her daughters-in-law would be better off staying in Moab. She tried to dissuade them from going with her by saying, "No, my daughters; for it grieves me very much for your sakes that the hand of the Lord has gone out against me!" But God was not against her. He proved this by wonderfully providing for her and Ruth after they returned to Israel. (Read the book of Ruth—it's short.)

God hasn't promised to keep us from problems. But He has proven that He is always "for us" as Christians by what He did through Jesus. Nothing, not even death, can separate us from His love. The Lord is always for us! —HVL

The One who died to save you will never be against you.

As the clay is in the potter's hand, so are you in My hand. Jeremiah 18:6

When I was a young woman, the Lord began convicting me of my negative, self-pitying, and bitter thinking. With the help of God's Word, I recognized my need for change in three main areas: my attitudes, actions, and reactions. But I feared I couldn't change. One day I read in Jeremiah 18 how the potter refashioned some marred clay (which is what I felt like) into a different vessel, as it pleased the potter. What I couldn't do, my great Potter could! I only needed to be cooperative clay.

Today this vessel is far from finished. But as I put myself in the Potter's hands, He keeps working on me and shaping my attitudes and actions. I call them Christ-attitudes, Christ-actions, and Christ-reactions. The great Potter can do the same for you. —JY

A change in the heart brings a change in behavior.

These things I have spoken to you, that My joy may remain in you, and that your joy may be full. John 15:11

Writer C. W. Metcalf was working as a hospice volunteer when he met thirteen-year-old Chuck, who was terminally ill. One day Chuck gave Metcalf half a dozen sheets of paper with writing on both sides and said, "I want you to give this to my mom and dad after I die. It's a list of all the fun we had, all the times we laughed." Metcalf was amazed that this young boy on the verge of death was thinking about the well-being of others.

Metcalf delivered the list. Years later he decided to make a list of his own. At first he found it difficult to compile his "joy list." But as he began looking each day for the moments of laughter, satisfaction, and joy, his list began to grow. Why not begin your own joy list today. It can be a good reminder of the Lord's faithful love and the gladness of heart He brings. —DCM

To multiply your joy, count your blessings.

MARCH 30

Jesus turned, and seeing them following, said to them, "What do you seek?"
John 1:38

How would you answer if Jesus were to ask you, "What do you seek?" Would you ask Him for health and fitness? A better job? A happier marriage? Financial security? Vindication from a false accusation? Salvation for a wayward loved one? An explanation of some difficult theological concept?

I wonder how often we miss an opportunity to spend time with Jesus because we're seeking something other than His presence. I know from experience that the more time I spend with Jesus, the less desire I have for a lot of things that once seemed very important. —JAL

Jesus longs for our fellowship even more than we long for His.

MARCH 31

*Take My yoke upon you and learn from Me . . . and
you will find rest for your souls.* Matthew 11:29

Many Christians are anxious and troubled. A closer look at their anxiety can
reveal the reason for their distress. Having never learned to rest in the Lord,
they fail to experience the "quietness and confidence" (Isaiah 30:15) that comes
to those who daily fellowship with Him through Bible study and prayer.

Don't become a victim of fruitless fretting. Instead, set aside part of each day
to talk with God, thanking Him for who He is and what He has done for you.
Then, by reading His Word and believing His comforting promises, your faith
will grow stronger and a supernatural peace will flood your soul. —HGB

*When we put our problems in God's hands,
He puts His peace in our hearts.*

APRIL 1

It may be that the Lord will look on my affliction, and that the Lord will repay me with good. 2 Samuel 16:12

Our natural inclination is to want to silence our critics, insist on fairness, and defend ourselves. We may ask our opponents to justify their charges, or we may counter them with steadfast denial. Or, like David, we can wait patiently until God vindicates us (2 Samuel 16:12). It is good to look beyond those who oppose us and look to the One who loves us with infinite love. It is good to be able to believe that whatever God permits is for our ultimate good. And as we grow in our awareness of God's protective love, we become less concerned with what others say about us and more willing to entrust ourselves to our Father.

You are in God's hands, no matter what others are saying about you. —DHR

We can endure life's wrongs because we know that God will make all things right.

When they looked up, they saw that the stone had been rolled away.
Mark 16:4

As the women approached the place of Jesus' burial, the practical difficulty of moving the heavy stone that sealed His tomb brought them anxiety. But their fears were groundless; the stone had already been moved.

We too are often needlessly concerned over prospective difficulties that God graciously removes or helps us overcome. Let us exercise greater faith in facing possible obstructions on the pathway of duty. We may be sure of the Lord's assistance in such matters when we press on in His name and for His glory. Whatever difficulty we may face, God will move the stone. —HGB

If God doesn't remove an obstacle, He'll help you find a way around it.

APRIL 3

The Son of Man did not come to be served, but to serve, and to give His life a ransom for many. Mark 10:45

One of Shakespeare's most well-known characters is Macbeth, a man who wanted so much to be king that he resorted to murder and paid for it with his life. We may not use such evil methods to achieve our goal, but we allow ambition to cloud our thinking. Instead of leaving matters in God's hands, we take them into our own.

Another example of too much ambition is found in the conversation James and John had with Jesus in Mark 10. Their goal was to sit in the positions of greatest prestige and power in the kingdom. They weren't content to wait and see if Jesus would bestow that honor on them; they boldly requested it. Ambition is not always wrong. But when it consumes us so that we can't wait for God, we display a lack of faith as the disciples did. —DB

Be ambitious for the Lord, but be cautious about your motives.

APRIL 4

Render to Caesar the things that are Caesar's, and to God the things that are God's. Mark 12:17

During a trip to London, I visited the Bank of England Museum and the Clockmakers' Museum. At some point, it struck me that both money and time have been important commodities as far back as anyone can remember. Yet they present one of the great dilemmas of life. We trade our valuable time working for money, and then we spend our money to make the most of our time off. We seldom possess the two with any degree of balance.

In contrast, our Lord never seemed perplexed by money or time. Regarding the payment of taxes, he said, "Render to Caesar the things that are Caesar's, and to God the things that are God's." And even with great demands on His time, Jesus spent early mornings and late nights in prayer, seeking to know and do His Father's will. —DCM

Spend time and money wisely; they both belong to God.

APRIL 5

He came to them, walking on the sea.
Mark 6:48

When a helicopter crashed in a cold, mountainous wilderness, the pilots survived but were seriously injured. The situation seemed hopeless—until a rescue helicopter appeared, its searchlights illuminating the darkness. The rescuers spotted the wreckage, landed nearby, and carried the injured pilots to safety. The homing device on the aircraft had gone off automatically when it went down. All the rescuers had to do was follow it.

The disciples of Jesus also experienced the joy of being rescued when Jesus came to them, walking on the water and calming the sea. When we're trapped, hurt, lonely, or discouraged, Jesus knows it. Our cries of grief are beacons that bring Him to our side—right when we need Him most. —DCE

Jesus hears even the faintest cry for help.

APRIL 6

When the people complained, it displeased the Lord.
Numbers 11:1

Two boys were eating some grapes. One of them remarked, "Aren't they sweet!" The other replied, "But they're full of seeds." Wandering into a garden, the first boy exclaimed, "Look at those big, beautiful red roses!" The other commented, "They're full of thorns!" It was a warm day, so they stopped at the store for a soft drink. After several swallows, the second youngster complained, "My bottle's half-empty already." The first quickly responded, "Mine's still half-full!"

No matter who you are or what your circumstances, there's always something to be grateful for. Instead of complaining about thorns, be thankful for the roses. —RDH

Instead of grumbling because you don't get what you want, be thankful you don't get what you deserve.

Rejoice in the Lord always. Again I will say, rejoice!
Philippians 4:4

Several years ago I read a story about a ninety-two-year-old woman who was legally blind. In spite of her limitation, each morning she would meet the new day with eagerness. After her husband of seventy years died, she had to go to a nursing home. As the attendant took her to her room, she began describing it to the woman. "I love it," the woman declared. "But you haven't seen your room yet," the attendant replied. "That doesn't have anything to do with it," she said. "Whether I like my room or not doesn't depend on how it's arranged. It's how I arrange my mind."

Remind yourself often of all that Jesus has given to you and be thankful. That's how to arrange your mind. —DHR

The happiness of your life depends on the quality of your thoughts.

Their eyes were opened and they knew Him; and He vanished from their sight.
Luke 24:31

When our dreams are shattered, we may feel that all has been lost. It takes the touch of God to open our eyes to the greater glory of His plan. When the crucified and risen Christ joined two disciples on the road to Emmaus, they were grieving over His death. But Jesus, whom they didn't recognize, said, "Ought not the Christ to have suffered these things and to enter into His glory?" Later they realized they had been talking with Jesus. He was alive!

In our times of loss, the risen Lord comes to us with comfort and peace, revealing His glory and the eternal gain that is ours because of His cross. —DCM

Present pains can lead to permanent gains.

Cast your burden on the Lord, and He shall sustain you.
Psalm 55:22

A poor man in Ireland was plodding along toward home, carrying a huge bag of potatoes. A horse and wagon drew up alongside him on the road, and the driver invited the man to climb aboard. After getting on the wagon, he sat down but continued to hold the heavy bag. When the driver suggested that the man set the bag down in the wagon, he replied, "I don't want to trouble you too much, sir. You are giving me a ride already, so I'll just carry the potatoes."

Sometimes we do the same thing when we attempt to bear the burdens of our lives in our own strength. Rather than trying to bear your burdens by yourself, set them down in God's hands. —HGB

God invites us to burden Him with what burdens us.

APRIL 10

I say to you, ask, and it will be given to you. Luke 11:9

I heard a woman say that she never prayed more than once for anything. She didn't want to weary God with her repeated requests. The Lord's teaching on prayer in Luke 11 contradicts this notion. He told a parable about a man who went to his friend's house at midnight and asked for some bread to feed his unexpected visitors. At first the friend refused, for he and his family were in bed. Finally he got up and gave his friend the bread—not out of friendship but because the caller was so persistent.

If a reluctant and irritated neighbor will give in to his friend's persistence and grant his request, how much more readily will our generous heavenly Father give us all we need! —JY

Don't worry about wearying God. He will never tire of your persistent prayer!

*When tribulation or persecution arises because
of the word, immediately he stumbles.*
Matthew 13:21

A friend of actress and comedienne Gracie Allen once sent a small, live alligator to her as a gag. Not knowing what to do with it, Gracie put it in the bathtub and then left for an appointment. When she returned home, she found a note from her maid. "Dear Miss Allen: Sorry, but I have quit. I don't work in houses where there is an alligator. I would have told you this when I started, but I never thought it would come up."

Some people who say they'll serve Christ are quick to leave when trouble comes. If we let difficulties shake our faith, we are breaking the spirit of the trust that brought us to Christ in the first place. —MRD

Tough times can teach us to trust.

Depart from me, all you workers of iniquity;
for the Lord has heard the voice of my weeping.

Psalm 6:8

Sometimes it doesn't take much to get us down. An unkind remark
from a friend, bad news from the auto mechanic, a financial setback,
or a misbehaving child can put a cloud of gloom over everything, even
on the sunniest day. We know we should be joyful, but everything
seems to be against us, making simple tasks a struggle.

David knew what to do when he was down. He looked up and trusted God
to take care of him and to see him through. When we look up and focus on
God, we get our eyes off ourselves and gain a new appreciation of Him. —DB

When life knocks you to your knees, you're in a good position to pray.

May the God of hope fill you with all joy and peace in believing,
that you may abound in hope by the power of the Holy Spirit.
Romans 15:13

Grant Murphy of Seattle was the active type, a man who ran at full throttle. Idling and coasting were not in his nature. Then multiple sclerosis began to slow him down. First he needed crutches to get around. Then he was limited to sitting in a chair. Finally he was confined to a bed. Near the end, he was hardly strong enough to talk. However, as one of his friends recalls, "He expressed only joy and thankfulness with a constant anticipation of being in the Lord's presence." Not long before he died, Grant whispered Romans 15:13 to a friend. He repeated the words "in believing," then added, "I can't do anything now."

It's when we can't do anything that *God does everything*. Faith is simultaneously an exercise of our will and the impartation of divine strength. —DJD

No one is hopeless whose hope is in God.

Do you think that they were worse sinners . . . ?
I tell you, no; but unless you repent you will all likewise perish.
Luke 13:4–5

Some Christians are quick to declare that disasters such as a terrorist attack, an earthquake, or a flood are the result of divine judgment. In reality, a complex array of factors lies behind most disasters. Instead of reading divine judgment into tragedies, we should see them as a call to personal repentance. Calamities in themselves are never good, but they can fulfill God's purposes when they serve as a wake-up call to believers, and when they bring unbelievers to repentance and faith in Jesus. Let's not ask, "Who's to blame?" but "Lord, what are you saying to me?" —HVL

In alarming situations, listen for God's wake-up call.

Clouds and darkness surround Him . . . .
His lightnings light the world; the earth sees and trembles.
Psalm 97:2, 4

It had been a long Michigan winter and my three-year-old granddaughter had forgotten all about thunderstorms. So she was frightened one spring afternoon when the sky grew dark, lightning flashed, thunder rolled, and rain came pouring down. She climbed onto her dad's lap. He reassured her that God knows all about thunderstorms, and he used the occasion to tell her about God's awesome power.

We've all witnessed the power of a thunderstorm, and sometimes we are afraid. But each storm that rolls across the sky can bring to mind great truths: God is awesome in power, He judges His foes, and His glory fills the earth. —DCE

When we trust God, His power is not a danger but a comfort.

APRIL 16

Rest in the Lord, and wait patiently for Him.
Psalm 37:7

A Christian couple was deeply distressed because their married son and his family had quit going to church and were giving God no place in their lives. As their friend, I advised them to continue showing love, to pray, and to avoid starting arguments. But at the family's annual Christmas gathering, the father gave his son a lecture in the presence of the other siblings. The son and his family left in anger and broke off all contact with his parents.

It's hard to rely on prayer alone when you want something to happen right now. It's not always easy to be patient. But God can be trusted. Wait patiently for Him. —HVL

Delay is not denial—pray on!

Do not worry about tomorrow.
Matthew 6:34

The phrase "One Day at a Time" can be found on bumper stickers, plaques, and refrigerator magnets. The slogan is often used by recovering alcoholics as a reminder that a person doesn't have to stay sober forever—just for today. A month, or even a week, without alcohol may seem impossible for them. But the key to success is to trust God for the strength to say no to a drink *today*.

The thread of living "one day at a time" is woven throughout the fabric of Scripture. God supplied the Israelites with manna daily. Our heavenly Father's mercies are new every morning. Jesus taught His followers to ask for their "daily bread" and to refuse to worry about tomorrow. Daily bread. Daily light. Daily strength. —DCM

God doesn't ask us to bear tomorrow's burdens with today's strength.

[I pray] that He would grant you, according to the riches of His glory, to be strengthened with might through His Spirit in the inner man. Ephesians 3:16

A large company uses suction to extract contaminating substances from steel drums. Powerful pumps draw the materials out of the barrels, but the workers must carefully regulate the force of these pumps. If they take out too much air, the drums will collapse like paper cups, because the outer pressure will exceed the inner pressure.

When adversity comes into our lives, God must empower us from within if we are to withstand the pressures from without. If we neglect the Scriptures and prayer, we'll grow weak and vulnerable. Then we will be unable to withstand the pressures of temptation or trouble. —DCE

The power of Christ within you is greater than the pressure of troubles around you.

[Cast] all your care upon Him, for He cares for you. 1 Peter 5:7

I recall walking along a Texas creek many years ago with my brother-in-law Ed and his three-year-old son David. David had been collecting smooth, round stones from the stream while we walked. He called them "piggies" because their rounded shape reminded him of little pigs. David stuffed his pockets full and then began carrying more stones in his arms. Ed said, "Here, let me help carry your piggies." Reluctance clouded David's face for a moment, and then it lit up. "I know," he said. "You carry me and I'll carry my piggies!"

I've often thought of that incident and my own childish insistence that I must carry my own load. How foolish it is to try to carry all your burdens on your own when Jesus asks you to cast "all your care upon Him, for He cares for you." —DHR

God cares.

APRIL 20

Alleluia! For the Lord God Omnipotent reigns! Let us be glad and rejoice and give Him glory. Revelation 19:6–7

When Senator Robert Kennedy was assassinated in Los Angeles in 1968, people everywhere, regardless of their political affiliation, were numb with grief and horror. Coming so soon after the assassination of his brother, President John F. Kennedy, made it even more tragic. Yet after Senator Kennedy's funeral in St. Patrick's Cathedral, the walls echoed with the triumphant words of Handel's *Messiah*: "The Lord God Omnipotent reigneth . . . and He shall reign for ever and ever."

In spite of such events, God is at work bringing good out of evil, light out of darkness, and life out of death. —HVL

The more clearly we see God's sovereignty, the less perplexed we are by man's calamities.

We love Him because He first loved us.
1 John 4:19

At times I struggle with pride, so I tend to believe that I have earned any love I receive. At other times, deep down inside, I know that I don't deserve the love I get. My motives are never pure, and I fear I will be rejected if they are exposed. When I consider my relationship with God, therefore, I tend to feel that His affection for me is based on my performance. When I do well, He loves me; but if I foul up, then I expect only His scorn. Yet God does not love us because we deserve it. He loves us in spite of what we are. Because of what Jesus Christ has done for us, we know we are always loved by God. That simple truth shatters our pride and dispels our fear. —HWR

No one is beyond the reach of God's love.

APRIL 22

God has not given us a spirit of fear, but of power and of love and of a sound mind.
2 Timothy 1:7

The silence awakened me at 5:30 one morning. There was no gentle whir of fan blades, no reassuring hum from the refrigerator downstairs. A power outage had left our neighborhood without electricity just as everyone was preparing for work. Alarm clocks did not sound. Coffee makers, toasters, hair dryers, and other appliances were useless. Beginning a day without power was an inconvenience and a disruption of routine—but it felt like a disaster.

Then I thought of how often I rush into the day without spiritual power. I spend more time reading the newspaper than the Bible. Talk radio replaces listening to the Spirit. Our power outage was short-lived, but the lesson remained: I need to begin each day by seeking the Lord. —DCM

The human spirit fails us unless the Holy Spirit fills us.

APRIL 23

Set your hearts on all the words which I testify
among you today . . . . It is your life.
Deuteronomy 32:46–47

Advances in medical science are making it possible for more and more people to live longer and better. Yet in spite of this, none of us can avoid growing old. One day aging will overtake all of us, and our bodies will shut down. What is preventable, however, is an attitude of bitterness and regret as we grow older.

As we grow older, we can dwell on the failures and hardships of our past, or we can remember God's faithfulness, accept His discipline, and keep looking to the future in faith. It's the only way to avoid a bitter attitude. —DJD

We cannot avoid growing old, but we can avoid growing cold.

APRIL 24

I was at ease, but He has shattered me. Job 16:12

Ground squirrels hibernate near our home during the winter and reappear when the snow melts in the spring. My wife and I enjoy watching them scurry from one hole to another, while others stand like tiny sentries watching for predators. In mid-May, a man from a nearby golf course arrives on a little green tractor with a tank loaded with lethal gas to eliminate these little critters because they dig holes in the fairways. Some survive, but most do not. It always makes us a little sad to see the tractor arrive. If I could, I'd chase the little animals away and force them to settle someplace else. I'm sure they would resent my interference, but my actions would be solely for their good.

So it is with God. He may break up our comfortable nests now and then, but He always is working for our ultimate good (Romans 8:28). —DJD

Behind every difficult change is God's love and eternal purpose.

Some men's sins are clearly evident . . . . Likewise, the good works of some . . . cannot be hidden. 1 Timothy 5:24–25

A woman had been maligned and misrepresented by an envious co-worker. She was frustrated because her attempts to confront her in private had only made matters worse. So she decided to swallow her pride and let the matter go. She said, "I'm glad the Lord knows the true situation." She expressed a profound truth that both warns and comforts.

Paul pointed out that nothing can be concealed forever. We can hide nothing from God—that's a solemn warning! But it's also a great comfort, for our heavenly Father knows about every encouraging smile, every kind word, and every loving deed done in Jesus' name. And someday He will reward us. —HVL

Neither vice nor virtue can remain a secret forever.

Teach me Your way, O Lord, and lead me in a smooth path.
Psalm 27:11

Unfamiliar roads can sometimes lead to trouble. I know a teenager who decided to take a different way to work one morning. As he tried to navigate unfamiliar city streets, he went through an intersection without seeing the red octagonal sign that said Stop. Within a few seconds, he was pulled over by a policeman, who reminded him that he should have stopped. It cost him eighty dollars to learn about unfamiliar roads.

In life, we often have to walk down unfamiliar paths—paths that may feel threatening. So how do we do that without making costly mistakes? We take Someone along who knows the way, and we say, "Teach me Your way, O Lord, and lead me in a smooth path." Does your path today seem unfamiliar? Ask your Father to travel the road with you. —DB

The Spirit within us will faithfully guide us.

APRIL 27

Let us search out and examine our ways, and turn back to the Lord.
Lamentations 3:40

A man shouted the same three words each day from his street-corner newsstand. "Ain't it awful!" he would say to passersby while extending a newspaper. People bought a paper because they just had to know what terrible thing had occurred.

Tragedy and dire predictions always make the front page, but if we become preoccupied with bad news, we will succumb to what a friend of mine calls "awfulizing"—a pervasive pessimism that clouds every situation with gloom. Disobedience to God can cause great pain, but the doorway out of discouragement leads to the Lord, who "is good to those who wait for Him" (Lamentations 3:25). —DCM

Awful circumstances cannot alter the goodness of God.

He shall be like a tree planted by the waters, which spreads out its roots by the river. Jeremiah 17:8

In the summer of 1992, a fire blackened 4,500 acres of forest about thirty-five miles north of Atlantic City. One homeowner saw a fireball with sixty-foot flames come roaring up across the street from his house before veering away. The fire was difficult to contain because of dry conditions.

The dry-tree condition behind this fire has a parallel in the history of Israel and for us. Jeremiah said that his countrymen had become like dry shrubs rather than green trees by a river (Jeremiah 17:6–8). They had aroused the fire of God's anger by departing from the Lord (vv. 4–5). Life's fiery trials threaten to scorch our souls if we're trusting in our own strength. —MRD

The fires of life will not destroy you if you're watered by the River of Life.

Turn away my eyes from looking at worthless things,
and revive me in Your way. Psalm 119:37

As a young boy, one of my favorite pastimes was hunting frogs along the banks of a pond near our home, but they seemed to elude me so easily. Later I learned that the frog's optical field is like a clean blackboard; the only images it receives are objects that directly concern it. Frogs are never distracted by unimportant things, but are aware only of whatever may be dangerous to them.

We frequently allow our lives to become so cluttered with materialistic and insignificant concerns that we lose perspective of the things that endure. Take a lesson from the frog's "blackboard" and center your gaze on Christ and His will for your life. —MRD

The more attracted we are to Christ, the less
we'll be distracted by the world.

*This also comes from the Lord of hosts, who is
wonderful in counsel and excellent in guidance.*
Isaiah 28:29

During times of hardship, I often feel like whining, "Who needs this pain? I certainly don't!" But Isaiah 28 and my own experience tell me this is a shortsighted reaction. Isaiah gives us the "poetic parable" of a farmer who skillfully plows the ground, plants his crops, and threshes the harvest (vv. 23–28). If the soil could talk, it might whine, "Who needs this painful plowing?" But the pain is not pointless. The farmer works in measured and well-timed ways, handling delicate crops with care and others more vigorously, but always with a sure harvest in view. Our reassurance during tough times is that in God's hands, hardship is an effective tool to bring about our much-needed growth. —JY

When you trust in God, pain is an opportunity for progress.

MAY 1

We also rejoice in God through our Lord Jesus Christ.
Romans 5:11

Author Lloyd Ogilvie tells of a Christian friend who was physically and emotionally depleted because of extreme pressures. When Ogilvie asked him how he was doing, he said grimly, "Well, joy's certainly no option!" Ogilvie replied, "You're right! Joy is no option. It's your responsibility." Shocked, the friend retorted, "You talk about joy as if it were a duty." Ogilvie responded, "Right again!" We have a duty to God, ourselves, and others to overcome our moods and to battle through to joy.

We have peace with God through Christ, access into grace, and hope of future glory. Fill your mind with these truths, and, no matter what your circumstances, you can choose joy. —JY

For the Christian, joy is a choice.

You are all sons of God through faith in Christ Jesus. Galatians 3:26

Have you ever experienced an identity crisis? Teens often wonder who they are, trying to fit in while trying to learn the meaning of life. During middle age some people struggle with identity, perhaps out of disappointment for not having achieved all they had hoped. In later years people realize that life is approaching its final stages, and they wonder what kind of person they have become.

It's always good to review who God says we are because of our relationship to Christ: forgiven, new creations, joint heirs with Christ, and God's witnesses and ambassadors. Such wonderful truths should leave no doubt about who we really are and why we are here! —DB

When we know we are identified with Christ, we will have no identity crisis.

MAY 3

Our citizenship is in heaven, from which we also eagerly wait for the Savior, the Lord Jesus Christ. Philippians 3:20

In the 1940s, Samuel Beckett wrote a play called *Waiting for Godot*, which is now regarded as a classic. Two men stand on an empty stage, hands in their pockets, staring at each other. There is no action, no plot; they just stand there waiting for Godot to come. As the play ends, those men are still standing on the stage doing nothing, just waiting. When the fiftieth anniversary of the play was celebrated, someone asked Beckett, "Now will you tell us who Godot is?" He answered, "How should I know?"

Waiting for Godot is a parable of many people's lives—empty and meaningless, a pointless matter of waiting. And without the God of love, grace, and wisdom, then life really is a hopeless waiting for empty time to pass. —VCG

The greatest joy on earth is to have the sure hope of heaven.

MAY 4

Command those who are rich in this present age not to . . .
trust in uncertain riches but in the living God.
1 Timothy 6:17

Publisher Frank Doubleday had a one-of-a-kind, leather-bound book that he called the *Book of the Law and the Profits*. Unlike the portions of the Bible that we call the Law and the Prophets, Doubleday's book was an account of his business dealings and his financial profits. According to author George Doran, the book contained Doubleday's morning prayers and evening vespers. In other words, it seemed that he worshiped money.

Our Lord warned, "What profit is it to a man if he gains the whole world, and loses his own soul?" (Matthew 16:26). Money can't bring us true and lasting profit. Only by trusting the living God and living in obedience to His Word will we have eternal profit. —VCG

None are so poor as those whose only wealth is money.

MAY 5

*In the shadow of Your wings I will make my
refuge, until these calamities have passed by.*

Psalm 57:1

It is believed that David wrote Psalm 57 while fleeing from King Saul. David ducked into a cave and was safe temporarily, but the threat was still there.

We've all, at some time, been pursued by something that strikes fear into our hearts. We wish that God would swoop in and whisk us to safety—just as David may have wished for a quick end to Saul's pursuit. We plead with God to stop the pain, to make the road to tomorrow smooth and straight, to eliminate our struggle. But the difficulty remains. It is then that we have to take refuge in God as David did. "In the shadow of Your wings I will make my refuge, until these calamities have passed by." —DB

We learn the lesson of trust in the school of trial.

MAY 6

His compassions fail not. They are new every morning;
great is Your faithfulness. Lamentations 3:22–23

Recently, as I read Lamentations, I was so caught up in the destruction
and desolation described by Jeremiah that a familiar passage took me
by surprise. "Through the Lord's mercies we are not consumed, because
His compassions fail not. They are new every morning; great is Your
faithfulness." Those verses are so often quoted alone that I had forgotten
the bleak context in which they were penned. In the midst of Jeremiah's
dark night of the soul, they shine as an unexpected ray of hope and light.

In our times of deepest sorrow, we are often surprised by the
light of God's never-failing love. Then, by His grace and mercy,
we can echo the words of Jeremiah: "'The Lord is my portion,'
says my soul, 'therefore I hope in Him!'" —DCM

Life's darkest trial cannot dim the light of God's love.

Go and learn what this means: "I desire mercy and not sacrifice."
Matthew 9:13

The mother of four growing children went to a counselor because she felt that she was a failure. She had trained for ministry and had hoped to serve the Lord as a missionary overseas. Instead, she fell in love and married a widower with four children. Busy with her duties as wife and mother, she was not able to engage in any formal ministry. She wrongly concluded that God was subjecting her to well-deserved chastisement.

A Christian counselor pointed her to Micah 6:8, which asks, "What does the Lord require of you?" Immediately that question is answered, "To do justly, to love mercy, and to walk humbly with your God." Those requirements she could meet without going to a foreign mission field. And meet them she did! —VCG

What God requires, God provides.

MAY 8

When I am weak, then I am strong. 2 Corinthians 12:10

My mother lives alone now. It's been eight years since my dad died. She can't get out by herself except to take brief walks. She's having a terrible time with her short-term memory. Conversations are limited to a few repeated comments. Yet she recently told me something profound. "I was thinking the other day about my troubles, and I decided that I don't have anything to complain about. God's taking care of me and I've got people who are helping. My only trouble is that I can't remember anything, and I've got plenty of pencils and paper to write everything down."

Our struggles may be related to age, finances, or a myriad of other difficulties. But if we trust God and are thankful even in the midst of our troubles, we'll acknowledge that we "don't have anything to complain about." —DB

God uses weakness to reveal His great sufficiency.

Thanks be to God, who gives us the victory through our Lord Jesus Christ.
1 Corinthians 15:57

"You have cancer." These words bring a chill to the heart. Although great progress is being made in treating this disease, recovery can be long and painful, and many people do not survive. An enthusiastic believer in Christ, Dan Richardson lost his battle with cancer. But his life demonstrated that even though the physical body may be destroyed by disease, the spirit can remain triumphant. This poem was distributed at his memorial service:

Cancer is so limited . . . it cannot cripple love, it cannot shatter hope, it cannot corrode faith, it cannot eat away peace, it cannot destroy confidence, it cannot kill friendship, it cannot shut out memories, it cannot silence courage, it cannot invade the soul, it cannot reduce eternal life, it cannot quench the Spirit, it cannot lessen the power of the resurrection. —DCE

Our greatest enemy is not disease but despair.

MAY 10

I enjoy my job, so usually I am eager to get out of bed and go to work. But one day I became discouraged when I thought about my family's financial security. Was I providing enough? Other people seemed to be doing so much better. I grew fearful as I thought about the future, and those fears sapped my zest for life.

How can we find courage at such times? Certainly not through measuring our achievements or by trying to boost our self-confidence. As God's people, our confidence comes from our relationship with Him. He is with us. We are His people. As we keep these truths in mind, we will find courage to continue working in a way that pleases Him and brings us joy. —AL

We find courage to stand when we kneel before the Lord.

MAY 11

Commit your way to the Lord, trust also in Him, and He shall bring it to pass.

Psalm 37:5

During a terrible ocean storm, a small passenger ship rolled precariously in the roaring tempest. Many thought the vessel was doomed. Finally, a passenger determined to find out if there was any hope for survival and set out to see the one who was in command. Clinging to the walls and handrails, he made his way to the wave-lashed deck, up a ladder, and into the wheelhouse. The ship was nearing land, between some jagged rocks, and it was apparent that the captain was trying to reach the safety of a calm bay up ahead. Knowing he could not make himself heard above the roar of the wind and waves, the captain turned and smiled. Reassured, the man returned to the others and said, "Don't be afraid. All is well. I've seen the captain's face, and he smiled!" —HGB

God may calm the storm around you, but more often He'll calm the storm within you.

MAY 12

[Abraham] did not waver at the promise of God through unbelief.
Romans 4:20

Promises are the hope of our heart. A child's security depends on a parent's promise to keep him or her safe. A spouse can live with confidence because of a mate's promise of fidelity, loyalty, and love. Businesses depend on promises from employees, vendors, and clients. Countries remain safe when neighbors keep their promise to honor their borders.

There is one Promise-Maker, though, who can be trusted completely and without fear. That one is God. He has given us hundreds of promises in His Word, and He keeps every one of them. —DB

The future always looks bright when viewed through the window of God's promises.

Plead my cause, O Lord, with those who strive with me. Psalm 35:1

My friend Ron wasn't having a good week. His new job had thrust him in the midst of some people who were foul-mouthed, rude, and obnoxious. After two months of working in that environment, Ron wasn't sure he could tolerate any more ungodly, uncouth behavior.

Perhaps you too are in an environment that is not friendly to godliness—either at work, at home, or elsewhere. Here are some suggestions that may help you survive and even thrive: *Concentrate on God's goodness and depend on it. Stay true to your convictions. Immerse yourself in the Bible. Do good for those who oppose you. Trust God to be your companion.* When it's just you and God, that's enough. —DB

With God behind you and His arms beneath you, you can face whatever is before you.

MAY 14

Oh, taste and see that the Lord is good; blessed is the man who trusts in Him!
Psalm 34:8

Mary was a widow, poor and housebound because of her ailments in old age. Because of her crippling pain, it took Mary a long time to inch her way through the house. So when her pastor visited her, he would call on the telephone and tell her that he was on his way and what time he would get there. Mary would then begin the slow, arduous journey to the door, reaching it about the time he arrived. Without fail, she would greet him with these triumphant words: "God is good!"

Over the years Mary had come to savor with deep gratitude every good thing God sent her way. She knew that the Lord is good, even when life isn't. —JY

When you taste God's goodness, His praise will be on your lips.

Hope does not disappoint.
Romans 5:5

Writing in *Texas Co-Op Power* magazine, Donna Chapman described the excitement generated on her family's farm in the 1940s by the arrival of the Montgomery Ward catalog. Often called "the wish book," its pages were filled with images of items ranging from clothing and cook stoves to furniture and tools. The catalog's warm, friendly tone invited people to picture themselves as they lived, worked, and dressed at the time, and as they hoped to become.

The Bible is not a spiritual mail-order catalog, but in its pages we vividly see ourselves both as we are today and as we hope to be. The Bible is God's book of hope. —DCM

No one is hopeless whose hope is in God's Word.

MAY 16

We are hard-pressed on every side, yet not crushed; we are perplexed, but not in despair.
2 Corinthians 4:8

Explorer Samuel Hearne (1745–1792) was on an expedition in northern Canada when a crucial piece of charting equipment broke, so he had to turn back. Then, thieves stole most of his supplies. Hearne responded in an unexpected way. In his journal he wrote, "As the ravagers had materially lightened my load . . . this part of the journey was the easiest and most pleasant of any I had experienced since my leaving the fort."

How did you respond the last time something went wrong? Did you fall apart? When things go wrong, ask God for patience and a positive perspective to handle life's setbacks. Then thank Him for working to increase your faith. —DCE

Tough times teach trust.

*Having been justified by faith, we have peace
with God through our Lord Jesus Christ.*

Romans 5:1

Lucky Lawrence thought he had it all. But like so many who seek fulfillment in money and fame, he struggled to find real joy. His real name was Larry Wright, and he was the number one rock-and-roll radio personality in Phoenix in the 1960s. But his family life was a mess, and he was fast becoming an alcoholic. The solution came when his wife, Sue, trusted Jesus as her Savior. Larry noticed the peace and joy in her life and the obvious change in her attitude toward him. Soon he too asked Jesus to forgive him and be his Savior. Gone was the frustrating search for peace. In its place was the joy and peace of God. Larry and Sue have now served the Lord for more than thirty years. —DB

No God, no peace; know God, know peace.

As cold water to a weary soul, so is good news from a far country. Proverbs 25:25

What's the good news today? I ask that question sometimes of people I know. If the person is a Christian, he might smilingly reply, "The same as it was yesterday. God loves us." And both he and I rejoice that it will be the same tomorrow. Those who don't know Christ, though, may sound like the pessimistic novelist T. C. Boyle: "If God doesn't exist . . . and you have no purpose on Earth, then it's a mighty mean place, ruled by accident . . . I'd like to have a lot better news for everybody, but I don't."

Faith in our Lord Jesus Christ gives a realistic reason for hope. That's the good news we can proclaim. That's the answer to the riddle of our existence. —VCG

The good news is not that Jesus lived and died, but that He died and lives.

This hope we have as an anchor of the soul, both sure and steadfast.
Hebrews 6:19

Two women. Both dedicated moms of young children. Both missionaries. Then suddenly, within the space of a month, both were dead. Sharon Fasick died in a car accident. Roni Bowers died with her daughter Charity when their plane was shot down over the jungles of Peru.

Their deaths filled many people with inexpressible sorrow. But there was something else—hope. Both women's husbands had the confident expectation that they would see their wives again in heaven. Jeff Fasick and Jim Bowers have spoken about the peace God has given them. They have testified that this kind of hope has allowed them to continue on in the midst of their unspeakable pain. —DB

The hope of heaven is God's solution for sorrow.

MAY 20

The effective, fervent prayer of a righteous man avails much. James 5:16

For many years, researchers have tried to determine if prayer has any effect on physical healing. An assistant professor at George Washington University School of Medicine says that "trying to scientifically determine prayer's effect on health is nearly impossible."

The writer of the book of James discussed prayer and healing in the context of a fellowship of believers. "Confess your trespasses to one another, and pray for one another, that you may be healed. The effective, fervent prayer of a righteous man avails much." While speaking of physical healing, James also included a call for restoration to spiritual health through repentance and confession. Science tries to prove cause and effect. Faith directs us to our loving God, whose ways we can rarely understand but can always trust. —DCM

Prayer is the soil in which hope and healing grow best.

Do not be overcome by evil, but overcome evil with good. Romans 12:21

A few days after arriving on the campus of Texas A&M University in 1984, Bruce Goodrich was awakened at 2:00 a.m. Upperclassmen roused him out of bed to initiate him into the Corps of Cadets, a military-style training program. Bruce was forced to exercise and run several miles in hot and humid conditions. When he eventually collapsed, he was told to get up and keep going. He collapsed again, went into a coma, and died later that same day. The students who mistreated Bruce were put on trial and charged with causing his death.

In the letter that Bruce's father wrote to the administration, faculty, and student body, he said, "[Bruce] is now secure in his celestial home. When the question is asked, 'Why did this happen?' perhaps one answer will be, 'So that many will consider where they will spend eternity.'" —HWR

Trusting God's sovereignty can turn outrage into compassion.

Tribulation produces perseverance; and perseverance,
character; and character, hope. Romans 5:3–4

Bristlecone pines are the world's oldest living trees. Several are estimated to be 3,000 to 4,000 years old. In 1957, scientist Edmund Schulman found one he named "Methuselah." This ancient, gnarled pine is nearly 5,000 years old! It was an old tree when the Egyptians were building the pyramids. Bristlecones grow atop the mountains of the western United States at elevations of 10,000 to 11,000 feet and have survived some of the harshest living conditions on earth: arctic temperatures, fierce winds, thin air, and little rainfall. Their brutal environment is actually one of the reasons they've survived for millennia. Hardship has produced extraordinary strength and staying power. —DHR

God uses our difficulties to develop our character.

MAY 23

Within a chip shot of our house is a golf course. When I stand in my backyard, I see ponds waiting hungrily for my next errant shot. At times I can imagine sand traps and trees joking about my bad days. I like to golf occasionally, but living so close to the course reminds me of my failures in playing the game.

A similar problem can occur in marriage when we lose sight of the hopes and dreams we once shared with our spouse and become irritated over our past failures and disappointments. But if we focus together on Christ, our flaws and failures fade, and we can rediscover our love for each other in the light of our Lord's great love for us. —MRD

Marriages may be made in heaven, but they have to be worked out on earth.

I will walk in my integrity; redeem me and be merciful to me. My foot stands in an even place.
Psalm 26:11–12

At times when I've been falsely accused of something, I have followed the example of David in Psalm 26 as he responded to his critics. Appealing directly to the Lord, David asked God to vindicate him and acknowledged his own need for mercy.

Have the painful barbs of critics or the accusations of your conscience filled you with fear and self-doubt? Talk to the Lord. If you need to confess sin, do it. Then put your hope and trust in God. He will replace your insecurity and doubt with His supernatural peace. He has done that for me. He will do the same for you. —HVL

Feeding your faith will starve your doubts.

MAY 25

If anyone sins, we have an Advocate with the Father, Jesus Christ the righteous.
1 John 2:1

Inventor Charles Kettering has suggested that we must learn to fail intelligently. "Once you've failed, analyze the problem and find out why, because each failure is one more step leading up to the cathedral of success. The only time you don't want to fail is the last time you try." Kettering then gives these suggestions for turning failure into success: (1) Honestly face defeat; never fake success. (2) Exploit the failure; don't waste it. Learn all you can from it. (3) Never use failure as an excuse for not trying again.

Kettering's practical wisdom holds a deeper meaning for the Christian. Failure is never final. We can make a new start, because Jesus died to pay the penalty for all our sins and is our "Advocate with the Father." Knowing how to benefit from failure is the key to continued growth in grace. —DJD

Failure is never final for those who begin again with God.

*The generous soul will be made rich, and he
who waters will also be watered himself.*
Proverbs 11:25

A *U.S. News & World Report* cover story explored the subject of happiness. According to the article, scientists have found that "strong marriages, family ties, and friendships predict happiness, as do spirituality and self-esteem. Hope is crucial, as is the feeling that life has meaning." But what if some of these elements are missing in our lives? Researchers say that "helping people be a little happier can jump-start a process that will lead to stronger relationships, renewed hope, and general upward spiraling of happiness."

What we give, more than what we get, produces joy in our lives. Is there some small way you can help someone else be happier today? —DCM

It is more blessed to give than to receive. — *Jesus*

MAY 27

*When they began to sing and to praise, the Lord set
ambushes against the people . . . who had come against Judah.*
2 Chronicles 20:22

Visitors to the Military Museum in Istanbul, Turkey, can hear stirring music
that dates back to the early years of the Ottoman Empire. Whenever their
troops marched off to war, bands accompanied them. Centuries earlier,
worship singers led the people of Judah into battle, but there was a big
difference. Whereas the Ottomans used music to instill self-confidence
in their soldiers, the Jews used it to express their confidence in God.

No matter what battles we may face today, we can march ahead
with confidence in God's power and sing praise to Him. —JAL

Praise is the voice of faith.

*Sorrow is better than laughter, for by a sad
countenance the heart is made better.*
Ecclesiastes 7:3

Sorrow can be good for the soul. It causes us to think earnestly about ourselves. It makes us ponder our motives, our intentions, our interests. Sorrow also helps us to see God as we've never seen Him. Job said, out of his terrible grief, "I have heard of You by the hearing of the ear, but now my eye sees You" (Job 42:5).

Those who don't let sorrow do its work, who deny it, trivialize it, or try to explain it away, remain shallow and indifferent. They never understand themselves or others very well. In fact, I think that before God can use us very much, we must first learn to mourn. —DHR

We can learn more from sorrow than from laughter.

Be anxious for nothing, but in everything by prayer and supplication, with thanksgiving, let your requests be made known to God.

Philippians 4:6

I hate to admit it, but I'm a worrier. And because there are a lot of people just like me, Jesus addressed this problem in Matthew 6:25–34 when He said: "Do not worry." Don't worry about the basic needs of life—food, clothing, shelter—and don't worry about tomorrow.

Worry may be a symptom of a bigger problem. Sometimes it's a lack of gratitude for the way God has cared for us in the past. Or perhaps it's a lack of faith that God really is trustworthy. Or it may be a refusal to depend on God instead of ourselves. Don't let worries hold you back from what God may be trying to teach you. He invites you to bring your anxious thoughts directly to Him. —CHK

To be anxious about nothing, pray about everything.

MAY 30

Looking for the blessed hope and glorious appearing of our great God and Savior Jesus Christ. Titus 2:13

PEACE TALKS FALL APART AGAIN - UNEMPLOYMENT
RATE RISES - TORNADO RIPS THROUGH TOWN

Newspaper headlines like this can lead us to despair. There doesn't seem to be any hope for this world. Yet according to the Scriptures, the dream of abolishing war is not merely wishful thinking. The idea of prosperity for all is more than a political gimmick. The Bible tells us that the eventual taming of nature is a certainty.

The hope for this world, however, is not to be found in human efforts but in the return of Jesus Christ. Because we have this hope, we can be optimistic even in the deepening gloom of this age. —RDH

The only hope for world peace is the coming of the Prince of Peace.

MAY 31

Sing to the Lord a new song, and His praise in the assembly of saints.
Psalm 149:1

An old Jewish legend says that after God had created the world He
called the angels together and asked them what they thought of it.
One of them said, "The only thing lacking is the sound of praise to the
Creator." So God created music, and it was heard in the whisper of the
wind and in the song of the birds. He also gave man the gift of song.
And throughout all the ages, music has blessed multitudes of people.

Good music is a blessing from the Lord. It's a soothing tonic for
troubled hearts. It can motivate us to live for Christ, and through
it we can lift our hearts in praise to the Lord. —RDH

Hearts in tune with God will sing His praises.

JUNE 1

I do not want you to be ignorant, brethren, concerning those who have fallen asleep, lest you sorrow as others who have no hope. 1 Thessalonians 4:13

It was to be an exciting summer for our family, including a trip to Florida to help our daughter Julie begin her teaching career. Instead, the summer of 2002 began with tragedy when our teenage daughter Melissa was killed in an automobile accident on the last day of school. Our summer of hope turned into a nightmare, but I began to pray that the loss of our daughter could have a positive impact—first among her friends and then in ever-widening ways.

Toward the end of the summer, we did take that Florida trip to get Julie started, heavy-hearted as we were. As she began teaching, Julie told her classes about her sister and her faith. One day, a student talked to Julie after class. "I'm scared," she said, "because I'm not a Christian like Melissa was." Julie then led her to faith in Jesus Christ. I imagined Melissa rejoicing in heaven. —DB

Even in life's darkest hour, Christians have the brightest hope.

JUNE 2

Teach us to number our days, that we may gain a heart of wisdom. Psalm 90:12

Author Victor Hugo said, "Short as life is, we make it still shorter by the careless waste of time." There's no sadder example of wasted time than a life dominated by fretting. Take, for example, an American woman whose dream of riding a train through the English countryside came true. After boarding the train she kept fretting about the windows and the temperature, complaining about her seat assignment, rearranging her luggage, and so on. To her shock, she suddenly reached her journey's end. With deep regret she said to the person meeting her, "If I'd known I was going to arrive so soon, I wouldn't have wasted my time fretting so much."

Instead of fretting, strive to grow in God's wisdom every day. Stay focused on eternal values. —JY

Worry casts a big shadow behind a small thing.

JUNE 3

Do not let sin reign in your mortal body, that you should obey it in its lusts.
Romans 6:12

A friend wrote to me about certain "reservations" in his life—areas of secret sin that he reserved for himself and into which he frequently withdrew. These "reserves" are like the large tracts of wilderness in my home state of Idaho. It may sound exciting to wander around these untamed regions by oneself, but it's dangerous.

We can set up perimeters that keep us from wandering into "the wild." (1) Remember that we are dead to sin's power (Romans 6:1–14). We do not have to give in to it. (2) Resist temptation when it first attracts us. (3) Find a person who will commit to hold us accountable each week by asking, "Have you gone where you should not go?" If we long for holiness and ask God for help, He will give us victory. —DHR

Beware — the more you look at temptation, the better it looks!

JUNE 4

Good and upright is the Lord; therefore He teaches sinners in the way. Psalm 25:8

The phrase "God is good, all the time; all the time, God is good" is repeated by many Christians almost like a mantra. I often wonder if they really believe it or even think about what they're saying. I sometimes doubt God's goodness—especially when it feels as though God isn't hearing or answering my prayers.

Do you ever feel as though God isn't answering your prayers? Are you tempted to doubt His goodness? When I feel this way, I have to remind myself that my circumstances aren't the barometer of God's love and goodness—the cross is. We can't rely on our feelings. But day by day as we choose to trust Him more, we learn to believe with confidence that God is good—all the time. —AC

Circumstances aren't the barometer of God's love and goodness — the cross is.

JUNE 5

Underneath are the everlasting arms. Deuteronomy 33:27

On August 27, 1960, US Air Force Captain Joseph Kittinger Jr. sat in a gondola suspended from a high-altitude balloon. When the balloon reached 102,800 feet above the surface of Earth (more than 19 miles), Kittinger jumped out. Four minutes and 36 seconds later his main parachute opened at 18,000 feet, but not before he had attained a velocity of 614 miles per hour! Kittinger carefully planned his record-setting descent.

In the spiritual realm, we're more likely to find that life is filled with unexpected free falls. The loss of a loved one, a broken relationship, or a terminated job can make us feel as if we're dropping into the unknown. But for believers, there is a spiritual "parachute"—the loving arms of God. —DF

With God behind you and His arms beneath you, you can face whatever lies ahead of you.

When they had prayed, the place where they
were assembled together was shaken.
Acts 4:31

Peter and John were in danger. The religious leaders in Jerusalem opposing the gospel had warned them to cease their missionary efforts. When the apostles reported this to the other believers, they immediately held a prayer meeting. First they praised God. Then they asked for boldness that they might continue the work. The results were dramatic. The house shook, and the believers were filled with the Holy Spirit. They boldly witnessed, enjoyed spiritual unity, and gave unselfishly to those in need.

I've never felt a building shake at a prayer meeting, but I have seen God's power at work. When we pray sincerely, praising God and seeking His glory, great things happen. —HVL

Sincere intercession is the key to God's intervention.

To those who have no might [God] increases strength.
Isaiah 40:29

Jonah Sorrentino was deeply hurt at age six when his parents separated. As a result, he held a lot of anger and bitterness inside. At fifteen, Jonah learned of God's love for him and became a believer in Jesus Christ. Jonah, also known as recording artist KJ-52, admits that he used to live like a victim of circumstances. In an interview with *Christianity Today*, he explained how he began to experience healing: "You definitely have to acknowledge that, no, you're not okay. You also have to reach a point of saying, 'I'm not going to dwell on everything of the past . . . on anger or bitterness or hurt. I'm going to move forward because God is going to give me the strength to do that.'"

God helped Jonah to forgive his parents and to write song lyrics that encourage others. —AC

Those who wait on the Lord shall renew their strength.

Man who is born of woman is of few days and full of trouble.
Job 14:1

Why is there suffering? Many of us ask that question when we hear of hurricanes, mudslides, earthquakes, and other disasters taking people's lives. Job asked that question too. Why is there so much pain in this world?

As Job discovered, this world is a fallen place. When we see suffering, however, we can use it as an opportunity to serve God by helping others, to trust Him in spite of the difficulty, and to grow in our faith in Him. When trouble hits, let our first reaction be to trust the Lord and care for the needs of others. —DB

Our response to suffering can either make us or break us.

JUNE 9

We have no power against this great multitude that is coming against us; nor do we know what to do, but our eyes are upon You.

2 Chronicles 20:12

During the years that I taught junior high students in an overcrowded school, I used to say (only slightly in jest) that my morning prayer was 2 Chronicles 20:12: "We have no power against this great multitude that is coming against us; nor do we know what to do, but our eyes are upon You."

When Judah's King Jehoshaphat spoke those words, however, it was a matter of life and death. As a coalition of armies marched against Jerusalem, the people of Judah gathered to seek God's guidance and help. During threatening times of disruption and change, we too can pray, "Lord, we don't know what to do, but our eyes are on you. What do you want to do with this moment?" —DCM

Faith ends where worry begins, and worry ends where faith begins.

JUNE 10

Marcie (not her real name) had broken up with her boyfriend, and now he was harassing her. He followed her, stared at her, and intimidated her in subtle ways. She was a cheerleader, and during one game, he stood at field level right in front of the cheerleading squad and stared at her as she did her routines. Her mom and stepdad, sitting in the stands, saw him there and realized what was happening. At a break, she ran into the stands, her eyes filled with panic. "Do you see him over there?" she blurted out. "Yes, I do," her stepdad said. "I'm watching, and I will not take my eyes off you." Marcie was relieved that he saw what was going on, understood how she was feeling, and was watching over her. —DCE

His eye is on the sparrow, and I know He watches me. — *Martin*

JUNE 11

Casting all your care upon Him, for He cares for you.
1 Peter 5:7

Emilie, wife of nineteenth-century German pastor Christoph Blumhardt, envied his ability to pray for his parishioners and then effortlessly fall asleep. So one night she pleaded, "Tell me your secret!" He answered, "Is God so powerless that my worrying would help the well-being of our parish? There comes a moment each day when we must simply drop what weighs on us and hand it over to God."

When worries begin to gnaw at your mind, surrender them to the Lord and don't take them back again. That's the secret of soul-serenity when we're on life's storm-tossed sea. —VCG

Drop what weighs you down by giving it to God.

He who calls you is faithful, who also will do it.
1 Thessalonians 5:24

During one hectic week, Pastor A. J. Gossip didn't have his customary amount of time to prepare his sermon. As he walked to the pulpit that Sunday morning, he felt guilty about the scanty sermon notes in his hand. It seemed that the Lord was asking him, "Is this the best you could do for me this week?" And Gossip honestly replied, "Yes, Lord, it is my best." He told a friend later that Jesus took that ill-prepared piece of work and in His hands "it became a trumpet" to his congregation.

When pressure-periods come and we just don't have the time we feel we need, we should do the best we can and then prayerfully trust God's faithfulness. —VCG

Be faithful—and leave the results to God.

JUNE 13

The floods have lifted up their voice; the floods lift up their waves.
Psalm 93:3

Trouble comes our way, according to Psalm 93, in relentless waves
that surge and pound against our souls and break upon them
with furious force. Yet above the deafening tempest we hear the
psalmist's refrain: "The LORD on high is mightier than the noise
of many waters, than the mighty waves of the sea" (v. 4).

The storm will not last forever. Yet while it rages, you can cling to the
Lord's promises of love and faithfulness, for His "testimonies are very
sure" (v. 5). Waves of trouble and grief may sweep over you, but you will
not be swept away. Our Father in heaven is holding your hand. —DHR

*When adversity is ready to strike us, then
God is most ready to strengthen us.*

JUNE 14

You comprehend my path and my lying down, and are acquainted with all my ways. Psalm 139:3

In today's world of inexpensive, high-tech spying devices, total privacy has become a rare and precious thing. A special agent for the Georgia Bureau of Investigation says, "Don't assume that you are alone, not ever." Cameras are used to monitor people in public places like banks and shopping malls. In addition, tiny wireless video cameras that sell for less than one hundred dollars are being used by ordinary people for less than honorable purposes.

It might seem odd, therefore, to hear someone celebrate a complete lack of privacy, until we realize that the One watching his every move was almighty God. After stating that God knew each thought, word, and action before it happened, David said, "Such knowledge is too wonderful for me" (139:6). —DCM

He is not alone who is alone with Jesus.

He is the Rock, His work is perfect; for all His ways are justice.
Deuteronomy 32:4

When I was coaching high school freshman girls' basketball, I was surprised at how many times I heard, "That's not fair!" If I asked some girls to do a defensive drill while others shot free throws, I heard, "Not fair." If I allowed one group to play offense longer than another group, I heard, "Not fair."

So many situations in life shout, "Not fair!" But we are not the arbiters of fairness. God is, and He knows far more than we do about His plans and purposes. In the end, it's not about fairness; it's about trust in a faithful God who knows what He is doing. —DB

Life is not always fair, but God is always faithful.

JUNE 16

As the mountains surround Jerusalem, so the Lord surrounds His people.
Psalm 125:2

I recall preaching at the funeral service of a young friend. From where I stood I could see the Rocky Mountains towering over the western horizon. The scene prompted me to consider how I will one day follow that friend through the valley of the shadow of death, and yet those peaks will still be thrusting themselves skyward. Eventually they will crumble into dust, but the God who made them will exist forever in undiminished glory. I also remember thinking that my deceased friend and I will, by God's grace, live with Him forever and ever.

That truth inspires us with hope. If by faith we belong to Jesus Christ the Savior, who is from everlasting to everlasting, we will one day rejoice in heaven in unending praise to Him. —VCG

To see God's hand in everything makes life a great adventure.

Their sins and their lawless deeds I will remember no more.
Hebrews 8:12

One Sunday I heard a sermon that revolutionized my thinking. The speaker caught my attention when he said, "The idea that God forgets my sins isn't very reassuring to me. After all, what if He suddenly remembered? In any case, only imperfection can forget, and God is perfect." As I was questioning the biblical basis for such statements, the pastor read Hebrews 8:12, "Their sins and their lawless deeds I will remember no more." Then he said, "God doesn't say He'll forget our sins—He says He'll remember them no more! His promise not to remember them ever again is stronger than saying He'll forget them. Now that reassures me!" —JY

To enjoy the future, accept God's forgiveness for the past.

JUNE 18

Now we see in a mirror, dimly.
1 Corinthians 13:12

When I was a child, I had to wear glasses. Interestingly, my vision improved, and from high school until age forty I didn't need them. My vision was better than 20/20. Now, because of the natural degeneration of the eyes with age, I wear bifocals. Without glasses, my vision is impaired.

About our "spiritual vision" the apostle Paul said, "Now we see in a mirror, dimly, but then face to face." In the ancient world, they didn't have the clear glass mirrors we have today. Instead, mirrors were made of polished metal and provided a reflection that was dim and distorted. In other words, our current spiritual vision is impaired, but in eternity we will see clearly. —DF

We now see Jesus in the Bible, but then, face to face.

JUNE 19

Bless the Lord, O my soul, and forget not all His benefits.
Psalm 103:2

Some days we awaken with aching joints or dull spirits and wonder how we can shake off our lethargy and make it through the day. Here's an idea: Like David, try lifting up your thanks to God. Use mind and memory to rekindle thankfulness for all God's "benefits." Gratefulness will lead to joy.

Thank God for His forgiveness. Thank Him for redeeming your life from destruction. Thank Him for crowning your life "with loving kindness and tender mercies" (103:4). Thank the One who, each day, renews your strength and vigor. "Forget not all His benefits." —DHR

Gratitude is the memory of a glad heart.

His delight is in the law of the Lord, and in His law he meditates day and night.
Psalm 1:2

In a quest for greater productivity and efficiency, many of us over-schedule our days, then rush through meals, drive impatiently, and wonder why the joy of living eludes us. Carol Odell, who writes a business advice column, says that slowing down can positively affect our lives at work and at home. Rushing can cloud our judgment and cause us to overlook important things and valuable people. Odell encourages everyone to slow down, and even suggests the radical idea of welcoming red traffic lights and using the waiting time to meditate.

Isn't it time for all of us to slow down and live? —DCM

Come apart and rest awhile or you may just plain come apart! —Havner

JUNE 21

*I have come that they may have life, and that they
may have it more abundantly.* John 10:10

On a family visit to Disneyland, I noticed the sign over the entrance arch that read, "Welcome to the happiest place on earth." However, for the rest of the day as I looked at the faces of the people around me, I was impressed by the small number who were actually smiling during their visit to "the happiest place on earth."

Living life to the fullest is very different than merely existing, than just going through the motions. In fact, Jesus said that part of His mission was to enable us to live life to the fullest: "I have come that they may have life, and that they may have it more abundantly" (John 10:10). This is life lived not according to the standards of a fallen world, but life as it was intended to be. It is life according to the designs and desires of the Creator of life. —BC

To know God puts a song in your heart and a smile on your face.

JUNE 22

He makes me to lie down in green pastures; He leads me beside the still waters.
Psalm 23:2

Our office is a busy place, often involving meeting after meeting, hallway conferences, and an avalanche of e-mail. In the midst of this, I sometimes need to escape, to decompress. On those days, I retreat to the quiet of my car. I grab some lunch and sit in my car, where I can read, listen to music, think, pray—and be refreshed.

The essence of the "still waters" the shepherd-psalmist points to in Psalm 23:2 is a quiet place, a retreat from the pressures of life, where you can rest in the presence of the Shepherd of your heart and be strengthened for what lies ahead. —BC

When we draw near to God our minds are refreshed and our strength is renewed!

JUNE 23

Whatever you ask in My name, that I will do, that the Father may be glorified in the Son. John 14:13

Five-year-old Randy wanted a toy stagecoach for Christmas. While shopping with Mom, he found just the one he wanted. "Mommy, I want this one. Pleeeease!" he begged, insisting that he get this stagecoach for Christmas. "We'll see," Mom said. On Christmas morning, Randy unwrapped the stagecoach he had begged for. He was so pleased. But then his older brother said, "You really did a dumb thing to insist on getting *that* coach. Mom bought you a much bigger one, but when you begged for that little one, she exchanged it!"

Sometimes we're like that with God. We beg and plead— and God may even give us exactly what we ask for. But He may have had something better in mind. —AC

Large asking results in large receiving.

You have turned for me my mourning into dancing.
Psalm 30:11

After receiving his second Academy Award, Denzel Washington said to his family, "I told you, if I lost tonight, I'd come home and we'd celebrate. And if I won tonight, I'd come home and we'd celebrate." Denzel, a Christian, was trusting God, whether in blessing or in disappointment.

Are you facing a situation in which you could be disappointed? Why not set up a celebration to count your blessings no matter what the outcome? —DF

The pain of disappointment is soothed by a heart of gratitude.

Shall we indeed accept good from God, and shall we not accept adversity? Job 2:10

When Jeremy was seventeen, he struggled with a question that theologians have wrestled with for centuries. For him the problem was not theoretical but practical. He was trying to understand why his mother had to have brain surgery. He asked, "Why do good people suffer, Mom?" She told him, "Suffering is part of living in a sin-cursed world, and good people suffer like anybody else. That's why I'm glad we have Jesus. If I die, I'll go to a better place, and I'll long for the day when I can see you again." She then said that she could understand his frustration, but she told him not to put the blame on God.

God didn't explain to Job what He was doing but said that He could be trusted to do what is right (Job 38–42). —DJD

God is not obligated to give us answers,
but He promises us His grace.

*Be still, and know that I am God; I will be exalted
among the nations, I will be exalted in the earth!*

Psalm 46:10

When God spoke to Elijah on Mount Horeb, He could have done so in
the wind, earthquake, or fire. Instead, He spoke with a "still small voice"
(1 Kings 19:12). God asked, "What are you doing here, Elijah?" (v. 13), as
he hid from Jezebel who had threatened to kill him. Elijah's reply revealed
what God already knew—the depth of his fear and discouragement. He said,
in effect, "Lord, I have been most zealous when others have forsaken You.
What do I get for being the only one standing up for You?" (see v. 14).

Both the clashing cymbals of our fears and failures and the loud trumpeting
of our successes can drown out God's still small voice. It's time for us to
quiet our hearts to listen for Him as we meditate on His Word. —AL

To tune in to God's voice we must tune out this world's noise.

Now I know that there is no God in all the earth, except in Israel.
2 Kings 5:15

When I rear-ended a truck with my nearly new car, positive thoughts did not immediately come to mind. I was thinking primarily of the cost, the inconvenience, and the injury to my ego. But I did find some hope in this thought, which I often share with other writers: "In every bad experience, there's a good illustration."

Finding the good can be a challenge, but Scripture confirms that God uses bad circumstances for good purposes. Even when we don't know why something bad has happened, we know that God has the power to use it for good. —JAL

God is the master of turning burdens into blessings.

JUNE 28

Arise, go over this Jordan . . . I will not leave you nor forsake you.
Joshua 1:2, 5

John Wesley wrote, "Among the many difficulties of our early ministry, my brother Charles often said, 'If the Lord would give me wings, I'd fly.' I used to answer, 'If God bids me fly, I will trust Him for the wings.'"

After the death of Moses, Joshua was thrust into a position of great responsibility—to lead the children of Israel into the Promised Land. The enormity of the challenge made him tremble with fear. But the Lord gave him an assuring promise: "I will not leave you nor forsake you." Then He said, "Be strong and of good courage; do not be afraid, nor be dismayed, for the Lord your God is with you wherever you go" (v. 9). Such reassurances were the backing Joshua needed. —RDH

Where God guides, God provides!

God remembered Noah, and every living thing,
and all the animals that were with him in the ark.
Genesis 8:1

A Chinese festival called *Qing Ming* is a time to express grief for lost relatives. Customs include grooming gravesites and taking walks with loved ones in the countryside. Legend has it that it began when a youth's rude and foolish behavior resulted in the death of his mother. So he decided that henceforth he would visit her grave every year to remember what she had done for him. Sadly, it was only after her death that he remembered her.

How differently God deals with us! God remembers us wherever we are. Our concerns are His concerns. Our pain is His pain. The all-seeing God remembers us as a mother remembers her children, and He waits to meet our needs. —CPH

To know that God sees us brings both conviction and comfort.

Be imitators of God . . . and walk in love.
Ephesians 5:1–2

In the middle of carting seventy pieces of luggage, an electronic piano, and other equipment through airports and on and off a tour bus, it's easy to wonder, "Why are we doing this?" Taking twenty-eight teenagers on an eleven-day ministry trip to a land across the ocean is not easy. But at the end of the trip our bus driver, who had carted us all over England and Scotland, grabbed the bus microphone and in tears thanked the kids for how wonderful they had been. Then after we got home, he e-mailed us to say how much he appreciated the thank-you cards the kids had written to him—many of which contained the gospel.

Whose life are you affecting? Sometimes it's not our target audience that we impact most. Sometimes it's the bus drivers of the world. —DB

Witnessing is not just something a Christian says, but what he is.

JULY 1

I have blotted out, like a thick cloud, your transgressions.
Isaiah 44:22

What is memory? By what process are events recorded, stored, and preserved in our brain to be brought back again and again? Much is still mystery.

We do know that memories can be blessings—full of comfort, assurance, and joy. Old age can be happy and satisfying if we have stored up memories of purity, faith, fellowship, and love. But memory can also be a curse and a tormentor. Many people would give all they possess to erase from their minds the past sins that haunt them. What can a person do who is plagued by such remembrances? Just one thing. Take them to the One who is able to forgive them and blot them out forever. —MRD

The best eraser is honest confession to God.

JULY 2

Through the Lord's mercies we are not consumed, because
His compassions fail not . . . . Great is Your faithfulness.
Lamentations 3:22–23

Hudson Taylor, the humble servant of God to China, demonstrated extraordinary trust in God's faithfulness. In his journal he wrote: "Our heavenly Father . . . sustained three million Israelites in the wilderness for forty years. We do not expect He will send three million missionaries to China; but if He did, He would have ample means to sustain them all . . . Depend on it, God's work done in God's way will never lack God's supply."

Our strength for the present and hope for the future are not based on the stability of our own perseverance but on the fidelity of God. No matter what our need, we can count on the Father's faithfulness. —PVG

He who abandons himself to God will never be abandoned by God.

JULY 3

I am with you always, even to the end of the age.
Matthew 28:20

One of my earliest memories of hearing good music was when a male quartet rehearsed at our home. I was about ten years old, and I was especially attentive to my dad, who sang first tenor. One of the quartet's favorites was titled, "I Am with You." Even at that tender age, I not only appreciated the music but I "got the message."

Those words of Jesus to His disciples just before He ascended—"I am with you always"—became precious to me as the quartet sang, "In the sunlight, in the shadow, I am with you where you go." Wherever I may be today, I know I am not alone. He will never leave me. —RBC

First make sure you are with Him; then you can be sure He'll be with you.

JULY 4

The God of peace will be with you.
Philippians 4:9

It's natural for us to be fearful in a storm (literal or figurative). The disciples had Jesus right there in the boat with them, yet they were afraid (Matthew 8:23–27). He used the calming of the storm as a lesson to show them who He was—a powerful God who also cared for them.

We wish that Jesus would always calm the storms of our life as He calmed the storm for the disciples that day. But we can find moments of peace when we're anchored to the truth that He's in the boat with us and He will take care of us. —AC

To realize the worth of the anchor, we need to feel the stress of the storm.

JULY 5

Lo, I am with you always, even to the end of the age.
Matthew 28:20

Jesus told His disciples that He would be with them "always." Literally, the Greek word here for *always* means "all the days." Jesus didn't simply say "always," but "all the days." That takes into account all our various activities, the good and bad circumstances surrounding us, the varied responsibilities we have through the course of our days, the storm clouds and the sunshine. Our Lord is present with us no matter what each day brings.

Practice God's presence, stopping in the midst of your busy day to say to yourself, "The Lord is here." —DHR

Pray that you will see Him who is invisible— and see Him everywhere.

JULY 6

*Whatever you do in word or deed, do all in the
name of the Lord Jesus.* Colossians 3:17

I was watching an episode of *Dirty Jobs* on the Discovery Channel, where
the host Mike Rowe was talking to an industrial painter. "There's really
no glory in what you do," he said. "No," the painter agreed, "but it's a job
that needs to be done." He paints the inside of the Mackinac Bridge towers
in Northern Michigan. His unnoticed job ensures that the steel of the
magnificent suspended structure won't rust from the inside out, compromising
the integrity of the bridge. Most of the twelve thousand people who safely
cross the Straits of Mackinac each day aren't even aware that they are
depending on workers like this painter to faithfully do their jobs well.

Though we may think our deeds—big and small—sometimes go unnoticed,
they are being observed by the One who matters most. —CHK

Daily work takes on eternal value when it is done for God.

JULY 7

Command those who are rich in this present age not to be haughty, nor to trust in uncertain riches but in the living God, who gives us richly all things to enjoy.
1 Timothy 6:17

Dream holidays, shopping, food, clothes, friends, cars—my guess is that if you perked up at the mention of shopping, holidays, or cars, you might have felt a twinge of guilt. We often view the joy of temporal things as less than spiritual and show our discomfort by apologizing for nice things. As if real Christians never eat quiche, drive cool cars, or wear designer clothes!

God's greatest gift to us is our relationship with His Son Jesus. It's a gift beyond comparison. But the enjoyment of "things" can be a positive spiritual experience. When we recognize that He "gives us richly all things to enjoy," our hearts should be full of thankfulness and praise. Enjoy the Giver and the gifts. —JS

Our heavenly Father delights in bringing us delight.

Fight the good fight of faith, lay hold on eternal life. 1 Timothy 6:12

Tolkien's classic *The Lord of the Rings* trilogy came to life in recent years on film. At one point in the epic story, the hero, Frodo, reaches a point of despair and wearily confides to his friend, "I can't do this, Sam." As a good friend, Sam gives a rousing speech: "It's like in the great stories . . . Full of darkness and danger they were . . . Folk in those stories had lots of chances of turning back, only they didn't. They kept going. Because they were holding on to something." Which prompts Frodo to ask: "What are we holding on to, Sam?"

In life's battles, we can hold on to the fact that good will triumph over evil in the end, that one day we will see our Master and Leader face-to-face, and we will reign with Him forever. We are guaranteed a victorious ending! —JS

The trials of earth are small compared with the triumphs of heaven.

JULY 9

God is not unjust to forget your work and labor of love which you have showed toward His name, in that you have ministered to the saints. Hebrews 6:10

When Britain's oldest man turned 111, vintage aircraft did a flyover, and the Band of the Royal Marines played "Happy Birthday." According to the *Daily Mirror,* Henry Allingham was amazed by all of the attention. Until six years earlier, he had for eighty-six years kept secret the horrific memories of what happened in the trenches of World War I. Only when tracked down by the World War I Veteran's Association did this old man, who had been shelled, bombed, and shot, receive honor for what he had endured in behalf of his country.

The Scriptures show that everything we have done in faith and love will one day be honored by God. —MRD

God remembers the good we forget.

JULY 10

We were burdened beyond measure . . . so that we despaired even of life.
2 Corinthians 1:8

When I was a child, kids on the playground jokingly quoted Shakespeare's famous line: "To be or not to be—that is the question!" But we really didn't understand what it meant. Later I learned that Shakespeare's character Hamlet, who speaks these lines, is a melancholy prince who learns that his uncle has killed his father and married his mother. The horror of this realization is so disturbing that he contemplates suicide. The question for him was: "to be" (to go on living) or "not to be" (to take his own life).

Focusing on ourselves can lead to despair. But putting our trust in God gives us an entirely different perspective—a divine purpose "to be." —DF

Trials make us think; thinking makes us wise; wisdom makes life profitable.

Happy is he who has the God of Jacob for his help. Psalm 146:5

The foundation for happiness is a proper relationship with the Lord. But to fully experience that happiness, we must build on that foundation in practical ways. I found this list of Ten Rules for Happier Living:

1. Give something away. 2. Do a kindness. 3. Give thanks always. 4. Work with vim and vigor. 5. Visit the elderly and learn from their experience. 6. Look intently into the face of a baby and marvel. 7. Laugh often—it's life's lubricant. 8. Pray to know God's way. 9. Plan as though you will live forever—you will. 10. Live as though today is your last day on earth. —RDH

Trusting and obeying the Lord brings true happiness.

Let not the floodwater overflow me, nor let the deep swallow me up.
Psalm 69:15

The builders of sport utility vehicles (SUVs) like to advertise their products in mind-boggling situations. High on a mountain crag, where no truck could seemingly go. Or in a swamp so impassable you'd need a hovercraft to negotiate it. We're supposed to think that SUVs are invincible. That's why I found unintended humor in the disclaimer in a recent ad for a four-wheel-drive SUV. A photo showed the vehicle up to its headlights in water as it forged across a foreboding river. The ad said: "Traversing deep water can cause damage, which voids the vehicle warranty."

Deep water is a problem not only for cars but also for us. Fortunately, traversing deep water won't affect our spiritual warranty. God will always be there to guarantee His support. —DB

When trouble overtakes you, let God take over.

*God . . . has blessed us with every spiritual
blessing in the heavenly places in Christ.*
Ephesians 1:3

Tennis superstar Arthur Ashe died of AIDS, which he contracted from a blood transfusion during heart surgery. More than a great athlete, Ashe was a gentleman who inspired and encouraged many with his exemplary behavior on and off the court. Ashe could have become embittered and self-pitying in the face of his disease, but he maintained a grateful attitude. He explained, "If I asked, 'Why me?' about my troubles, I would have to ask, 'Why me?' about my blessings. Why my winning Wimbledon? Why my marrying a beautiful, gifted woman and having a wonderful child?"

Think about God's blessings and ask, "Why me?" Then
your grumbling will give way to praise. —VCG

With unwanted burdens come undeserved blessings.

JULY 14

Commit your way to the Lord, trust also in Him, and He shall bring it to pass.
Psalm 37:5

In her book *Beyond Our Selves*, Catherine Marshall wrote about learning to surrender her entire life to God through a "prayer of relinquishment." When she encountered situations she feared, she often panicked and exhibited a demanding spirit in prayer: "God, I must have thus and so." God seemed remote. But when she surrendered the dreaded situation to Him to do with it exactly as He pleased, fear left and peace returned. From that moment on, God began working things out.

Instead of trying to quell your fears with panic prayers, surrender yourself to God through a prayer of relinquishment, and see what He will do. —JY

Prayer is the bridge between panic and peace.

JULY 15

Fear God and keep His commandments, for this is man's all. Ecclesiastes 12:13

What's the point? This question came to mind as I watched my grandsons' dog fetch a ball for me again and again. What's the point? That's what the writer of Ecclesiastes asked as he thought about the monotonous cycle he observed in nature and in life—the same things happening year after year, generation after generation.

What's the point? Here it is. A few years before a friend of mine died, he said, "Life is a wonderful experience. It's marvelous to see that God keeps nature going in its pattern. It's wonderful to know that we're here to love God above everything and to love our neighbor as ourselves. It's comforting to believe that all our sins are forgiven because of what Christ did on the cross. And it's exciting to think about the eternity God has for us. It sure is great to be alive." —HVL

When we focus on Christ, everything else becomes clear.

JULY 16

Rejoicing in hope, patient in tribulation.
Romans 12:12

Friends gave us a piece of Raku pottery. "Each pot is hand-formed," the tag explained, "a process that allows the spirit of the artist to speak through the finished work with particular directness and intimacy." Once the clay has been shaped by the potter it is fired in a kiln. Then, glowing red hot, it is thrust into a smoldering sawdust pile where it remains until finished. The result is a unique product—"one of a kind," the tag on our piece insists.

So it is with us. We bear the imprint of the Potter's hand, and each of us is "one of a kind." But we're not yet finished. We must experience the kiln of affliction. Aching hearts, weary spirits, aging bodies are the processes God uses to finish the work He has begun. Be "patient in tribulation" and await the finished product. —DHR

Don't fear the furnace that surrounds you.

Fear not, for I am with you; be not dismayed, for I am your God.
Isaiah 41:10

On a bright Sunday morning one of my boys was walking to church with me. He was skipping on ahead when suddenly his carefree progress came to an end. A few yards away was a boxer dog looking at him. My son turned and rushed to my side. Only when his hand was securely in mine and he knew I was right beside him was he able to walk without fear past the boxer.

What a picture of our pilgrimage through this world! We're skipping along—until something strikes fear into our hearts. Then, by faith, we make our way to the Savior, realizing we dare not go forward without the assurance of His presence. As we completely trust in Him, He takes our hand and walks with us each step of the way. —DJD

If you can't find a way out, look up.

[God] delivered us from so great a death, and does deliver us; in whom we trust that He will still deliver us.

2 Corinthians 1:10

They were called the "lost boys" of Sudan. Thousands of them fled the civil war in that country and sought refuge from the chaos and killing. Many had been taught the gospel in churches founded by missionaries, but they knew little of the world beyond their villages.

A *National Geographic* article profiled one of these "lost boys" who is now resettled in the United States. He told a church congregation that he is grateful for the comforts of the US, but also for the faith he learned through hardship. "Americans believe in God," he told them, "but they don't know what God can do." In the crucible of testing, we move from theory to reality as we experience God's power. —DCM

By trusting God in hardship we learn what He can do in our lives.

A merry heart does good, like medicine. Proverbs 17:22

The Bible isn't a psychology textbook, but it gives us the wisest counsel for experiencing happiness here and now. Proverbs 17:22, for example, assures us that "a merry heart does good, like medicine, but a broken spirit dries the bones." That simple statement was corroborated by the extensive research of Dr. Daniel Mark, a heart specialist at Duke University, who says, "A healthy outlook helps heal the heart."

But Dr. Nancy Frasure-Smith, a heart specialist who has studied the effect of depression, anxiety, and anger, admits, "We don't know how to change negative emotions." Faith in God, however, can produce that change. People who look beyond their present difficulty and put their trust in God's goodness cannot help but be joyful. —VCG

No matter what happens, you can find joy in the Lord.

JULY 20

I will sing of the mercies of the Lord forever. Psalm 89:1

I was driving to work and listening to a Christian radio station when, amid the usual morning banter, came the song "I Could Sing of Your Love Forever." As soon as this uplifting praise song began, I felt tears running down my face. There I was, almost at work, and I could hardly see to drive because of a song. What was going on? Then it struck me. The song reminded me that while another day of normal activity was beginning here on earth, my daughter Melissa was fulfilling the ultimate hope of that song in heaven. I pictured her brightly singing of God's love—getting a head start on the rest of us in that forever song. It was a bittersweet moment of understanding Melissa's joy while being reminded again of our sadness in not having her with us. —DB

In the sad moments of life, we need the anticipation
of joy that comes from singing of God's love.

JULY 21

The Lord knows those who are His. 2 Timothy 2:19

Arctic sea birds called guillemots live on rocky coastal cliffs, where thousands of them come together in small areas. Because of the crowded conditions, the females lay their eggs side by side in a long row. It's incredible that a mother bird can identify the eggs that belong to her. And studies show that even when one is moved some distance away, she finds it and carries it back to its original location.

Our heavenly Father is far more intimately acquainted with each of His children. He is aware of every thought, emotion, and decision we make. From morning till night He gives personal attention to our daily affairs. Jesus told His disciples that the Father knows when a single sparrow falls to the ground. Because people are of so much greater value than the birds, God's children can be assured of His constant care. —MRD

With God, you're never lost in a crowd.

JULY 22

Little by little I will drive them out from before you, until you have increased, and you inherit the land. Exodus 23:30

When I was a little girl, I loved to read, and I loved one particular story. It was about a little boy with a small shovel. He was trying to clear a pathway through deep, new-fallen snow in front of his house. A man paused to observe the child's enormous task. "Little boy," he inquired, "how can someone as small as you expect to finish a task as big as this?" The boy replied confidently, "Little by little, that's how!" And he continued shoveling.

God awakened in me the seed of that story years later at a time when I was recovering from a breakdown. How could someone as inadequate as I expect to surmount so great a mountain as this? That little boy's reply became my reply: "Little by little, that's how!" And I did overcome—by depending on God. But it was one small victory after another. —JY

Trust God to move your mountain, but keep on climbing.

Let us run . . . looking unto Jesus.
Hebrews 12:1–2

Corrie ten Boom lived through the hellish life of Nazi concentration camps. She saw the face of evil up close and personal. She saw some of the most inhumane acts man can do to man. She survived to tell her story of unfaltering faith and tight-fisted hope in God, and she said this: "If you look at the world, you'll be distressed. If you look within, you'll be depressed. But if you look at Christ, you'll be at rest."

Where are you looking? Are you focusing on the world and its dangers? Are you gazing at yourself, hoping to find your own answers? Or are you looking to Jesus, the author and finisher of your faith? —DB

When your world is falling apart, trust Jesus to hold it together.

Be anxious for nothing, but in everything by prayer . . .
let your requests be made known to God. Philippians 4:6

You may have played the game when you were a child. You interlace your fingers with someone else's and try to bend the other's hands back until one or the other cries "Mercy!" The winner is the one who gets the other person to surrender.

Sometimes we try to play "Mercy" with God when we pray. We have a request that we desperately want answered in a certain way, so we try to "bend His fingers back" and get Him to give in. God does want honesty of heart. But occasionally in our honesty a demanding spirit comes out. Deep down we know that prayer is not meant to be a contest with God that we try to win. Instead of praying with grudging resignation, "Lord, You always win," surrender to Him. Say "Mercy!" —AC

Prayer isn't a time to give orders but to report for duty.

JULY 25

Our whole being is dried up; there is nothing at all except this manna before our eyes! Numbers 11:6

Many of our recurring complaints focus not on what we don't have, but on what we do have and find uninteresting. Whether it's our work, our church, our house, or our spouse, boredom grumbles that it's not what we want or need. This frustration with sameness has been true of the human spirit since the beginning. Remember the protest of God's people about their menu in the wilderness? God provided exactly what they needed each day, but they wanted something more exciting. Oswald Chambers said: "There are times when there is . . . no thrill, but just the daily round, the common task . . . Routine is God's way of saving us between our times of inspiration. Do not expect God always to give you His thrilling minutes, but learn to live in the domain of drudgery by the power of God." —DCM

Drudgery is our opportunity to experience the presence of God.

JULY 26

*He who trusts in his own heart is a fool, but
whoever walks wisely will be delivered.*
Proverbs 28:26

The local TV meteorologist occasionally points to a map and says something like this: "I'm afraid that things are going to get worse before they get better."

Even when we are obedient to the Lord, the skies of adversity may not always clear immediately. Circumstances may get worse before they improve. But praise God, His grace will sustain us, and the storm will pass. —MDH

It's always darkest before the dawn.

He counts the number of the stars; He calls them all by name.
Psalm 147:4

A team led by an Australian astronomer calculated the number of stars in the known universe to be seventy sextillion—seven followed by twenty-two zeros. That unfathomable number is said to be more than the grains of sand in every beach and every desert on earth.

Having an estimate of the number of stars can help us praise God with greater awe and wonder. Psalm 147 says: "He counts the number of the stars; He calls them all by name. Great is our Lord, and mighty in power; His understanding is infinite." This psalm not only presents God's majesty, but it also affirms His personal concern for each of us. Let's praise the great God of stars and sand who knows and cares for each one of us. —DCM

All creation points to the almighty Creator.

Bless the Lord, O my soul, and forget not all His benefits. Psalm 103:2

As a minister was addressing a group, he took a large piece of paper and made a black dot in the center of it. Then he held up the paper and asked them what they saw. One person replied, "I see a black mark." "Right," the preacher said. "What else?" Silence prevailed. "I'm really surprised," he said. "You have completely overlooked the most important thing of all—the sheet of paper."

How often we are distracted by small, dot-like disappointments
and forget the innumerable blessings we receive from the Lord.
But like the sheet of paper, the good things are far more important
than the adversities that monopolize our attention. —RDH

*Spend your time counting your blessings —
not airing your complaints.*

Let us not grow weary while doing good, for in
due season we shall reap if we do not lose heart.
Galatians 6:9

If you love someone who struggles with a substance-abuse problem, you know that your emotions and his can be like riding a roller coaster—up and down. Today he wants help; tomorrow he's drinking or is high on drugs again. Today she's being honest; tomorrow she's running from the truth. The Holy Spirit helps us learn how to love people like that, even in their sins and struggles. Here are a few principles we can put into practice:

Treat the person with respect. Remember that you do not have the power to change another person. Reach out in love. Depend on God. Making some of these choices can help to slow down the roller coaster ride of changing emotions. —AC

Love helps people even when it hurts.

JULY 30

To you it has been granted on behalf of Christ, not only to believe in Him, but also to suffer for His sake. Philippians 1:29

When people tell me life is hard, I always reply, "Of course it is." The path by which God takes us often seems to lead away from what we perceive as our good, causing us to believe we've missed a turn and taken the wrong road. That's because most of us have been taught to believe that if we're on the right track, God's goodness will always translate into a life free of trouble. But when we come to the end of all our dark valleys, we'll understand that every circumstance has been allowed for our ultimate good. "No other route would have been as safe and as certain as the one by which we came," Bible teacher F. B. Meyer said. "If only we could see the path as God has always seen it, we would have selected it as well." —DHR

No trial would cause us to despair if we knew God's reason for allowing it.

JULY 31

I am like a broken vessel.
Psalm 31:12

Few of us can fulfill our hopes and plans without some interruption and disappointment along the way. But man's disappointments are often God's appointments, and the things we believe are tragedies may be the very opportunities through which God chooses to exhibit His love and grace.

Has the dearest thing in your life been torn away? Then remember that if you could see the purpose of it all from God's standpoint, you would praise the Lord. The best things that come to us are not those that accrue from having our way, but by letting God have His way. Remember, we have the Lord's promise: "No good thing will He withhold from those who walk uprightly" (Psalm 84:11). —MRD

For a Christian, wholeness always comes after brokenness.

AUGUST 1

Consider Him who endured such hostility . . .
lest you become weary and discouraged in your souls.
Hebrews 12:3

A man took home a cocoon so he could watch the emperor moth emerge. As the moth struggled to get through the tiny opening, the man enlarged it with a snip of his scissors. The moth emerged easily—but its wings were shriveled. The struggle through the narrow opening is God's way to force fluid from the moth's body into its wings. The "merciful" snip, in reality, was cruel.

Hebrews 12 describes the Christian life as a race that involves endurance, discipline, and correction. We never get beyond the need of a holy striving against self and sin. Sometimes the struggle is exactly what we need to become what God intends us to be. —JY

We experience God's strength in the strain of our struggle.

Keep sound wisdom and discretion . . . Then you will walk safely in your way.
Proverbs 3:21, 23

A frustrated homeowner had a yard full of moles. He tried everything he knew to defeat his underground enemy, but he was losing the battle. Finally a friend informed him that he was trying to solve his problem the wrong way. The moles weren't the true culprits. The real problem was the grubs that the moles were feeding on. Get rid of them and the moles would have no reason to stay.

Proverbs 3 gives us a parallel situation. Instead of moles, the problem is fear—the kind that robs us of strength during the day and sleep at night. We can eliminate our fears only by attacking the "grubs" that attract it—our self-sufficiency and foolish ways. What's important is to know the real problem so that we can work on it. —MRD

Keep your eyes on God and you'll soon lose sight of your fears.

AUGUST 3

I am the Lord, I do not change.
Malachi 3:6

I've learned to manipulate our bathroom scale in a self-satisfying manner. The little adjustment knob serves to vary the register, and if that becomes too much bother, I just lean a certain way. The idea is to get a favorable reading—hopefully one that is a few pounds less.

We live in an age when many people believe there are no absolutes. Self-serving behavior is rampant and tramples the moral law given for the protection of society. But there is a God of absolutes who says, "I am the Lord, I do not change." This should put steel into our spiritual backbone, giving us confidence in the face of difficulty and the assured fulfillment of every divine promise. —PVG

Earth changes, but God and His Word stand sure! — *Browning*

AUGUST 4

*I have surely seen the oppression of My people
who are in Egypt, and have heard their cry.*

Exodus 3:7

When we are experiencing deep sorrow or difficult circumstances, we may feel offended if a well-meaning person tries to encourage us to trust God's promises. We may perceive this as insensitive or even unrealistic. There also are times when our hurts and fears can close our ears to the hopeful words of God. But the Lord doesn't stop speaking to us, even when it's hard for us to hear. He continues working on our behalf just as He did in delivering His people from Egypt. As we experience God's compassion and His loving care, we can begin to hear again even as the hurt continues to heal. —DCM

*Even when we don't sense God's presence,
His loving care is all around us.*

AUGUST 5

In the world you will have tribulation; but be of good cheer, I have overcome the world. John 16:33

There's a lake near our home in the mountains that is known for good fishing. To get there, I had to hike two miles up a steep ridge—a hard climb for an old-timer like me. But then I discovered that it's possible to drive within a half-mile of the lake. I spent most of a day driving several mountain roads until I found the one that got me the closest. Then I carefully mapped the road so I could find it again. Several months later, I drove the road again. I came to a section that was much worse than I remembered—rocky, rutted, and steep. I wondered if I had missed a turn, so I stopped and checked my map. There, penciled alongside the stretch on which I was driving, were the words: "Rough and steep. Hard going." I was on the right road. If you're following Christ and experiencing some bumpy times, take heart—you're on the right road! —DHR

Following Jesus is always right — but not always easy.

AUGUST 6

The Lord said to [Gideon], "Peace be with you; do not fear."
Judges 6:23

It was ten-year-old Cleotis's first time fishing, and as he looked into the container of bait he seemed hesitant to get started. Finally he said to my husband, "Help me, I-S-O-W!" When my husband asked him what the problem was, Cleotis responded, "I-S-O-W! I'm Scared of Worms!" His fear had made him unable to act.

We all have fears of various kinds—from worms to wars. But we can be confident of this: If God asks us to do something, He'll give us the strength and power to do it. —AC

To take the fear out of living, put your faith in the living God.

AUGUST 7

God is my salvation, I will trust and not be afraid.
Isaiah 12:2

I have an ancient leaf blower that I use to clean up our patio. It sputters, rattles, smokes, and is excessively noisy. But our dog is utterly indifferent to the racket. When I start up the blower, she doesn't even raise her head. That's because she trusts me. A young man who occasionally mows our yard uses a similar blower, but when he enters the backyard, we have to put the dog in the house because she growls, barks, and snarls at him. Years ago, when she was a puppy, he teased her with the machine and she has never forgotten. Same set of circumstances, but the hands that use the blower make all the difference.

The hands that control the universe—God's hands—are wise and compassionate. We can trust them and not be afraid. —DHR

God is in control, so we have nothing to fear.

AUGUST 8

*David arose from the ground . . . and he went
into the house of the Lord and worshiped.*
2 Samuel 12:20

Children are so lovable and innocent—until their parents say no to their demands. When that happens, some kids scream uncontrollably, insisting on what they want. When our children were little, my wife and I thought it was important for them to learn to accept no for an answer. We felt this would help them to handle the disappointments of life more effectively. We prayed that it would also help them submit to God's will.

Likewise, we sometimes must accept no from God as the answer to our pleas. We should seek God's help and deliverance, but we must still trust Him if He does not answer our prayers the way we want Him to. —AL

Have we learned to take no for an answer?

When you pass through the waters, I will be with you. Isaiah 43:2

I'll never forget my first experience using an automatic car wash. Approaching it with dread, I pushed the money into the slot, nervously checked my windows, eased the car up to the line, and waited. Powers beyond my control began moving my car forward. When a thunderous rush of water, soap, and brushes hit my car from all directions, I thought irrationally, *What if I get stuck in here or water crashes in?* Suddenly the waters ceased, the car was dried, and I was propelled into the outside world again, my car clean and polished.

Sometimes I feel the same way about life—a victim of forces beyond my control. "Car-wash experiences," I now call them. And when I come out on the other side, which I always do, I say with joy and confidence, "He is a faithful God!" —JY

A tunnel of testing can produce a shining testimony.

AUGUST 10

Your Father knows the things you have need of before you ask Him. Matthew 6:8

As a child, C. S. Lewis enjoyed reading the books of E. Nesbit, especially *Five Children and It*. In this book, brothers and sisters on a summer holiday discover an ancient sand fairy who grants them one wish each day. But every wish brings the children more trouble than happiness because they can't foresee the results of getting everything they ask for.

Toward the end of his life, C. S. Lewis wrote, "If God had granted all the silly prayers I've made in my life, where should I be now?" The Bible tells us to make our requests known to God. But prayer is much more than telling God what we want Him to do for us. Prayer is placing ourselves in the presence of God to receive from Him what we really need. —DCM

Our highest privilege is to talk to God; our highest duty is to listen to Him.

AUGUST 11

*God . . . has begotten us again to a living hope through
the resurrection of Jesus Christ from the dead.*
1 Peter 1:3

The morning after my mother died, I was reading the Bible and talking to the Lord about my sadness. The Bible-in-One-Year reading for that day was John 6, and when I came to verse 39, the Lord whispered comfort to my sad heart: "This is the will of the Father who sent Me, that of all He has given Me I should lose nothing, but should raise it up at the last day." Mom's spirit was with the Lord already, but I knew that one day she would be raised and given a new body. As I continued reading, I noticed three other times in John 6 that Jesus said He will raise His people from the dead at the last day. He was repeating this truth to those who were listening long ago as well as to my heart that day.

The resurrection is our living hope. —AC

The risen Christ will come from heaven to take His own to heaven.

AUGUST 12

I will heal them and reveal to them the abundance of peace and truth. Jeremiah 33:6

On May 18, 1980, Mount St. Helens erupted in one of the greatest natural disasters of modern times. The top of the mountain was blown into the atmosphere and became a dark plume of pulverized rock eleven miles high. Avalanches of rock, mud, and ice swept down the mountain destroying everything in their path, clogging rivers, and stopping ships. Since that time, the US government has spent over a billion dollars on Mount St. Helens' recovery and long-term improvements of the area. Much of the engineering and construction work is unseen because "it takes the form of floods that will not happen, homes and communities that will not be destroyed, [and] river traffic that will flow smoothly."

True spiritual recovery often takes time. But as we allow the Lord to clean up our lives, He can safeguard us against future failures. —DCM

Christ's cleansing power can remove the most stubborn stain of sin.

AUGUST 13

I have heard your prayer . . . surely I will heal you.
On the third day you shall go up to the house of the Lord.
2 Kings 20:5

A runner at a school track meet crossed the finish line just ahead of his nearest rival. A bystander, noticing that the winner's lips were moving during the last couple of laps, wondered what he was saying. So he asked him about it. "I was praying," the runner answered. Pointing to his feet, he said, "I was saying, 'You pick 'em up, Lord, and I'll put 'em down.'" That athlete prayed for God's help, but he also did what he could to answer his own prayer.

When we ask the Lord to do something, we must
also be ready to do our part. —RDH

Pray as if everything depends on God; work
as if everything depends on you.

*Jacob said to Pharaoh, ". . . Few and evil
have been the days of the years of my life."*
Genesis 47:9

Jacob's life was full of trials. And as it was for the old patriarch, so it is for us.
Life buffets and restricts us, makes demands on us that we do not want to bear.
We want the quick fix. But there are no shortcuts that can accomplish God's
ultimate purpose for us. The only way to grow into Christ's likeness is to submit
each day to the conditions God brings into our lives. As we accept His will
and submit to His ways, His holiness becomes ours. Gradually but inexorably,
God's Spirit begins to turn us into kinder, gentler men and women—sturdier,
stronger, more secure and sensible. The process is mysterious and inexplicable,
but it is God's way of endowing us with grace and beauty. —DHR

God often empties our hands to fill our heart.

Jesus . . . has abolished death and brought life and immortality to light through the gospel. 2 Timothy 1:10

Crowds gathered each week to hear the soul-stirring sermons of Joseph Parker, the famous pastor of London's City Temple in the late nineteenth century. Then a crisis hit him hard. His wife died after an agonizing illness. A heartbroken husband, Parker confessed publicly that for a week he had even denied that God existed. But Parker's loss of faith was only temporary. From that experience he gained a stronger personal trust in Jesus' death-destroying resurrection and began to testify: "I have touched the bottom, and it is sound."

Death is our most venomous enemy, robbing us of joy and hope—
unless the triumph of Christ's resurrection reverberates in our
heart. As we believe in the mighty Victor over death, doubt is
banished and light drives away the darkness. —VCG

Because of Christ's empty tomb, we can be full of hope.

AUGUST 16

You are with me; Your rod and Your staff, they comfort me. Psalm 23:4

When my eight-year-old grandson, Jacob, visited me in the hospital, he brought me a custom-made "Get Well" card. It was an 8 1/2" x 11" piece of stiff white paper folded in half. On the front he had written, "Hope you feel better soon." On the inside, in large block letters, was this message: "I will be with you wherever you go." There was no Scripture reference, but Jacob had added these words: "God said that." He wanted to be sure I didn't expect *him* to be at my side during my entire hospital stay.

That added note brought a smile to my face and comfort to my heart. A hospital can be a lonely place. It's a world of unfamiliar faces, first-time medical procedures, and uncertain diagnoses. But I had God's assurance that He would go with me down every hall, through every new door, into any unknown future. God said that! —DJD

No danger can come so near the Christian that God is not nearer.

AUGUST 17

This is the day the Lord has made; we will rejoice and be glad in it. Psalm 118:24

I was in a convenience store one day, standing in line behind a man paying for his groceries. When he was finished, the clerk sent him off with a cheery "Have a great day!"

To the clerk's surprise (and mine) the man exploded in anger. "This is one of the worst days of my life," he shouted. "How can I have a great day?" And with that he stormed out of the store.

I understand the man's frustration; I too have "bad" days over which I have no control. Then I remember these words: "This is the day the Lord has made." Now, when people give me the parting admonition to have a great day, I can reply, "That's beyond my control, but I can be grateful for whatever comes my way, and rejoice—for this is the day the Lord has made." —DHR

A smile is a curve that can set things straight.

Look at the birds of the air . . . Are you not of more value than they?
Matthew 6:26

When you shift your mind into neutral and just let it idle, where do your thoughts go? Do you worry about money? We are to be careful with money, but Jesus taught that we are not to be full of care about it. If you have put your faith in the Lord, you don't have to worry about life's necessities. God himself has assumed responsibility for your food and clothing—and all your needs.

Whether or not you live only for money, you'll ultimately leave it or it will leave you. But if you focus your life on God and doing His will, all these other things will be provided. —HWR

Poverty of purpose is far worse than poverty of purse.

AUGUST 19

Come to Me, all you who labor and are heavy laden, and I will give you rest.
Matthew 11:28

In the fifth century BC, King Ahasuerus of Persia refused to allow mourners to enter his gates (Esther 4:1–2). One commentator suggests that the king preferred to surround himself with people who were awed by his wealth and were eager to attend his lavish parties. His reluctance to be bothered by bad news nearly resulted in the annihilation of the Jewish people.

Ahasuerus ruled his kingdom by allowing only happy people to enter his presence. Jesus builds His kingdom by welcoming the burdened and sorrowful into His presence. Jesus has the willingness and the power to turn our most troubling circumstances into a celebration of praise. —JAL

The gospel is bad news to those who reject it
and good news to those who receive it.

AUGUST 20

Help us, O Lord our God, for we rest on You.
2 Chronicles 14:11

An ancient Indonesian fable tells of a turtle that could fly. He would hold on to a stick with his mouth as it was carried by geese. When the turtle heard the onlookers on the ground saying, "Aren't those geese brilliant!" his pride was so hurt that he shouted, "It was *my* idea!" Of course he lost his grip. His pride became his downfall.

God is looking for those who will allow Him to show himself strong in their lives. Living a humble, God-dependent life is truly a brilliant idea! —AL

No one is stronger than the one who depends on God.

AUGUST 21

God has caused me to be fruitful in the land of my affliction. Genesis 41:52

Have you ever heard anyone say, "Who needs all this grief?" But consider, for a moment, the origin of pearls. Each pearl is formed by an oyster's internal response to a wound caused by an irritant, such as a grain of sand. Resources of repair rush to the injured area. The final result is a lustrous pearl. Something beautiful is created that would have been impossible without the wound.

In today's Bible reading, we see the patriarch Joseph in a position of influence. But how did he become influential? It began with a wound—being sold into slavery—which produced a pearl of usefulness. Because Joseph drew on God's resources when humiliated, he became better, not bitter. Author Paul E. Billheimer says of Joseph, "If human pity could have rescued him from the sad part of his life, the glorious part that followed would have been lost." So if you're suffering, remember: No wounds, no pearls! —JY

Adversities are often blessings in disguise.

AUGUST 22

Bless the Lord, O my soul, and forget not all His benefits. Psalm 103:2

There's a legend about a day the sun didn't rise. At six in the morning it was dark. At seven it was still night. Noon came and it was like midnight. By four in the afternoon, people flocked to the churches to beg God for the sun. The next morning, huge crowds gathered outdoors to face the eastern sky. When the first rays of sunlight pushed open the door of the morning, the people burst into cheers and praised God for the sun.

Because God's goodness is as constant as the sun, we are in danger of forgetting what He showers on us each day. If we count our blessings one by one, we'll never get finished. But if we jot down a list of ten or twenty gifts God gives us each day, something will happen to our hearts. —HWR

If you want to be rich, count all the things you have that money can't buy.

Through the Lord's mercies we are not consumed.
Lamentations 3:22

Not long ago I received a letter from a woman who told me that when their second son was born with Down syndrome, their initial response was "grief, shock, and disbelief." Yet the same day he was born, God used Philippians 4:6–7 to put peace in their hearts and give them an undying love for their precious son. It says: "Let your requests be made known to God; and the peace of God, which surpasses all understanding, will guard your hearts."

Nine years later, their fourth son was diagnosed with cancer. Before he reached his third birthday, he was gone. Shock, pain, and sadness again broke into their world. And again, they found help from God and His Word. "When the grief overwhelms us," says this mom, "we turn to God's Word and His gift of eternal life through Jesus Christ." —DB

Feeling hopeless reminds us that we are helpless without God.

AUGUST 24

Do not worry about your life. Matthew 6:25

I heard about a woman who kept a box in her kitchen that she called her "Worry Box." Every time something troubled her, she would write it down on a piece of paper and put it in the box. She resolved not to think about her problems as long as they were in the box. She knew they could be dealt with later. Occasionally she would take out a slip of paper and review the concern written on it. Because she had not been drained by anxiety, she was relaxed and better able to find the solution to her problem. Many times she discovered that a specific worry no longer existed. Writing your worries on paper and putting them in a box may be helpful, but how much better it is to place them in the hands of God who promises to meet our needs. —RDH

When we put our cares in God's hands,
He puts His peace in our heart.

AUGUST 25

Even to your old age, I am He, and even to gray hairs I will carry you! I have made, and I will bear; even I will carry, and will deliver you.

Isaiah 46:4

Years ago I heard about an elderly gentleman who was suffering from the first stages of dementia. He lamented the fact that he often forgot about God. "Don't you worry," said a good friend, "He will never forget you."

Growing old brings losses. We lose our strength, our looks, our friends, our job. We may lose our wealth, our home, our health, our spouse, our independence, and perhaps the greatest loss of all, our sense of dignity and self-worth. But there is one thing that you and I will never lose—the love of God. —DHR

God's love never grows old.

AUGUST 26

Blessed is the man who endures temptation; for when he has been approved, he will receive the crown of life.

James 1:12

A pastor placed this sign on his door: "If you have problems, come in and tell me all about them. If you don't have any problems, come in and tell me how you avoid them." Having endured many trials and facing a new struggle with cancer, *Our Daily Bread* author Joanie Yoder said this: "I have relinquished my destiny to God's will. Nothing, praise God, not even cancer, can thwart His will. I may have cancer, but cancer doesn't have me—God alone has me. So in this light, I would value your prayers that Christ may be magnified in my body, whether by life or by death." —AL

We can endure trials in this life because of the joys in the life to come.

My Presence will go with you, and I will give you rest.
Exodus 33:14

After winning a bronze medal in the 2004 Olympics in Athens, wrestler Rulon Gardner took off his shoes, placed them in the center of the mat, and walked away in tears. Through that symbolic act, Gardner announced his retirement from the sport that had defined his life for many years.

Times of "walking away" come to all of us, and they can be emotionally wrenching. A child moves away from home. We leave a job or a community and it feels as if we've left everything behind. But when we know the Lord, we never have to walk into an unknown future alone. Because He goes with us, we can walk into the future with confidence. —DCM

Every loss leaves a space that only God's presence can fill.

AUGUST 28

Though an army may encamp against me, my heart shall not fear.
Psalm 27:3

During the US Civil War, fierce fighting took place near Moorefield, West Virginia. Because the town was close to enemy lines, it was controlled one day by Union troops and the next by Confederates. In the heart of the town lived an elderly woman. One morning several enemy soldiers knocked on her door and demanded breakfast. When the food was ready, she said, "It's my custom to read the Bible and pray before breakfast. I hope you won't mind." They consented, so she took her Bible, opened it at random, and began to read Psalm 27, "The Lord is my light and my salvation; whom shall I fear?" . . . and on to the end. When she finished, she said, "Let us pray." While she was praying, she heard sounds of the men moving around in the room. When she said "amen" and looked up, the soldiers were gone. —HWR

If you are facing enemies, God will use His Word to help you.

AUGUST 29

It is good for me that I have been afflicted, that I may learn Your statutes.
Psalm 119:71

I was in my early thirties, a dedicated wife and mother, a Christian worker at my husband's side. Yet inwardly I found myself on a trip nobody wants to take—the trip downward. I was heading for that certain sort of breakdown that most of us resist, the breakdown of my stubborn self-sufficiency. Finally I experienced the odd relief of hitting rock bottom, where I made an unexpected discovery: The rock on which I had been thrown was none other than Christ himself. Cast on Him alone, I was in a position to rebuild the rest of my life, this time as a God-dependent person rather than the self-dependent person I had been. My rock-bottom experience became a turning point and one of the most vital spiritual developments of my life. —JY

When a Christian hits rock bottom, he or she finds that Christ is a firm foundation.

AUGUST 30

One of them, when he saw that he was healed, returned, and with a loud voice glorified God. Luke 17:15

An unkempt, poorly adjusted youth named Tim (not his real name) was converted to Christ in an evangelistic crusade. Several days later, still unkempt but bathed in the love of Christ, he was sent to my home so that I could help him find a good church. And so it was that he began attending with me. Though Tim needed and received much loving help in personal grooming and basic social graces, one characteristic has remained unchanged—his untamed love for his Savior. One Sunday after church Tim rushed to my side, looking somewhat perplexed. He exclaimed, "Why me? I keep asking myself, why me?" Oh, no, I thought, he's become another complaining Christian. Then, with arms outstretched, he said, "Out of all the people in the world who are greater and smarter than I am, why did God choose me?" With that he joyfully clapped his hands. —JY

Gratitude should be a continuous attitude.

AUGUST 31

Weeping may endure for a night, but joy comes in the morning.
Psalm 30:5

That sinister stranger called sorrow comes knocking on your door. You must let him in, for he knocks insistently and will not go away. You believe no one sees your tears and you feel all alone. But God sees them—and He understands. "All night I make my bed swim; I drench my couch with my tears," David said. But "the Lord has heard the voice of my weeping" (Psalm 6:6, 8).

When God's love comes into our thoughts, our feelings of sorrow and dread flee. We can rise to greet the day with shouts of ringing praise for His mercy, guidance, and protection. No matter our circumstances, let's sing to the Lord once again! —DHR

Praise is the voice of a soul set free.

SEPTEMBER 1

Set your mind on things above, not on things on the earth.
Colossians 3:2

Popularity and success do not guarantee a happy life. Presidents and prime ministers may have extremely high approval ratings for a while, but they don't last. Twenty years ago several top executives were highly successful because of their winning personalities and outstanding abilities. Yet they lost their high-salaried positions because they could not keep up with the rapid changes their jobs demanded. Today, because of company mergers and corporate downsizing, many of their replacements have also lost their positions.

How we view popularity and success depends on what we value most. If we set our hearts on earthly things, we will eventually be disappointed. But if we set our hearts on Christ and live for Him, we will find that He is faithful to provide for our every need. —HVL

The master key to success is knowing the Master.

Set your mind on things above, not on things on the earth.
Colossians 3:2

In the movie *Gladiator*, as a general challenges his troops to give their very best in battle, he says, "What we do in life echoes in eternity." These words from a fictional military leader convey a powerful concept that is of particular significance to believers in Christ. We are not just taking up time and space on a rock that's floating in the universe. We are here with the opportunity to make an eternal difference with our lives.

How can we learn to set our minds "on things above"? A good way to begin is to discover what our eternal God values. Throughout the pages of the Bible, He reminds us that He values people above possessions and our character above our performance. Those are the truths that last forever. Embracing them can bring an eternal perspective to our daily living. —BC

What we do in this life echoes in eternity.

Faith is the substance of things hoped for, the evidence of things not seen.
Hebrews 11:1

When I mail a letter, it's an exercise of trust. I need the help of the postal service. But for them to do their part, I have to drop my letter in the mailbox. I have to let it go. Then I must trust the postal service to take over until my letter is delivered to my friend's home.

Likewise, when we recognize our need for God's help, first we must go to Him in prayer. Until that moment, we're still holding on to our problem. We know the situation won't get resolved until we let go and commit it into God's hands. Once we let go, we then must trust God to take over until the problem is resolved in His way. —JY

Trusting God turns problems into opportunities.

SEPTEMBER 4

Come aside by yourselves to a deserted place and rest a while. Mark 6:31

The Red Baron and his counterparts in World War I flew planes that were not equipped with throttles for slowing down or speeding up. Flying at constant full speed took its toll on the life of the engines, and takeoffs and landings were an edge-of-danger adventure.

God did not create us to run at full speed all the time. We may race for a while with open throttle through our Christian lives, packing our time with one activity after another, but if we don't slow down occasionally we are headed for burnout or a crash landing. We need times of rest not only for physical renewal but also for spiritual refreshment through reflection, Bible reading, and prayer. —DCE

*Come apart and rest a while, or you may
just plain come apart.* —Havner

In all your ways acknowledge Him, and He shall direct your paths. Proverbs 3:6

Former college basketball coach Don Callan was in Nepal, looking for ways to assist the people of that land. Don flew to Pokhara in the heart of Nepal, praying for God's guidance as he went. He had been given the name of a man in Pokhara who could serve as a guide, although the man did not know Don was coming. Not knowing the city, Don randomly chose a hotel and took a taxi from the airport to its location. He walked into the hotel lobby feeling unsure of himself. He didn't know anyone and couldn't speak the language. A group of men were standing at the front desk, so Don ventured over to them and said, "I'm looking for Jeevan." What a surprise when one of the men said, "I'm Jeevan." Obviously, God had directed Don's path. —DB

God does not ask you to go where He does not lead.

God will provide for Himself the lamb.
Genesis 22:8

It is easy to make a profession of faith. But the real test of obedience comes when God asks us to lay our dearest treasures on the line, as He did with Abraham. A businesswoman lost a high-paying job because she wouldn't compromise her standards. A pastor was driven from his church when he obeyed God's Word and spoke out about racism in his congregation. Shouldn't these people have been rewarded when they did the right thing? Faith meets its toughest test when we feel that the Lord has not rewarded our faithfulness.

You may be faced with giving back to God something you feel He has given you. Learn to see this test as an opportunity to demonstrate your faith in the One who always keeps His promises—even when you don't understand. —HWR

Faith is the ability to see God in the dark.

At midnight Paul and Silas were praying and singing hymns to God.
Acts 16:25

Gray skies and blue moods—the two seem to go together. In fact, some weather forecasters describe the amount of cloudy days a region can expect during its winter season as "the gloom index." Other factors might be figured into a gloom index. Think, for instance, of what Paul and Silas, those two first-century co-workers for Christ, endured (Acts 16). Any one of their troubles was enough to ruin the sunniest day. But they were able to rise above their circumstances because they were motivated by a desire to obey God and spread the message of Christ.

We too can overcome the gloom index of discouraging circumstances by relying on our Lord and Savior, Jesus Christ. —MRD

No day is dark when you live in the light of God's Son.

Our light affliction . . . is working for us a far more exceeding and eternal weight of glory. 2 Corinthians 4:17

Sometimes it's easy to feel that everything and everyone is against us. We know we're supposed to trust God, but it's hard to understand why He would allow our circumstances to become so difficult and confusing. A friend of mine who has experienced many setbacks offered a fresh look at the role of our difficulties. "We think our afflictions are working *against* us," he said, "but God says they are working *for* us. They're producing a glory that will last forever. Compared to our trials, the glory is always greater. That's why we don't lose heart."

From God's perspective, our deepest disappointments and sorrows are "but for a moment." By faith, we can embrace His perspective today. —DCM

God can weave the thorns of life into a crown of glory.

SEPTEMBER 9

Thus says the Lord of hosts: "Consider your ways!"
Haggai 1:7

During one semester in college, my grades dropped dramatically, I got in trouble in the dorm, and I was called into the Dean's office. I went back to my room and thought seriously about my situation. The problem was not schoolwork or the guys in the dorm. I was the problem. When I changed my attitude and my behavior, things began to go better.

Not all our troubles are of our own making. But when difficulties arise, it's wise to consider our ways. Like the people of Haggai's day, we may find that our disobedience is blocking God's blessing. —DCE

The way of obedience is the only way of blessing.

As many as are led by the Spirit of God, these are sons of God. Romans 8:14

By nature we all have a desire to control our world. From infancy we turn to our own independent way, trying to control circumstances, the future, people—and even God if we could. Our need to be in control is rooted in excessive self-love. For example, when people we love are sick, we often want them to get well so we can get some rest and not have to worry about them. "Boil it down to this," a Bible teacher once said, "we are madly in love with ourselves!"

In Romans 8, the apostle Paul called this self-centeredness "the flesh." He then offered an effective alternative: We can be led and controlled by God's Spirit (v. 14). Human control shackles us; God's control gives us freedom. Human control insists on immediate results; God's control allows for a lifelong process of change. —JY

To be under Christ's control is to have true freedom.

You saw how the Lord your God carried you, as a man carries his son.
Deuteronomy 1:31

Kelsey's daddy was reading to her before she went to sleep. She had picked the zoo book, and to her active imagination it was as if she and Daddy were there. She looked happily at the pages with the giraffes, zebras, and elephants. But when they got to the page with the grizzly bears, she said, "You would have to carry me." She said the same thing when she saw the gorillas on the next page. Curious, her dad asked her why he would have to carry her. "Because I'd be scared," came her straightforward reply.

The Lord will do the same for us when we are afraid. When the scary times come, when we are called on to do the hard things life demands, God will lift us up and carry us along. He gives us His strength in Christ. —DCE

With God's arms beneath us, we need not fear what lies before us.

I have begun to give Sihon and his land over to you. Begin to possess it.
Deuteronomy 2:31

After forty years in the wilderness, Moses was told that it was time for the people to take possession of the land God had promised them. The first order of business was to decide what to do about a king named Sihon who stood between the Israelites and the land of Canaan. God's command was, "Begin to possess it, and engage him in battle" (Deuteronomy 2:24). God certainly could have eliminated Sihon without anyone's help, but He commanded His people to take the first step. When difficult circumstances or broken relationships persist for months or years, we may feel that nothing we do will make a difference. But the Lord says, "Begin." We must make the first move—speak a kind word, ask forgiveness, pay some of what we owe. We must be the initiators. Is there a first step you should take today? —DCM

Nothing can be accomplished until we take the first step.

SEPTEMBER 13

We wanted to come to you . . . but Satan hindered us.
1 Thessalonians 2:18

The apostle Paul told the believers at Thessalonica that he and his co-workers wanted to visit them but Satan hindered them. Does it disturb you to read that a child of God can be blocked by the devil from doing what he believes to be the will of God? If it does, remember that nothing happens without God's knowledge nor apart from His direct or permissive will.

I'm reminded of Joseph's response to his brothers who had sold him into slavery: "You meant evil against me; but God meant it for good" (Genesis 50:20). What a comfort to know that nothing happens apart from the will of our heavenly Father! Under God's sovereign control, evil can be turned around to accomplish His good purposes. —RDH

God can bring showers of blessing out of storms of adversity.

God will wipe away every tear from their eyes. Revelation 21:4

If we consider what people thought years ago about life in the future, we realize how hard it is to know what's ahead. For instance, what if everyone had believed the patent office worker who, in 1899, said, "Everything that can be invented has been invented"? Or what if folks in the nineteenth-century had believed this memo from Western Union: "The telephone has too many shortcomings to be seriously considered as a means of communication"? Predictions about the future are usually bad guesses. When I was a kid, I read science magazines that said that by the end of the twentieth century we would all be flying around in air-cars and living in domed houses.

One source for what's ahead, however, is never wrong. It's God's Word. —DB

We can trust our all-knowing God for the unknown future.

SEPTEMBER 15

My God shall supply all your need according to His riches in glory by Christ Jesus.
Philippians 4:19

"Dad, can I have ten dollars?" "Dad, can you help me with my math?" "Dad, what's the capital of Maine?" "Dad, why can't we get another car?" "Dad, I didn't make the team." The questions and requests and needs of my children seem endless. Whether they are in junior high, in high school, in college, or married, they never stop needing help.

Often I can provide the help they need, but sometimes I am unable to come up with the answer or the solution. As much as I would like to, I don't have an answer or the resources for everything. But I know who does. I know that God supplies all of our needs. And He knows when our requests are genuine needs, or when He must redirect our thinking instead. —DB

God never tires of our asking.

SEPTEMBER 16

I hated all my labor in which I had toiled under the sun.
Ecclesiastes 2:18

A successful lawyer told me he often wonders why he works so hard. He said his sons and daughters had been misusing his money and making a mess of their lives. He knows they will probably waste everything he leaves them. Another man who had worked hard and managed his money well said sadly, "All my hard work! And my kids can hardly wait for me to die."

Solomon, too, realized that at his death his fortune would go to people who had not worked for it and might misuse it. However, he found meaning and satisfaction through faith in God. He said that inner contentment is a gift of God to His children. This enables them to enjoy the fruit of their labor (v. 24). God replaces frustration with contentment! —HVL

Contentment is the soil in which true joy thrives.

Whatever you do, do it heartily, as to the Lord. Colossians 3:23

A friend of mine has a view of life that is summed up in one of his favorite sayings: "Wherever you are, be all there." That is, whatever your situation, be the very best you can be. During his college years, my friend got a job one summer at a resort. He expected it to be exciting, but when he arrived he was told that he would be washing dishes. He could see only two options—leave and be happy or stay and be miserable. But a friend encouraged him to consider a third option: Stay and maintain the right attitude, then watch for positive results. He decided to stay and be the best dishwasher he could be, concluding that he was really working for the Lord. As a result, even in washing dishes, he was "all there."

We can't always choose our circumstances in life. We may not be able to change our job or location. But we can "be all there." —DCM

Wherever you are, be all there for God.

You have put gladness in my heart. Psalm 4:7

David Lykken, emeritus professor at the University of Minnesota, has developed what he calls a "set point" theory of happiness. He contends that most people return to their previous level of happiness within six months to a year after dramatic events occur in their lives, such as the sorrow of losing a loved one or the thrill of moving into a dream home. He calls that original reference point of happiness their "set point." The Christian, however, has a different kind of "set point"—one that does not depend on the normal highs and lows of human experience. The psalmist David praised the Lord, saying, "You have put gladness in my heart, more than in the season that their grain and wine increased." —DCM

We find our joy in the unchanging God rather than in our changing circumstances.

David strengthened himself in the Lord his God.
1 Samuel 30:6

Everything looked bleak to David and his men when they arrived at Ziklag (1 Samuel 30:1–6). The Amalekites had attacked the city and taken their wives and children captive. In the end, David's army rescued their families and defeated the Amalekites. But the story takes a great turn even before that when "David strengthened [encouraged, refreshed] himself in the Lord his God."

How can we *strengthen, encourage, or refresh ourselves in the Lord when we're feeling discouraged?* First, we can remember what God has done. We can list the ways He has cared and provided for us in the past. Second, we can remember what God has promised. —AC

Our greatest strength is often shown in our ability to stand still and trust God.

SEPTEMBER 20

By humility and the fear of the Lord are riches and honor and life. Proverbs 22:4

Becoming rich and famous does not guarantee contentment. If it did, multimillionaire athletes would not jeopardize their careers and their lives by using drugs. If it did, a wealthy lawyer would not have tearfully told me that he would gladly trade everything he had for a change in the behavior of his sons. If it did, multiple marriages among celebrities would not be commonplace. Obviously, contentment must come from a source other than wealth and fame.

Paul wrote that we are "not to be haughty, nor to trust in uncertain riches but in the living God, who gives us richly all things to enjoy" (1 Timothy 6:17). Only when we trust in the Lord will we find true and lasting satisfaction. —HVL

Discontentment makes rich men poor;
contentment makes poor men rich!

SEPTEMBER 21

*I also count all things loss for the excellence of the
knowledge of Christ Jesus my Lord.* Philippians 3:8

The airline had mangled Debbie's luggage. Then her purse disappeared. Instead of entering the airport through an enclosed corridor, she had to stumble off the plane in the pouring rain. She was drenched, far from home with no money, no identification, and no dry clothes. Under normal conditions Debbie would have been furious, but that night it didn't matter. She had just survived the crash of Flight 1420 in Little Rock, Arkansas. "When I walked off that plane," Debbie said, "I walked off with nothing. Then I stopped and thought, *I have everything*." Her life was more important than all she had lost.

It sometimes takes a dramatic turn of events to alter our perspective. That was true for Saul of Tarsus. When he met Christ on the Damascus road, his whole outlook changed. To have life in Christ is to have everything. —DCM

When we have nothing left but Christ, we find that Christ is enough.

Let not your heart be troubled; you believe in God, believe also in Me. John 14:1

Noted British preacher J. H. Jowett believed that inner peace comes not from tranquil circumstances but from an untroubled heart. He said: "If we were to hear one hundred people repeating the sentence, 'Let not your heart be troubled,' we should find that ninety-nine of them put the emphasis upon the word *troubled* . . . I feel led to believe that the purposed emphasis is on the word *heart* . . . The heart is to be clothed in serene regality even when hell is knocking and rioting at its very gates."

Jowett's perceptive words caused me to wonder if I'm spending more energy trying to avoid difficulties than on letting them help me get to know Christ better. We can focus on the trouble in the world and in our lives, or we can focus on the victory we have in Christ because His death was followed by His resurrection. —DCM

When we keep our mind on God, God gives us peace of mind.

He who trusts in the Lord, mercy shall surround him.
Psalm 32:10

While I was a guest at a home in Manila, I used my hostess's Bible one day for my devotions. When I opened it, I saw these words written on the flyleaf: *Acknowledgment. Acceptance. Adjustment.* Those words express the steps that believers in Christ need to take when they receive bad news.

Acknowledgment. When we are faced with a problem, whether it's the result of our sin or not, it's futile to run from the truth. *Acceptance.* We need to see difficulties as opportunities to trust God and to grow spiritually. *Adjustment.* We may need to ask the Lord for the ability to make a lifestyle change or to take some specific action. These three steps can help you handle bad news in a way that will please the Lord and result in good. —DCE

God takes us into His darkroom to develop our character.

Do not worry about tomorrow, for tomorrow will worry about its own things.
Matthew 6:34

Ralph Easter had driven many times from Calgary, the foothills city of Alberta, to Banff, high in the Canadian Rockies. But it was his first trip that left an indelible impression on him. As the road wound westward from Calgary over rolling hills, there always loomed before him a range of snow-capped peaks that seemed to block the highway. He recalls wondering how he would ever pass over such an insurmountable barrier, but he drove steadily on. Finally, as he reached the point where it looked as if the road would stop, he came to a sharp bend and the highway stretched on as before. Many such turns kept him progressing upward and forward until he came to the other side of the range. As we travel the road of life, obstacles often loom up before us, filling us with apprehension. But as we keep on by faith, God opens a new way before us. —RDH

Worry is a burden that God never meant for us to bear.

Jesus wept.
John 11:35

As I think of Jesus' tears at Lazarus' grave, I believe He wept for Lazarus as well as for Mary and Martha and their grief. Later, Jesus wept over Jerusalem (Luke 19:41–44). And He knows and shares our grief today. But as He promised, we will see Him again in the place He's preparing for us (John 14:3). In heaven, our grief will end. "God will wipe away every tear from [our] eyes; there shall be no more death, nor sorrow, nor crying" (Revelation 21:4).

Until then, know that God weeps with you. —DHR

If you doubt that Jesus cares, remember His tears.

SEPTEMBER 26

Men always ought to pray and not lose heart.
Luke 18:1

George Müller (1805–1898), pastor and orphanage director, was known for his faith and persistent prayer. Whenever he prayed for specific needs for his orphanage, God sent exactly what was required. Yet for more than forty years he also prayed for the conversion of a friend and his friend's son. When Müller died, these men were still unconverted. God answered those prayers, however, in His own time. The friend was converted while attending Müller's funeral, and the son a week later!

Do you have a special burden or request? Keep on praying! Trust your loving heavenly Father to answer according to His wisdom and timing. God honors persistent prayer! —JY

Failure to pray is the line of least persistence.

SEPTEMBER 27

While I was speaking in prayer, the man Gabriel . . . reached me.
Daniel 9:21

Daniel prayed regularly, and it got him thrown into the lions' den. But we can learn important lessons from Daniel about how God answers our prayers today. In Daniel 9, we learn that Daniel prayed that God would not delay the end of the Israelites' captivity. He confessed Israel's sin and asked for God's intervention. Then, while Daniel was still praying, God not only sent an answer but He also sent His angel Gabriel to deliver it. Before Daniel had even finished his prayer, God heard it and immediately sent Gabriel with the answer. Yet, on another occasion when Daniel prayed, Scripture tells us that the messenger God sent with the answer took three weeks to arrive (10:12–13).

Sometimes God sends the answer immediately. Sometimes the answer is delayed. Either way, He always answers. —DB

There are three possible answers to prayer: Yes, No, or Wait.

SEPTEMBER 28

The Lord said to Satan, "Have you considered My servant Job?"
Job 1:8

My Sunday school class was studying one book of the Bible each week. Beginning with Genesis, we looked at the theme, structure, and uniqueness of each book. Then two women in my class told me how eager they were to get to the book of Job. They were nurses who daily confronted the problem of human suffering, and they were often asked hard questions about God's role in it.

Job's three friends who came to sit with him told Job that he deserved the suffering because of his sin. But the real reason Job was suffering was that Satan was trying to get him to turn from God. As in Job's case, sometimes suffering is part of a larger, cosmic struggle. If we endure suffering with our trust in the Lord unshaken, we will thwart Satan's efforts and glorify our God. —DCE

When your world is shaking, run to the Rock.

*Pray for one another, that you may be healed. The
effective, fervent prayer of a righteous man avails much.*
James 5:16

When we pray for others, we become partners with God in His work
of salvation, healing, comfort, and justice. God can accomplish those
things without us, but in His plan He gives us the privilege of being
involved with Him through prayer. When we intercede for a grandson
in trouble, a mother having surgery, a neighbor who needs Christ,
or a pastor who needs strength, we are asking God to provide for
that person what we can't provide. We are acting as go-betweens,
asking God to direct His power in a specific direction. —DCE

*The most powerful position on earth is kneeling
before the Lord of the universe.*

He gives His beloved sleep.
Psalm 127:2

I am often asked to speak on the subject of stress. I'm not an expert, just an experienced sufferer! I simply share counsel from God's Word that helps me live less stressfully and more restfully. However, I sometimes get blank looks when I make this particular recommendation: "Get more sleep!"

I'm not alone in linking spirituality to sleep. A godly Bible teacher was asked to share the key ingredient in his own life for walking in the Spirit. He studied the Bible and prayed regularly, but his surprising reply was this: "Get eight hours of sleep each night."

Sleep is not the full remedy for stress, but other solutions can become clearer to people who get adequate rest. —JY

We can sleep in peace when we remember that God is awake.

OCTOBER 1

I am the Alpha and the Omega, the Beginning and the End.
Revelation 1:8

Whether the company is Twentieth Century Fox in Hollywood or Twentieth Century Data in Dallas, time has caught up with these companies and they're a century behind. Should they change their names? Consultant Frank Delano says, "You can't do business in the twenty-first century with a twentieth-century name. You need a name that is really universal with no limitations."

Through the ages, Christians have known and worshiped a Savior who is not bound by time. Jesus Christ is the Master of time. Jesus Christ is Lord of eternity. Jesus Christ is "the same yesterday, today, and forever" (Hebrews 13:8). In every century His name is universal, without limitation. Jesus Christ is the timeless name. —DCM

Jesus is the Lord of time and eternity.

OCTOBER 2

A Christian who believed God had led him to take a daring step of faith remarked, "If God doesn't give me success in this matter, He'll certainly have a lot of explaining to do!" It's easy to judge this man's words, but have you ever said, "When I get to heaven, I expect God to explain why some of my prayers were not answered and why tragedies were not always prevented!" The story of Job reassures us that questioning God is common to human experience. Yet, when Job demanded that God justify His lack of intervention in his trials, God didn't comply. Instead, He bombarded Job with His own searching questions (Job 38–41). The Almighty does not have to explain himself or reveal His grand design. But we can rest in the assurance that He reveals himself and His plans to us in His way and in His time for our ultimate benefit. —JY

When we trust God's promises, we won't demand explanations.

It is good for me that I have been afflicted, that I may learn Your statutes.
Psalm 119:71

Lieutenant Paul Galanti, a US Navy pilot, spent six and a half years as a prisoner of war in North Vietnam. The experience has given him a heightened sense of ordinary privileges that most of us take for granted. Speaking of his life today, nearly three decades after being released, Galanti says, "There's no such thing as a bad day when there's a doorknob on the inside of the door." After 2,300 straight days in a locked cell, he understands the privilege of walking outside whenever he pleases.

When the days are dark and relief is out of sight, we need to cling to what we know to be true about the goodness and faithfulness of God. And then, when He brings us out into the light, we too will see the results and thank God for what we have learned through affliction. —DCM

Tough times teach trust.

OCTOBER 4

He could do no mighty work there . . . And He marveled because of their unbelief.
Mark 6:5–6

A child once asked, "What does God do all day?" If the answer to that question depended on how much we allow God to do in our individual lives, some of us would have to reply, "Not much!" Although God is constantly working, He allows us to set a limit on the degree of work He does on our behalf.

Strong Christians are those who unashamedly admit their weaknesses and draw on Christ's power. The more we learn to depend on God, the more opportunity this gives Him to be active in our life. Whenever I face a daunting task, I say, "Joanie and Jesus can do it!" So can you and Jesus. —JY

We must admit our weakness to experience God's strength.

*God has not given us a spirit of fear, but of power
and of love and of a sound mind.* 2 Timothy 1:7

Police found it hard to believe, but an unarmed housewife captured three burglars singlehandedly. The woman came home and found three men loading household items into their car parked in her driveway. She pulled her van behind their car and then ordered the men to carry her belongings back into the house and sit on the couch until the police arrived. Later, when asked why they didn't escape, she replied, "The Lord was with me. I wasn't going to move my van so they could get away. What was I to do? Run away?"

It's not easy to know when such boldness is wise or foolish. Only the Spirit can show us. But one thing is sure: Christians have reason to be courageous. God is our helper. And when we rely on Him, He'll enable us to stand firm no matter what danger we may face. —MRD

Courage is fear that has said its prayers.

OCTOBER 6

That you may be filled with all the fullness of God.

Ephesians 3:19

In the western panhandle of Texas is a small town named Texline. It began in the late 1800s as a thriving center along a new railroad line. Within a few years, though, most of the shops had closed and the town's population shriveled to about 400. In 2000, the population was still just over 500. One online description of Texline says that it has "a city limits sign at one end, another at the other end, and not much in between."

"Not much in between"—what a waste if the same description could be given of our spiritual journey! The journey of the Christian life on earth begins at the moment of faith in Jesus and ends when the believer goes to be with the Lord. But what happens in between? God desires to give us a marvelous beginning with salvation and a great ending in glory—with much in between. —DCE

A life given fully to God becomes a God-filled life.

The Lord is near to all who call upon Him, to all who call upon Him in truth.
Psalm 145:18

When I was seven years old, my grandfather was caretaker of a wooded estate. One fall evening I took my toy gun, called for my dog Pal, and headed down a path into the forest. I walked bravely into the woods. Soon, though, it began to get dark and I panicked. "Grandpa!" I shouted. "I'm right here," he said calmly, only a few yards away. He had seen me go into the woods and had followed me to make sure I was okay.

Sometimes we venture into unfamiliar territory. We try new things. We take on responsibilities that are bigger than we've ever attempted before. We risk rejection when we witness to friends about Christ. It can get pretty scary. But wherever we go, God is there. He will always hear our cry. —DCE

Dark fears flee in the light of God's presence.

The race is not to the swift, nor the battle to the strong. Ecclesiastes 9:11

The newspaper headline read, "Jockey Beats Horse over Finish Line." The jockey beat the pack by 20 lengths and his horse by one length when he was catapulted out of the saddle and over the finish line. His horse had tripped and followed soon after. But the victory went to the second-place finisher named Slip Up. A race official said that the jockey "was so far in front that only a freak accident would stop him . . . and that's what happened."

Life is filled with unpredictable experiences and events. A strong, healthy man drops dead. A rising young athlete contracts a crippling disease. A person of means suddenly loses everything in a bad deal. What can we learn from this? Not to trust our own strength, our own wisdom, or our own skill, but to depend on the Lord who alone knows the end from the beginning. Life's race is not over till He says it's over. —MRD

Living without faith in God is like driving in the fog.

OCTOBER 9

*You will keep him in perfect peace, whose mind
is stayed on You, because he trusts in You.*

Isaiah 26:3

For many years, a friend of mine has followed a simple guideline he refers to as HWLW, which stands for "His Word the Last Word." Every night, just before turning out the light, he reads a passage from the Bible or meditates on a verse he has memorized. Before he goes to sleep, he wants the last word he thinks about to be from God—not the evening news or the weather, not the late-night talk-show host, but a final word from the Lord.

Is it possible that the words of Isaiah 26:3 could apply to our subconscious as well as our conscious minds? Wouldn't "perfect peace" for the person "whose mind is stayed on" the Lord make for a good night's sleep? Try "His Word the Last Word" as spiritual preparation for a peaceful night's sleep! —DMC

Before you turn out the light, turn to the light of God's Word.

OCTOBER 10

He heals the brokenhearted and binds up their wounds. He counts the number of the stars; He calls them all by name. Psalm 147:3–4

Two Harvard astronomers have discovered a "great wall" of galaxies that they estimate to be 500 million light-years long, 200 million light-years wide, and 15 million light-years thick. (One light-year is 5.88 trillion miles.) Those numbers are mind-boggling.

Here's something even more amazing. God created all of those galaxies and sustains everything that exists by His powerful hands. Yet that same mighty God uses those hands to gently touch the lives of suffering men and women. The Lord not only knows all the stars by name, but He also "heals the brokenhearted and binds up their wounds." —VCG

Those who see God's hand in everything can leave everything in God's hand.

OCTOBER 11

It is enough! Now, Lord, take my life, for I am no better than my fathers.
1 Kings 19:4

Author Roger Barrett describes depression as "a wretched experience that leaves you exhausted, uninvolved, and in deep, hopeless despair . . . You feel doomed, trapped . . . It's awful!"

In every age, God's people have struggled with this crippling emotion. Elijah's cry "It is enough! Now, Lord, take my life!" is the cry of a despondent man. Others like Job and David knew similar agony of soul, but they emerged from it with stronger faith. That's encouraging! Depression can be rooted in spiritual, mental, or physical causes, and we should not be afraid to seek godly counsel and medical help. God loves us and longs to shine His light through the clouds that surround us. He is the God of hope. —DJD

No one is hopeless who knows the God of hope.

If anyone is in Christ . . . old things have passed away;
behold, all things have become new. 2 Corinthians 5:17

Rebecca McLain, who restores valuable paintings, says many works of art that seem hopelessly damaged can be saved by an expert. She has brought color and life back to dulled oil paintings by carefully removing dirt and discolored varnish. But she has also seen the damage done when people attempt to clean their own soiled art with oven cleaner or abrasive powders. If you value the art, she advises, take it to an expert in restoration. Our efforts at ridding ourselves of the guilt and defilement of sinful actions and attitudes often end in frustration and despair. When it comes to cleansing the canvas of our souls, only Jesus Christ, our redeemer, is the expert in restoration. —DCM

Only God can transform a sin-stained
soul into a masterpiece of grace.

OCTOBER 13

Do not grow weary in doing good.
2 Thessalonians 3:13

The teenager's mom, a bit exasperated by the failure of her youngest child to show the desired maturity, sighed and said, "Two more years of junior high." To which he, in typical style, replied with a smile, "Mom, why don't you just take the next two years off!"

Often there are things we would simply like to avoid by taking "time off." When children rebel and make parenting a struggle, we'd prefer a long vacation from the hassle. When it's not possible to "take the next two years off," we can gain hope from this advice: Keep doing good and keep casting your care on God. That's better than taking time off. —DB

When God stretches your patience He
is seeking to enlarge your soul.

I have been crucified with Christ; it is no longer I who live, but Christ lives in me.
Galatians 2:20

A young woman often complained to her friends about how difficult her home life was. She blamed her parents and the other members of her family for her unhappiness and discontent and threatened to move out as soon as she could afford to be on her own. One day, though, her face bore a happy smile, her eyes were sparkling, and there was a spring in her step. When a friend noticed the difference, she exclaimed, "Things must have improved at home. I'm so glad!" "No," the young woman responded, "I'm the one who's different!"

When we are confronted with irritating situations and we begin to feel sorry for ourselves, we should ask these questions: Is the trouble really with others? Or could it be me? Letting God change us is the best way to change our world. —RDH

When you stop changing, you stop growing.

OCTOBER 15

Bless the Lord, O my soul, and forget not all His benefits.
Psalm 103:2

Although forgetfulness sometimes increases with age, it's really common to us all. Even children have lapses of memory and excuse themselves by saying, "I forgot!" But there's one kind of forgetfulness that is inexcusable at any age—forgetting to be grateful to God. The psalmist David was determined not to fail the Lord in this way, so he exhorted his soul: "Forget not all His benefits."

When was the last time you openly and unashamedly praised God for helping you? Someone has said, "If Christians praised God more, the world would doubt Him less." Your example may encourage others to move from doubt to faith as you praise Him. —JY

An attitude of gratitude can make your life a beatitude.

OCTOBER 16

The Lord has heard my supplication; the Lord will receive my prayer.
Psalm 6:9

During every morning worship service in a small church I attended, the congregation would share prayer requests. After each one, the pastor would say, "Lord, in your mercy," and the people would respond, "Hear our prayer." One Sunday, a four-year-old boy behind me became more intense after each request, until he finally shouted out, "Hear our prayer!"

We often make our requests quietly and confidently, but there are times when we cannot help but cry out to God. In that mysterious blend of confidence and crying out, we can bring everything to our loving heavenly Father, saying, "Lord, in your mercy, hear our prayer!" —DCM

In prayer, God hears more than just words —He listens to your heart.

OCTOBER 17

There is a river whose streams shall make glad the city of God. Psalm 46:4

In the autumn of 2001, a violent storm blew across Lake Michigan for thirty-six hours straight. Sustained winds of sixty miles per hour, with gusts much stronger, whipped up the highest waves in fifteen years. One frothing roller after another, some up to eighteen feet high, crashed over the breakwaters and pounded the shore with great fury.

The writer of Psalm 46 must have experienced a sustained spiritual and emotional crisis like the incessant pounding of a giant storm, for he wrote of troubled waters and roaring seas. If that describes how life feels to you right now, let the Lord quiet the storms in your heart. He says, "Be still, and know that I am God" (v. 10). —DCE

God does not shield us from life's storms;
He shelters us in life's storms.

Cast your burden on the Lord, and He shall sustain you;
He shall never permit the righteous to be moved.

Psalm 55:22

Anxiety is a leading mental health problem today. When David composed Psalm 55, his mind was agitated by the same types of situations we struggle with today. He recoiled in horror from the violence, anger, and abuse that stalked the city streets (vv. 9–11). He suffered the anguish of being betrayed by a close friend (vv. 12–14). He longed to leave and escape to a place of peace (vv. 4–8). Thankfully his prescription for relief can be ours as well. "I will call upon God, and the Lord shall save me," he said. "Cast your burden on the Lord, and He shall sustain you" (vv. 16, 22). If your heart is weighed down with anxiety, the Lord is ready to bear every burden you give Him. —DCM

God invites us to burden Him with what burdens us.

OCTOBER 19

The peace of God . . . will guard your hearts and minds through Christ Jesus.
Philippians 4:7

The eighteenth-century author Samuel Johnson was noted for his wit, sensitivity, and encyclopedic knowledge. He found solitude depressing, so he often took in the poor and homeless so that he could be surrounded by people. He confessed that he had a deep fear of dying. Biographical information, however, also speaks of Johnson's "zest for living."

I have known many believers with a disposition like that. Most of them went through repeated cycles of joy and gloom. But they kept living for God and praying, and their faith prevailed. The "peace of God" filled their heart. That's good news for all of us, especially for those who go through times of doubt and despair. —HVL

When life is filled with shadows, face the sunshine of God's love.

The angel of the Lord encamps all around those who fear Him, and delivers them.
Psalm 34:7

In a materialistic world like ours, we are tempted to conclude that the only real things are those we experience with our five senses. Yet there is another realm of reality, just as substantial as anything we see, hear, touch, taste, or smell in this world. It exists all around us—not out there "somewhere," but "here." There are legions of angels helping us, for which the world has no countermeasures (Hebrews 1:14).

Faith is the means by which we are able to "see" this invisible world. Faith is to the spiritual realm what the five senses are to the natural realm. By faith we recognize the existence of the spiritual world and learn to depend on the Lord for His help in our daily life. —DHR

Faith sees things that are out of sight.

OCTOBER 21

Which of you by worrying can add one cubit to his stature? Luke 12:25

Hans Christian Andersen, author of such well-known fairy tales as "The Emperor's New Clothes," had a phobia of being buried alive. As a result, he always carried a note in his pocket telling anyone who might find him unconscious not to assume he was dead. He often left another note on his bedside table stating, "I only seem dead."

Do we have fears that will someday look just as irrational? Is it possible that the day will come when we look back and marvel at our own anxieties? Will we one day wonder at our foolishness in choosing to worry rather than to pray? Worrying doesn't change anything. But trusting the Lord changes everything about the way we view life. —MRD

When we put our cares in God's hands,
He puts His peace in our hearts.

You are great, and do wondrous things; You alone are God.
Psalm 86:10

King Louis XIV, who liked to be referred to as Louis the Great, had ruled France from 1643 to 1715 with absolute power and incredible splendor. His funeral was held in a magnificent cathedral that was lit by a single candle alongside the ornate coffin. When it was time for Jean-Baptiste Massillon to begin his funeral sermon, he reached out and extinguished the flame. Then he broke the silence with the unexpected declaration, "Only God is great."

We may appropriately admire some of our fellow mortals who excel as philosophers and theologians, scientists and inventors, and in other fields of endeavor. But only God is truly great. —VCG

In a world of empty superlatives, God is the greatest.

OCTOBER 23

May the God of all grace . . . after you have suffered a while, perfect, establish, strengthen, and settle you. 1 Peter 5:10

In his early years of ministry, the English preacher Charles Simeon (1759–1836) was a harsh and self-assertive man. One day he was visiting a friend and fellow pastor in a nearby village. When he left, his friend's daughters complained to their father about Simeon's manner. So the father took the girls to the backyard and said, "Pick me one of those peaches." It was early summer, and the peaches were green. The girls asked why he wanted green, unripe fruit. He replied, "Well, my dears, it is green now, and we must wait; but a little more sun, and a few more showers, and the peach will be ripe and sweet. So it is with Mr. Simeon." Simeon, in due time, did change. The warmth of God's love and the "showers" of misunderstanding and disappointment were the means by which he became a gentle, humble man. In time, He too will "perfect, establish, strengthen, and settle" us. —DHR

Growth is the labor of a lifetime.

I called on the Lord in distress; the Lord answered me.
Psalm 118:5

"Come quick! My baby is going to die," the young mother called to missionary Gale Fields. Gale looked at the malaria-stricken child and realized she didn't have the right medicine to help the infant. "I'm sorry," she told the mother, "I don't have any medicine for babies this small." Gale paused, then said, "I could pray for her though." Gale prayed for the baby and then went home feeling helpless. Soon she again heard the mother cry out, "Gale, come quick and see my baby!" Expecting the worse, Gale saw that the dangerous fever was gone!

We shouldn't be surprised when God answers our prayers.
His power is great and His resources are endless. —DB

*The most powerful position on earth is kneeling
before the Lord of the universe.*

OCTOBER 25

The earth is full of the goodness of the Lord. Psalm 33:5

One Saturday my life came perilously close to being permanently altered. My brother and my nephew stopped by to pick up a desk. After loading it on the truck, they chatted for a few minutes and then drove off. I went into the house while my husband, Jay, pulled our car into the garage. Moments later I heard a loud crash, so I raced out to the garage. Jay was staring at the overhead garage door, which had suddenly slammed down. If the spring had broken a few minutes earlier, someone would have been hit by the two-hundred-pound door—and would have been seriously injured, or even killed. It was not simply a matter of luck or coincidence that no one was hurt in that garage. God's protective hand was there—one more reminder of His goodness. —JAL

If you know that God's hand is in everything,
you can leave everything in God's hand.

OCTOBER 26

My brethren, count it all joy when you fall into various trials.
James 1:2

British counselor Selwyn Hughes reminds people that trials are our friends only if our goal is to become more like Jesus. If our goal is to avoid difficulties or mishaps, our trials will seem more like intruders. He recalls a time when he and his wife had pulled off to the side of the road to look at a map. Then a truck swerved and slammed into their car. They escaped injury, but their car was totaled. Then it started to rain! Hughes immediately battled with frustration, apprehension, and anger toward the other driver, and found it extremely difficult to "count it all joy." But as they waited for the police, he began to focus on how God could use the trial to make him more like Jesus. Gradually, the crisis became his friend. —JY

God chooses what we go through; we choose how we go through it.

OCTOBER 27

The Lord preserves all who love Him.
Psalm 145:20

A young girl traveling on a train for the first time heard that it would have to cross several rivers. She was fearful as she thought of crossing the water. But each time the train came to a river, a bridge was always there to provide a safe way across. After passing safely over several rivers and streams, the girl settled back in her seat with a sigh of relief and said to her mother, "I'm not worried anymore. Somebody has put bridges for us all the way!"

When we come to the deep rivers of trial and the streams of sorrow, we too will find that God in His grace "has put bridges for us all the way." Even though we may not understand how He will meet our needs, we can be sure that He will provide a way. —HGB

Where God guides, He provides.

OCTOBER 28

All we like sheep have gone astray; we have turned, every one, to his own way; and the Lord has laid on Him the iniquity of us all. Isaiah 53:6

When we went on a weekend road trip with friends, we had our first experience using a Global Positioning System. The GPS has a female voice, so our friends call her Gladys. We programmed our destination into the GPS, and Gladys plotted our course. "Turn right in .2 miles," Gladys said confidently. She was right—Gladys is always right. When we made an unexpected detour to get gas, she got a bit insistent: "Please make a U-turn at your earliest convenience!" Gladys had calculated a route for us, but we had gone a different way. That was our choice, but if we had continued going our own way, we would have become lost.

No matter how far you've traveled in the wrong direction, it's not too late to turn around. God is ready to forgive and restore. —CHK

No matter how far you've run from God, He's only a prayer away.

OCTOBER 29

Jesus Christ is the same yesterday, today, and forever. Hebrews 13:8

Peter Marshall, whose dynamic preaching attracted crowds of people, died suddenly on the morning of January 25, 1949, at the age of forty-six. In one of his sermons he had said: "When the clock strikes for me, I shall go, not one minute early, and not one minute late. Until then, there is nothing to fear. I know that the promises of God are true, for they have been fulfilled in my life time and time again. Jesus still teaches and guides and protects and heals and comforts, and still wins our complete trust and our love."

Some anxiety about the process of dying is normal. Yet, by the grace of God and by the comfort of His Spirit, we can face tomorrow's terrors with courage. —VCG

Worry can do a lot of things to you; prayer can do a lot of things for you.

*He who comes to God must believe that He is, and that He is
a rewarder of those who diligently seek Him.* Hebrews 11:6

A *National Geographic News* survey reported that many young Americans
are geographically illiterate. According to the survey, 63 percent of
Americans aged 18–24 failed to correctly locate Iraq on a map of the
Middle East. The results for US geography are even more dismal.
Half could not find New York State on the map, a third could not find
Louisiana, and 48 percent could not locate the state of Mississippi.

Understanding geography is helpful in daily life, but "God-
ography" (finding God) is infinitely more crucial—for now and for
eternity. Finding God is a matter of faith—confidence in Him and
commitment to Him. And those who seek Him will find Him because
God will give them a heart to recognize Him as Lord. —MW

To find God, we must be willing to seek Him.

This is the day the Lord has made; we will rejoice and be glad in it. Psalm 118:24

In Edith Schaeffer's book *The Tapestry*, she describes a summer when her husband, Francis, was away in Europe for three months. During that time of missing him greatly, Edith and her sister Janet took their children to live in a former schoolhouse on Cape Cod. On a shoestring budget they shared the rent, lived without a car, and created daily adventures for the five young children. Looking back years later, Edith said of that summer: "Never again have I spent time of that sort with my own children or my sister and nephews. The sudden precious moments in life need to be recognized for the unique periods they are, not wasted by wishing for something else." —DCM

You don't have to worry about eyestrain from looking on the brighter side of life.

NOVEMBER 1

By this all will know that you are My disciples, if you have love for one another.
John 13:35

'Tis the season to receive catalogs in the mail. Every trip to the mailbox ends with an armload of slick holiday catalogs. Each one claims to offer me something I need—and the lure works. I open the pages and discover things that suddenly seem essential, even though a few minutes earlier I didn't know they existed. Manufacturers use catalog illustrations to create desire for their products. In a way, Christians are God's catalogs. His work in our lives makes us a picture of qualities that people may not know they need or want until they see them at work in us. As you browse holiday catalogs, consider what the "catalog" of your life says about God. Do people see qualities in you that make them long for God? —JAL

As a Christian, you are "God's advertisement." Do people want what they see in you?

NOVEMBER 2

The eternal God is your refuge, and underneath are the everlasting arms.
Deuteronomy 33:27

After a pre-concert rehearsal in New York City's Carnegie Hall, Randall Atcheson sat on stage alone. He had successfully navigated the intricate piano compositions of Beethoven, Chopin, and Liszt for the evening program. With only minutes remaining before the doors opened, he wanted to play one more piece for himself. What came from his heart and his hands was an old hymn: *"What have I to dread, what have I to fear, leaning on the everlasting arms? I have blessed peace with my Lord so near, leaning on the everlasting arms."*

What a gift we have in our own arms and hands—they can swing a hammer, hold a child, help a friend, or play a magnificent musical composition. But while our strength is limited, our security and peace are in His everlasting arms. —DCM

The heavenly Father's arms never tire of holding His children.

NOVEMBER 3

As a father pities his children, so the Lord pities those who fear Him. Psalm 103:13

Several mothers of small children were sharing encouraging answers to prayer. One woman admitted that she felt selfish when she troubled God with her personal needs. "Compared with the huge global needs," she explained, "my circumstances must seem trivial to Him." Moments later, her little son pinched his fingers in a door and ran screaming to his mother. She didn't say, "How selfish of you to bother me with your throbbing fingers when I'm busy!" No, she showed him great compassion and tenderness. As that child ran freely to his mother, so may we run to God with our daily problems. Our compassionate God doesn't neglect others to respond to your concerns. He has limitless time and love for each of His children. No need is too trivial for Him. —JY

God bears the world's weight on His shoulder, and He holds His children in the palm of His hand.

*Your words have upheld him who was stumbling, and
you have strengthened the feeble knees.* Job 4:4

The local newspaper reported that a mother is devastated because her twenty-one-year-old son, who had always seemed like an upright young man, had been arrested for dealing drugs. Also in our community, the parents and siblings of a fifteen-year-old are grieving because he was killed in a gun accident. An aged friend is heartbroken because her only daughter, the person she depended on more than all others, died from cancer.

People who are hurting need to be assured that tragedy and grief are not a mark of God's disfavor but that He weeps with them, He loves them, and He will never leave those who are His. —HVL

*God doesn't comfort us to make us comfortable,
but to make us comforters.*

NOVEMBER 5

The Word of God is living and powerful . . . a discerner of the thoughts and intents of the heart. Hebrews 4:12

A friend of mine recently underwent a laryngoscopy. I winced as he explained how his doctor took a camera with a light on the end and stuck it down his throat to try to find the cause of his pain. It reminded me, however, of the exploratory nature of God's Word. It invades the unseen areas of our lives, exposing the diseased and damaged spiritual tissue that troubles us. If you're wincing at the thought of how uncomfortable this divine procedure might be, consider Jesus' words: "Everyone practicing evil hates the light and does not come to the light, lest his deeds should be exposed" (John 3:20). Internal intrusions may be uncomfortable, but do you really want the disease?

Welcoming God's Word to penetrate the deep, dark places of our hearts is the only way to find true healing and spiritual health. —JS

Let God's Word explore your inner being.

A man who bears false witness against his neighbor is like a club, a sword, and a sharp arrow. Proverbs 25:18

In some offices you can get fired for gossiping. According to a 2002 survey, the average employee gossips sixty-five hours a year. One Chicago firm decided to become a "gossip-free zone." They require that employees never talk badly about co-workers behind their backs. If you're caught, you lose your job.

A ministry for people in the entertainment industry takes a refreshing alternative to gossip. They combat it with prayer. Instead of putting down famous people who get in trouble with bad choices, they encourage people to pray for them. Gossip feeds into our natural desires to feel superior to others and to belong or fit in, so combating it in our personal lives can be a challenge. But if we choose to love through prayer, our lives can be a gossip-free zone. —AC

You can never justify gossip.

This is the day the Lord has made; we will rejoice and be glad in it.
Psalm 118:24

World-famous cellist Pablo Casals once gave this challenging testimony: "For the past 80 years I have started each day in the same manner . . . I go to the piano and I play two preludes and fugues of Bach. I cannot think of doing otherwise. It is a benediction on the house. But that is not its only meaning for me. It is a rediscovery of the world of which I have the joy of being a part."

If that is how a dedicated musician daily started his waking hours, we Christians—by the enabling grace of the Holy Spirit—can surely dedicate each new day to our Lord. No matter where we are or what our situation may be, each day we can resolve to dedicate the hours before us to God's praise. —VCG

If you know Jesus, you always have a reason to rejoice.

Whenever I am afraid, I will trust in You.
Psalm 56:3

In the comic strip *Peanuts,* Lucy broke the news to Linus that children cannot live at home forever. Eventually they grow up and move away. Then she said that when he left she would get his room. But Linus quickly reminded her that at some time she too would have to leave home. When this realization hit Lucy, she was shocked, but she quickly came up with a solution. She turned the TV up loud, crawled into her beanbag chair with a bowl of ice cream, and refused to think about it.

We may try to hide from or avoid unpleasant realities, but life has a way of catching up with us. Facing up to difficulties may seem frightening at first, but when we trust God and draw close to Him, we'll experience real deliverance. —PVG

When troubles call on you, call on God.

[God] heals the brokenhearted and binds up their wounds. He counts the number of the stars; He calls them all by name.

Psalm 147:3–4

The psalmist tells us that God "counts the number of the stars" and even "calls them all by name." Would He care for the stars, which are mere matter, and not care for us, who bear His image? Of course not. He knows about our lonely struggles, and He cares. It is His business to care.

The stars will fall from the sky someday. They are not God's major concern—you are! He "is able to keep you from stumbling, and to present you faultless before the presence of His glory with exceeding joy" (Jude 1:24). And He will do it! —DHR

Because God cares about us, we can leave our cares with Him.

He guides them to their desired haven.
Psalm 107:30

In the world of sailing vessels there were two great fears: a terrible gale, or no wind at all. In "The Rime of the Ancient Mariner," English poet Samuel Taylor Coleridge describes tempests and doldrums at sea. Two lines have become household words: *"Water, water everywhere, nor any drop to drink."* In doldrum latitudes, the wind dies down and a sailing ship remains stationary. Captain and crew are "stuck," and eventually, with no wind, their water supply runs out.

Sometimes life puts us to the test of tedium. We may feel stuck. But even when the spiritual wind has been taken out of our sails, we can trust the Lord, who is sovereign over changing circumstances. He will eventually guide us to our desired haven. —DF

God orders our stops as well as our steps.

NOVEMBER 11

It may be that the Lord will look on my affliction, and that the Lord will repay me with good for his cursing.
2 Samuel 16:12

It seems to me that as the years go by, we grow—as David did—in the awareness of God's protective love. We become less concerned with what others say about us and more willing to give ourselves over to our Father. We may, of course, ask our opponents to justify their charges, or we may meet them with steadfast denial if they charge us falsely. But when we have done all we can do, the only thing left is to wait patiently until God vindicates us.

In the meantime, it's good to look beyond the words of those who vilify us to the will of the One who loves us with infinite love. We're in God's hands, no matter what others say about us. —DHR

It takes the storm to prove the real shelter.

NOVEMBER 12

Give me neither poverty nor riches—feed me with the food allotted to me.
Proverbs 30:8

Prosperity and adversity are equal-opportunity destroyers. The extremes of life can be hazardous because a person with too much may encounter as much difficulty as one with too little.

The late Dr. Carlyle Marney, a prominent pastor, often said that most of us need to have our "wanter" fixed. Instead of always asking for more, we should seek the balance expressed in Proverbs 30. When we invite the Lord to place His mark of ownership on our lives, we acknowledge His wise and loving provision for all our needs. —DCM

Contentment is realizing that God has already given me all I need.

NOVEMBER 13

By grace you have been saved through faith, and that not of yourselves; it is the gift of God. Ephesians 2:8

Ayn Rand, an American philosopher who died in 1982, had a sizable following who read her books and attended her lectures, and still has followers today. An avid individualist, Rand said: "Now I see the free face of god and I raise this god over all the earth, this god who men have sought since men came into being, the god who will grant them joy and peace and pride. This god, this one word, *I*." When asked if she believed in God, she answered, "This god is myself, *I*." Egotism—faith in oneself—that was her belief and philosophy. Are we embracing the philosophy of egotism, which is really a confidence that will prove eternally self-destructive? Or have we embraced the self-sacrificing grace of Jesus Christ? —VCG

We are saved not by what we do but by trusting what Christ has done.

NOVEMBER 14

In the multitude of my anxieties within me, Your comforts delight my soul.
Psalm 94:19

Hudson Taylor (1832–1905) was the founder of the China Inland Mission and a great servant of God. But after the ferocious Boxer Rebellion of 1900, in which hundreds of his fellow missionaries were killed, Taylor was emotionally devastated and his health began to fail. Nearing the end of life's journey, he wrote, "I am so weak that I cannot work. I cannot read my Bible; I cannot even pray. I can only lie still in God's arms like a child and trust."

Have you been passing through a time when you are tired of body and sick of heart? Do you find it difficult to focus on biblical promises? Has it become hard for you to pray? When we experience such times, all we can do—indeed, all we *need* do—is lie still like a child in the arms of our heavenly Father. —VCG

When we have nothing left but God, we'll find that God is enough.

I will praise the name of God with a song . . .
The humble shall see this and be glad.

Psalm 69:30, 32

Ancient Israel's beloved songwriter and king often wrote about gladness. In three consecutive songs, David spoke of being glad: Psalms 68:3; 69:32; 70:4. His lyrics assure us that it's not the rich or the powerful who have reason to be glad but those who are humble and right with God. David expanded on this theme in another song: "Blessed is he whose transgression is forgiven, whose sin is covered . . . Be glad in the Lord and rejoice, you righteous; and shout for joy, all you upright in heart!" (32:1, 11).

If you are feeling poor and powerless today, you can still be glad. You can have something of far more value: a debt-free relationship with God. —JAL

Joy is the result of a right relationship with God.

God Himself will be with them and be their God.
And God will wipe away every tear from their eyes.
Revelation 21:3–4

Engaged couples often spend hours poring over travel brochures and vacation websites looking for just the right honeymoon spot. They can hardly wait for their romantic getaway. But it's not so much about the place; it's about being with the person they love. We get used to places no matter how glorious they are. But being with a person who loves us never gets old!

In Revelation, John paints a beautiful picture of what heaven will be like. But it's not really about the place—it's about the Person we'll be with. Make no mistake, the place—heaven—will be incredible beyond our dreams. But our greatest joy will be the experience of being with Jesus forever! —JS

The greatest aspect of heaven will be spending eternity with Jesus.

A man of understanding is of a calm spirit.
Proverbs 17:27

A Christian I know was angry with someone at his workplace over a perceived injustice. A colleague listened to his grievance and, sensing that his temper still ran high, gave him this wise advice to consider before confronting those involved: "Cooler heads prevail."

As we interact with others, disagreements are inevitable. The discerning believer understands his own heart and takes steps to deal with conflict diplomatically. This means keeping in check a multitude of opinions that could ignite further anger in others. Someone who displays wisdom will think before speaking, and then will share only insights likely to be helpful. The next time you become angry, stop and prayerfully reflect for a moment. Ask God for a calm spirit and the right words to say. Remember, cooler heads prevail. —DF

The best time to stop an argument is before it starts.

NOVEMBER 18

The peace of God . . . will guard your hearts and minds through Christ Jesus.
Philippians 4:7

I was scheduled to teach at a Bible conference outside the US and was waiting for my visa to be approved. It had been rejected once, and time was slipping away. Without the visa, I would lose an opportunity for ministry, and my colleagues in that country would have to find another speaker at the last minute. During those stressful days, a co-worker asked how I felt about it all. I told him I was experiencing "peaceful anxiety." When he looked at me rather quizzically, I explained: "I have had anxiety because I need the visa and there is nothing I can do about it. But I have great peace because I know that, after all, there is nothing I can do about it!" My inability to do anything about the problem was more than matched by my confidence in God, for whom all things are possible. As I prayed about the situation, my anxiety was replaced by His peace. —BC

When we keep our minds on God, God will keep our minds at peace.

God is our refuge and strength, a very present help in trouble.
Psalm 46:1

A survey titled "Care giving in the U.S." estimates that more than forty-four million Americans are unpaid caregivers, and a majority of them currently work or have worked while providing care. The survey also found that God, family, and friends were most often cited as sources of strength by people who are caring for others. Three-fourths of the respondents said they relied on prayer to deal with the demands of care giving. "Prayer is the best way to refresh yourself," said one person. "I find a quiet place and pray and cry and get relief. Then I can go back into the room calm."

Care giving is a high calling and a difficult task. But there is strength from the Lord to help us as we care for those who need us.—DCM

Prayer puts us in touch with God—our greatest caregiver.

NOVEMBER 20

As you are partakers of the sufferings, so also you will partake of the consolation.
2 Corinthians 1:7

After years of a remarkable and fruitful ministry in India, Amy Carmichael became a bedridden sufferer. As the courageous founder and dynamic heart of the Dohnavur Fellowship, she was instrumental in rescuing hundreds of girls and boys from a terrible life of sexual servitude and bringing many young people into spiritual freedom through faith in Jesus Christ. Then arthritis made Amy a pain-wracked invalid. Did she bemoan her affliction or question God? No. She was still the guiding inspiration of Dohnavur, and she wrote books, meditations, letters, and poems filled with praise to God and encouragement to her fellow pilgrims.

When we rely on the Lord, He will help us turn pain into praise. —VCG

Praise is the song of a soul set free.

The things which are impossible with men are possible with God.
Luke 18:27

Countless times I've heard myself say, "I'm going to bake a cake."
Then one day I realized that only my oven can do that. I simply
mix the right ingredients and allow the oven to do its part.

God used my oven musings to clarify a dilemma I once had after starting a
neighborhood Bible study. It was one thing to bring my neighbors together
to study the Bible, but seeing them believe and follow Christ was another.
I felt powerless. Suddenly I saw the obvious. I had blended the right
ingredients—an open home, friendship, love. Now I had to trust the Holy
Spirit, through His Word, to do His work. When I cooperated with that
division of labor, I had the joy of seeing others taste of God's goodness. —JY

We sow the seed, but God brings the harvest.

Make Your face shine upon Your servant; save me for Your mercies' sake.
Psalm 31:16

After the terrorist bombing in Bali in 2002, one man reacted by giving up traveling. Three years later, he finally took his family for a holiday in Bali. The trip ended in tragedy when his family was caught in a suicide bombing at a café on Jimbaran Beach.

In our world, perfect safety is not possible. But though our earthly security may be threatened, we can never lose God's eternal, unfailing love. To those who trust in the Lord, the psalmist David wrote these hope-filled words: "[The Lord] shall strengthen your heart" (Psalm 31:24). When we place our times in His hand, we can exchange the fear of terror for peace and praise. —AL

Putting your faith in the living God takes the fear out of living.

*The Lord does not see as man sees; for man looks at the
outward appearance, but the Lord looks at the heart.*
1 Samuel 16:7

No one watching *Britain's Got Talent*, a popular televised talent show, expected
much when mobile phone salesman Paul Potts took the stage. The judges
looked skeptically at one another when the nervous, unassuming, ordinary-
looking chap announced he would sing opera—until Potts opened his mouth.
He began to sing Puccini's "Nessun Dorma"—and it was magical! The crowd
roared and stood in amazement while the judges sat stunned in tearful silence.
It was one of the greatest surprises any such television program has ever
had, in large part because it came wrapped in such an ordinary package.

If we judge others only by their outer appearance, we might
miss the wonderful surprise of what's in their heart. —BC

It's what's in the heart that counts.

I commend to you Phoebe . . . for indeed she has been a helper of many and of myself also. Romans 16:1–2

Counting your blessings promotes good physical health, according to a study by some US doctors. Volunteers who kept weekly gratitude journals reported fewer aches and pains than those who recorded daily hassles or neutral events.

A "gratitude visit" was developed by Dr. Martin E. P. Seligman to promote strong emotional health. He asks people to think of someone who has made an important difference in their lives, then to write the story of how that person has helped them, and then to visit that person and read the story aloud. A year later the people who had done so were happier and reported fewer episodes of depression. And think of what it must have done for those who were thanked! Who has helped to shape your life? Could you make a gratitude visit—for their sake, and for yours? —AC

Gratitude should be a continuous attitude.

*You will keep him in perfect peace, whose mind
is stayed on You, because he trusts in You.*
Isaiah 26:3

Richard Fuller, a nineteenth-century minister, told of an old seaman who said, "In fierce storms, we must put the ship in a certain position and keep her there." Said Fuller, "This, Christian, is what you must do . . . You must put your soul in one position and keep it there. You must stay upon the Lord; and, come what may—winds, waves, cross seas, thunder, lightning, frowning rocks, roaring breakers—no matter what, you must hold fast your confidence in God's faithfulness and His everlasting love in Christ Jesus."

Fix your mind on the Lord. Ask for His help. Then trust Him to give you peace in your storm (Philippians 4:6–7). —RDH

The secret of peace is to give every anxious care to God.

NOVEMBER 26

Why have you despised the commandment of the Lord, to do evil in His sight?
2 Samuel 12:9

When I sat in my car at the start of the automatic car wash, I didn't know that my left front tire was not properly lined up with the track. The car wash started but my car wasn't moving, so I accelerated. That caused my tire to jump the track. Now I was stuck—I couldn't move forward or backward. Meanwhile, cars began lining up and waiting for me. I was glad when two workers at the station helped me get my car back on the track. Sometimes in our Christian lives we get off track too. King David did in a big way, and he needed help to get back on track. The Bible says that "the Lord sent Nathan to David" (12:1). He confronted David about stealing another man's wife, and David wisely repented (v. 13), even though his sin still had dire consequences. Does someone you know need your help to get back on track? —AC

True love dares to confront.

O Death, where is your sting? O Hades, where is your victory?
1 Corinthians 15:55

As I waited outside the Intensive Care Unit for changes in the condition of a loved one, I was reminded that death affects all of us: old and young, male and female, rich and poor.

In 1 Thessalonians 4, the apostle Paul comforted those who mourned the death of their loved ones. He told them that we need not weep like those who have no hope. Instead, we must rely on three certainties: The first is that the soul does not die. Second, Jesus will come for every believer. And third, there will be a joyous reunion. Knowing these certainties brings comfort to believers when their friends and loved ones depart. Although we are separated from them for a while, we will meet again in the presence of our Lord. —AL

Sunset in one land is sunrise in another.

NOVEMBER 28

Nevertheless I am continually with You; You hold me by my right hand.
Psalm 73:23

One of the joys of being with kids is holding their hands. We do it to keep them safe while crossing the street, or to keep them from getting lost in a crowd. And whenever they stumble and lose their footing, we grab their little hands tighter to keep them from falling.

That's what God does for us. Inevitably there are stones and cracks that trip us up on the sidewalks of life. That's why it's easy to identify with the psalmist, who said, "My steps had nearly slipped" (Psalm 73:2). So, next time you stumble, remember that the powerful hand of God is holding your hand and walking you through life—all the way home! —JS

Let God do the holding and you do the trusting.

Christ is risen from the dead, and has become
the firstfruits of those who have fallen asleep.
1 Corinthians 15:20

Konrad Adenauer, former chancellor of West Germany, said, "If Jesus Christ is alive, then there is hope for the world. If not, I don't see the slightest glimmer of hope on the horizon." Then he added, "I believe Christ's resurrection to be one of the best-attested facts of history."

When the Greek philosopher Socrates lay dying, his friends asked, "Shall we live again?" He could only say, "I hope so." In contrast, the night before author and explorer Sir Walter Raleigh was beheaded, he wrote in his Bible, "From this earth, this grave, this dust, my God shall raise me up." If we trust in Christ as our Savior, we won't say, "I hope so" about our own resurrection. Jesus' resurrection gives us a sure hope. —DJD

Christ's resurrection is the guarantee of our own.

NOVEMBER 30

Be anxious for nothing, but in everything by prayer . . .
let your requests be made known to God.
Philippians 4:6

A man was sitting on a park bench shredding old newspapers and spreading them around. "What are you doing?" asked a bystander. "I'm spreading this paper around to keep the elephants away." The visitor looked around the well-kept city park. "I don't see any elephants," he said. The man smiled. "Works pretty good, doesn't it?" he replied.

Worry is like that. We expend a lot of energy on problems that don't exist. One of the great challenges for worriers is to turn every care into a prayer and then to stop there, leaving it with God. Aren't you glad that our teacher, the Lord Jesus, is patient with us—even when we tear up papers and spread them around? —DJD

Worry is carrying a burden that God never intended us to bear.

DECEMBER 1

Bethlehem Ephrathah, though you are little among the thousands of Judah, yet out of you shall come forth to Me the One to be Ruler in Israel.

Micah 5:2

Jesus was born in Bethlehem, which means "house of Bread." He was laid in a manger, a feeding trough. He once said, "I am the living bread which came down from heaven. If anyone eats of this bread, he will live forever; and the bread that I shall give is My flesh" (John 6:51).

The prophet Micah indicated that One born in Bethlehem would rule over Israel. But not until Jesus came did anyone realize the uniqueness of this kingdom. Christ's rule would not be imposed upon anyone; it would be imparted to those who accepted this new citizenship. As we sing of Bethlehem's manger, let's remember that the heaven-sent infant King came so that we might "eat this bread" and partake of His divine nature. —JAL

Only Christ the Living Bread can satisfy our spiritual hunger.

DECEMBER 2

If we confess our sins, He is faithful and just to forgive us our sins and to cleanse us from all unrighteousness.
1 John 1:9

A number of computer games come with a special feature called the "Boss Key." If you're playing a game when you're supposed to be working, and someone (like the boss) walks into your office, you quickly strike the Boss Key. Your computer screen changes immediately, hiding what you've been doing.

Trying to hide from others when we've done something wrong comes naturally. We may feel guilty, but our desire to avoid admitting our responsibility is often stronger than our guilt. If you've been disobedient, it's time to come out of hiding. God is lovingly calling you and offering His cleansing, forgiveness, and restoration. —AC

Confession is the key that opens the door to forgiveness.

DECEMBER 3

I will lift up my eyes to the hills—from whence comes my help? My help comes from the Lord. Psalm 121:1–2

A woman whose work demanded constant reading began to have difficulty with her eyes, so she consulted a physician. "Your eyes are just tired," he said. "You need to rest them." She replied, "That is impossible in my type of work." The doctor asked, "Do you have windows at your workplace?" "Oh, yes," she said. "From the front windows I can see the Blue Ridge Mountains." The physician replied, "That is exactly what you need. When your eyes feel tired, go look at your mountains for ten minutes—twenty would be better—and the far look will rest your eyes!"

The eyes of the soul are often tired and weary from focusing on our problems and difficulties. The upward look—the far look—will restore our spiritual perspective. —HGB

For the right spiritual focus, fix your eyes on the Lord.

DECEMBER 4

He took [little children] up in His arms . . . and blessed them.
Mark 10:16

While Jesus lived on earth, He took little children in His arms and blessed them, and He is still in the child-embracing ministry today. Many of God's much older children have experienced His unseen everlasting arms around them and beneath them. Brother Lawrence, the seventeenth-century monk known for sensing the presence of God even amid the pots and pans of the monastery kitchen, spoke of being "known of God and extremely caressed by Him." And Hudson Taylor, the pioneer missionary to China, said as he neared the end of his life: "I am so weak . . . I can only lie still in God's arms like a child, and trust."

Whether we're young or old, strong or weak, God wants us to cuddle close to Him in childlike trust. Have you and God had a "hug of the heart" today? —JY

Jesus longs for our fellowship even more than we long for His.

DECEMBER 5

Behold, the glory of the God of Israel came from the way of the east. Ezekiel 43:2

I've seen an awe-inspiring nighttime launch of the space shuttle, the majesty of Mount Fuji in Japan, the sparkling beauty of ocean sea life off the coast of the Philippine Islands, and the gleaming midsummer spectacle of a night baseball game in a major league stadium. But nothing I've ever seen comes close to what some Old Testament people saw. Moses, the people he led, Ezekiel, and others witnessed the most breathtaking sight of all: They had a glimpse of the glory of God—a visible manifestation of the Lord's invisible being and character. Someday we who have been redeemed will see God's glory shine in the heavenly Jerusalem. And we will see our risen and glorified Savior. This hope encourages us to keep going, for nothing in this world compares to seeing God's glory! —DB

The world's greatest glory is but a spark compared to the radiance of God's glory.

*She will bring forth a Son, and you shall call His name Jesus,
for He will save His people from their sins.* Matthew 1:21

During an all-night festival in Paris, five drunken young people broke into the Orsay Museum and left a four-inch gash in a priceless painting by Claude Monet. One news headline read: "Monet Masterpiece Marred." To *mar* is to injure or damage; to spoil, disfigure, or impair. It's an apt description of sin's effect on us. We know well the results of our own choices made in ignorance or defiance of God.

As we approach Christmas, it's good to remember why Jesus was born. The Son of God did not come to establish a nostalgic, commercially successful holiday. Christmas began with a present from God to His sin-damaged world. The masterpiece of God's human creation, marred by turning away from Him, can be restored when we give our hearts to Christ. —DCM

Jesus came to earth to repair our sin-damaged lives.

Do not worry about tomorrow . . . Sufficient for the day is its own trouble.
Matthew 6:34

I once read about a paratrooper in the US Army who had made more than fifty successful parachute jumps without a single serious injury. But the first day back home after being discharged, he stumbled over a rug, fell against a table, and broke four of his ribs! He had worried a great deal about his parachute jumps, but then something happened he had never worried about: He tripped over a rug.

So why worry? Jesus said that it's futile to fret, for worrying can't change anything (Matthew 6:27). Our heavenly Father knows all about our situation and watches over us. He will take care of our needs no matter what tomorrow brings. So don't be a worrywart! —MRD

Worry doesn't improve the future, it only ruins the present.

DECEMBER 8

God is our refuge and strength, a very present help in trouble.
Psalm 46:1

Most homes are built to keep inhabitants safe from ill effects of the weather, but not the dwellings built for *Succoth*. During this Jewish holiday, also known as the Feast of Tabernacles, worshipers live in dwellings made of leaves and branches. One requirement is that the stars must be visible through the "roof." Obviously, this dwelling provides little protection from inclement weather. And that's the point. Living in this vulnerable shelter reminds the Jews of their dependency on God.

Succoth calls us to examine our lives to make sure that our security rests not on lies but on God's truth; it reminds us that all of life is sustained by God's goodness. When we make truth our refuge, no storm can threaten us. —JAL

God is a safe dwelling place in life's storms.

DECEMBER 9

A fool has no delight in understanding, but in expressing his own heart.
Proverbs 18:2

Mrs. Grumpty complained bitterly because her friends seemed to avoid her, and she just couldn't understand why. If only she could have heard a recording of her own voice, she would have known the reason for her unpopularity. She always talked about her complaints, weaknesses, aches, and pains, and she insisted on relating in wearying detail her stay in the hospital.

If you want to keep friends, don't be a grumbler. Most people have enough problems of their own and don't need to hear all of yours. Share your joys with others, and leave your troubles with the Lord. —MRD

Spend your time counting your blessings, not airing your complaints.

DECEMBER 10

*Whatever things you ask when you pray, believe
that you receive them, and you will have them.*
Mark 11:24

Lots of things are easier to do when they're bite-size. If you have a major task to get done, for example, it helps to divide it into smaller units and tackle them one at a time. Rosalind Rinker suggests that the same is true of prayer. She found that when she made very general, all-inclusive requests of God, it seemed that nothing happened. But when she began making specific, bite-size requests, she saw results.

Rinker recommends that we make our requests very specific and ask for what we really believe is according to God's will. As we see God's answers to relatively small requests, we will find that we are asking for bigger needs with a greater degree of faith. —DCE

Be specific in your prayers if you want specific answers.

DECEMBER 11

Surely I am more stupid than any man, and do not have the understanding of a man. Proverbs 30:2

In 1992, a Seattle man running for the office of Washington State's lieutenant governor legally changed his name to "Absolutely Nobody." He said he wanted to greet the voters, saying, "Hi, I'm Absolutely Nobody. Vote for me." He later admitted that the purpose of his campaign was to abolish the office of lieutenant governor.

The right kind of humility is healthy. But there's a downside to insisting that we are "nobody" if it is to avoid doing what God commands, as we are warned in the story of Moses (Exodus 4:1–17). When we do that, our motives make us into somebody who resists the loving purposes of God. Remember, God doesn't make nobodies. We can do anything He wants us to do—in His strength. —MD

God doesn't make nobodies.

DECEMBER 12

*In returning and rest you shall be saved; in
quietness and confidence shall be your strength.*
Isaiah 30:15

Some people are calm by nature; others are high-strung. But Christians,
regardless of their temperament, can come to God in prayer and learn to
renew their strength in quietness and confidence. Martin Luther said that he
could get so busy that he first needed to spend at least three hours a day in
prayer to get anything done. Often we reverse that order. We rush from task
to task feeling flustered because we haven't taken time to be with the Lord.

Let's learn the principle set forth in Isaiah 30:15: In quietness and confidence
before God we find the real source of strength to stay calm. —RDH

Never take on more work than you have time to pray about.

DECEMBER 13

When the fullness of the time had come, God sent forth His Son.
Galatians 4:4

Why is being on time so challenging for some of us? Even when we start early, something inevitably gets in our way to make us late. But here's the good news: God is always on time! Speaking of the arrival of Jesus, Paul said, "When the fullness of the time had come, God sent forth His Son." The long-awaited, promised Savior came at just the right time.

This should remind us that the Lord knows what time is best for us as well. If you're waiting for answered prayer or the fulfillment of one of His promises, don't give up. If you think He has forgotten you, think again. When the fullness of time is right for you, He'll show up—and you'll be amazed by His brilliant timing! —JS

God's timing is always perfect.

DECEMBER 14

*Do not be conformed to this world, but be transformed
by the renewing of your mind.* Romans 12:2

Farmers in Zentsuji, Japan, are preparing full-grown watermelons for shipment, only these are no ordinary melons—they're *square*! They were placed in tempered-glass cubes while they were still growing. Why would anyone want a square watermelon? They're much easier to store in a refrigerator!

It's amusing to think of how a naturally round watermelon can become square because of the shape of the container in which it's grown. But this also reminds me of the forces in the world that exert their influence on us and attempt to shape us. The external pressures of the world will try to shape our character, but they will not succeed if God's Word is changing us from within. —AL

*If we are being transformed by the Word,
we won't be conformed to the world.*

DECEMBER 15

To everything there is a season, a time for every purpose under heaven. Ecclesiastes 3:1

I grew up on the West Coast of the US, where the possibility of snow for Christmas was so remote that my mom would point to fog in the early morning as evidence that the holidays were just around the corner. I now live in the Midwest, where there's usually a lot of snow when the yuletide season comes around. I couldn't be happier with four distinct seasons. In Ecclesiastes 3:1–8, Solomon acknowledged the cycles of life. There is a time—a season—to sow and to reap, to weep and to laugh, to mourn and to dance, to gain and to lose, to keep silent and to speak, to love and to hate. Do we resist those seasons and complain about the "snowy" conditions on the horizon? Or do we trust God and thank Him for whatever He has planned for us? —DF

Rather than praying for a change in circumstances, pray for a change of heart.

DECEMBER 16

He has sent Me to heal the brokenhearted . . . to set at liberty those who are oppressed. Luke 4:18

During a December visit to New York City's Metropolitan Museum of Art, I paused to admire the magnificent Christmas tree. It was covered with angels and surrounded at its base by an elaborate eighteenth-century nativity scene. Nearly two hundred figures, including shepherds, the Magi, and a crowd of townspeople, looked in anticipation toward the manger or gazed up in awe at the angels. But one figure—a barefoot man with a heavy load on his back—looked at the ground. It struck me that this man, like many people today, was so weighed down that he couldn't see the Messiah.

Christmas can be a difficult time for those who carry the burden of hard work, stressful family situations, and personal loss. But Jesus came to lift our burdens, so we can raise our eyes to welcome Him at Christmas. —DCM

To find true joy, look to Jesus.

DECEMBER 17

A man's heart plans his way, but the Lord directs his steps. Proverbs 16:9

It was Christmas Eve in Oberndorf, Austria, in 1818. Joseph Mohr, the vicar of the church, had written a new song for the Christmas Eve service, and the organist Franz Gruber had set it to music. But the organ in the village church broke down. So Gruber grabbed a guitar and accompanied Mohr in the first-ever rendition of "Silent Night." The story doesn't end there, however. When a man came to fix the organ, Gruber tested it by playing the new song. The repairman liked the song so much that he took a copy of it back to his own village. There, four daughters of a village glove maker learned the song and began singing it in concerts all over the region. Because of that faulty organ, this new Christmas song blessed people all over Austria—and eventually the world. —DB

In the drama of life, God is the director behind the scenes.

DECEMBER 18

There has not failed one word of all His good promise.
1 Kings 8:56

As an avid baseball fan, my favorite team is the Chicago Cubs. The interesting thing about being a Cubs fan is that the team has a way of letting us down. They have not won a World Series since 1908. And while they often have great promise at the beginning of the season, they usually disappoint their loyal fans in the end. One die-hard fan had it right when he said, "If they didn't disappoint us, they wouldn't be our Cubs!"

Thankfully, God is not like the Cubs! You can count on Him. He will not disappoint you in the end. He always keeps His promises, and His Word provides comfort, hope, and wise advice that never fail. —JS

Looking for someone who won't disappoint you? Look to Jesus.

DECEMBER 19

God has revealed them to us through His Spirit.
1 Corinthians 2:10

Imagine Christmas morning without wrapping paper! The joy would be short-lived, for much of the excitement is the anticipation of tearing off the paper and finding out what's in the package.

Apparently God created us to enjoy the process of discovery. He could have revealed all truth to all people at the very beginning of time, but He chose to reveal himself gradually (1 Corinthians 2:7–8). Perhaps that's because we value things more when we have to search and wait for them. So don't be discouraged over what you don't know about God. Be excited about unwrapping all there is yet to discover. —JAL

God's gift of himself to us is a present we will always be unwrapping.

DECEMBER 20

The word which they heard did not profit them, not being mixed with faith.
Hebrews 4:2

In the 1960s, the Kingston Trio released a song called "Desert Pete." The ballad tells of a thirsty cowboy who is crossing the desert and finds a hand pump. Next to it, Desert Pete has left a note urging the reader not to drink from the jar hidden there but to use its contents to prime the pump. The cowboy resists the temptation to drink from the jar immediately and uses the water as the note instructs. In reward for his obedience, once he has primed the pump he receives an abundance of cold, satisfying water. Had he not acted in faith, he would have had only a single jar of unsatisfying, warm water to drink.

Sometimes life can seem like an arid desert. But when by faith we believe the promises of God's Word, we can experience rivers of living water and grace for our daily needs. —DF

Only Jesus, the Living Water, can satisfy our thirst for God.

DECEMBER 21

That you may know what is the hope of His calling . . . and what is the exceeding greatness of His power toward us who believe. Ephesians 1:18–19

My two-year-old grandson was fascinated by the bubbling mud pool, the result of geothermal activity in Rotorua, New Zealand. On moving to another spot and seeing no bubbles there, he remarked, "No batteries?" He was so accustomed to his electronic toys that he attributed even natural phenomena to battery power!

Christians can make a similar mistake. They look to their own puny power to live righteous lives, but the standards of a holy God prove impossible to live up to. The result is joyless Christians, hopelessly burdened and defeated. The power to live according to God's standards comes only when we plug into His inexhaustible power by daily seeking His face and asking Him to fill us with His Holy Spirit. —CPH

The Light of the World knows no power failure.

DECEMBER 22

Looking unto Jesus, the author and finisher of our faith. Hebrews 12:2

When my son Joe was a child, I took him to the local YMCA for swimming lessons. He took one look at the water, one look at the instructor, and started bawling. In the midst of his sobs and pleas to go home, I gave him a little pep talk: "You can do it, Joe! I'll come to all your lessons, and we'll have a signal. When you get scared you can look up at me, and when I hold my thumb up you'll know it's going to be okay because I'm here cheering you on." Joe finally agreed, and today he can swim circles around me. When we face situations that seem overwhelming and impossible, our first instinct may be to back away in fear. But that's exactly when we need to look to Jesus, who will raise His nail-scarred hand and say, "Stay with it. Run the race. I've run it before you, and in my power you can win. You can do it!" —JS

*Christ's victory in the past gives courage for
the present and hope for the future.*

DECEMBER 23

Behold, an angel of the Lord stood before them,
and the glory of the Lord shone around them.
Luke 2:9

Writer Anita Brechbill observed: "Most often the Word of the Lord comes to a soul in the ordinary duties of life." She cites the examples of Zacharias performing his duties as a priest, and the shepherds watching their flocks. They were at work as usual with no idea that they were about to receive a message from God.

Oswald Chambers said: "Jesus rarely comes where we expect Him; He appears where we least expect Him, and always in the most illogical situations. The only way a worker can keep true to God is by being ready for the Lord's surprise visits." On this ordinary day, the Lord may have a word of encouragement, guidance, or instruction for us, if we're listening and ready to obey. —DCM

God speaks to those who are quiet before Him.

DECEMBER 24

There was no room for them in the inn. Luke 2:7

Life was tough for Datha and her family. At age thirty-nine, she had a heart attack and bypass surgery and learned that she had coronary artery disease. A year later, her fifteen-year-old daughter Heather became paralyzed as the result of a car accident. Datha quit her job to take care of Heather, and the bills started piling up. Soon they would be facing eviction. Datha was so angry with God that she stopped praying.

Then came Christmas Eve 2004. A young girl knocked on Datha's door. The girl wished her a "Merry Christmas," gave her an envelope, and left quickly. Inside was a gift that would cover Datha's housing needs for the next year. The attached note read, "Please accept this gift in honor of the Man whose birthday we celebrate on this holy night. Long ago, His family also had a shelter problem." —AC

You do the casting, God will do the caring.

DECEMBER 25

*All those who heard it marveled at those things which
were told them by the shepherds.* Luke 2:18

Elmer Kline, a bakery manager in 1921, was given the job of naming the
company's new loaf of bread. While visiting the grounds of the Indianapolis
Motor Speedway, he stopped to watch the International Balloon Festival.
Later he described the sight of the beautiful hot-air balloons launching
into the Indiana sky as one of "awe and wonderment." The thought
stuck, and he called the new product Wonder Bread. To this day, the
packaging for Wonder Bread is brightened by colorful balloons. *Wonder*
is a word that captures the experience of all the people surrounding the
events of the coming of Jesus into the world—the angels, Mary, Joseph,
the shepherds, and all the people they told. As we celebrate Christmas,
may we be filled with wonder at His love and His coming! —BC

Look with wonder at the Christ of Christmas.

DECEMBER 26

I give them eternal life, and they shall never perish;
neither shall anyone snatch them out of My hand.
John 10:28

On December 26, 2004, an earthquake shook the whole earth. Many people didn't feel it, but the South Asian region and parts of Africa suffered a devastating tsunami as a result. According to reporter Randolph Schmid, however, "No point on Earth remained undisturbed." That earthquake "shook the ground everywhere on Earth's surface."

We too have had or possibly will have "earthquakes" in our lives. But it's comforting to know that under the worst of circumstances, our faith in God can—and will—hold us fast. No one, nor any disaster, can snatch us out of our heavenly Father's hands. His grip will hold us into all eternity. —VCG

Our unknown future is secure in the hands of our all-knowing God.

DECEMBER 27

Looking unto Jesus, the author and finisher of our faith,
who for the joy that was set before Him endured the cross.
Hebrews 12:2

As a boy, I was fascinated by the book *The Invisible Man.* The main character played an elaborate game of hide-and-seek. To have a physical presence, he wore clothes and wrapped his face in bandages. When it was time to escape, he simply removed everything and disappeared.

Sometimes we may feel that God is beyond our reach and invisible. And while it is true that we will never fully comprehend what God is like, He is accessible to us. Jesus came to "show us the Father" and to bring us close to Him, because "He is the image of the invisible God, the firstborn over all creation" (Colossians 1:15). —BC

God's presence with us is His greatest present to us.

DECEMBER 28

Will You not revive us again, that Your people may rejoice in You?
Psalm 85:6

Over thirty years ago, I bought a brand-new, professional-quality, five-string banjo. That banjo has accompanied me on ministry efforts around the world. But despite its excellent craftsmanship, eventually it needed to be refurbished. A master repairman pointed out how imperfections had worn into the banjo, but he was confident that his repairs would result in the instrument sounding better than new. I wasn't disappointed. The action on the strings and the clarity of the sound are astonishingly superior to its original condition when I purchased the instrument.

In a way, our lives are like that. Over time, life wears us down, and it's vital that we submit our souls to the Master's restorative touch. Why not set aside some time for spiritual retreat and ask the Lord to repair your heart? —DF

Time in Christ's service requires time out for renewal.

DECEMBER 29

Walk worthy of the Lord, fully pleasing Him.
Colossians 1:10

A story is told about a vendor who sold bagels for fifty cents each at a street corner food stand. A jogger ran past and threw a couple of quarters into the bucket but didn't take a bagel. He did the same thing every day for months. One day, as the jogger was passing by, the vendor stopped him. The jogger asked, "You probably want to know why I always put money in but never take a bagel, don't you?" "No," said the vendor. "I just wanted to tell you that the bagels have gone up to sixty cents."

Too often we treat God with that same kind of attitude. Not only are we ungrateful for what He's given us—but we want more. Of course, God doesn't owe us anything, yet He gives us everything. Our grateful response should be to live to please Him. —CHK

Life is a gift from God to be lived for God.

DECEMBER 30

Vindicate me, O Lord, for I have walked in my integrity. Psalm 26:1

As I was moving my laptop, cell phone, and assorted books and papers from one room to another, the "regular" phone rang. I hurriedly set down my stuff and rushed to answer the call before the answering machine kicked in. "Hello," I said. No reply. I said hello again and heard rustling, but still no response. So I hung up and went back to my stuff on the floor. When I picked up my cell phone I realized that I had accidentally speed-dialed my home phone number! I laughed at myself, but then wondered: How often are my prayers more like calling myself than calling on God? For example, when I am falsely accused, I plead with God for vindication. But then I get impatient with God and try to vindicate myself. I may as well be praying to myself. When we call on God, He will help us—but in His perfect time and in His perfect way. —JAL

The purpose of prayer is not to get what we want, but to become what God wants.

DECEMBER 31

Moses My servant is dead. Now therefore, arise.
Joshua 1:2

During our church's annual New Year's Eve Communion service, we say this prayer together: "Father, we surrender this past year and give it up to you. We give you our failures, our regrets, and our disappointments, for we have no more use for them. Make us now a new people, forgetting what lies behind and pressing on toward that which lies ahead of us. We give you all our hopes and dreams for the future. Purify them by your Spirit so that our wills shall truly reflect your will for us. As we stand on the threshold of another year, encourage us by our successes of the past, challenge us by the power of your Word, and guide us by the presence of your Holy Spirit."

In every transition, it's good to look both ways. With confidence in God, we can look back and look ahead, then walk boldly into a new year. —DCM

The victories of the past give courage for the future.